Poverty in World Politics

Whose Global Era?

Edited by

Sarah Owen Vandersluis
Department of International Relations
London School of Economics and Political Science

and

Paris Yeros
Department of International Relations
London School of Economics and Political Science

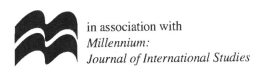

in association with
Millennium:
Journal of International Studies

First published in Great Britain 2000 by
MACMILLAN PRESS LTD
Houndmills, Basingstoke, Hampshire RG21 6XS and London
Companies and representatives throughout the world

A catalogue record for this book is available from the British Library.

ISBN 0–333–71379–6 hardcover
ISBN 0–333–71380–X paperback

First published in the United States of America 2000 by
ST. MARTIN'S PRESS, INC.,
Scholarly and Reference Division,
175 Fifth Avenue, New York, N.Y. 10010

ISBN 0–312–22314–5

Library of Congress Cataloging-in-Publication Data
Poverty in world politics : whose global era? / edited by Sarah
Owen Vandersluis and Paris Yeros.
  p. cm.
"In association with Millennium: Journal of International Studies."
Includes bibliographical references and index.
ISBN 0–312–22314–5
1. Poverty. 2. Social justice. 3. Political participation. 4.
Competition, International. 5. International economic relations. I.
Owen Vandersluis, Sarah, 1974– . II. Yeros, Paris, 1968– .
HC79.P6 P685 1999
362.5—dc21
                                                  99–11276
                                                       CIP

This book is printed on paper suitable for recycling and made from fully managed and
sustained forest sources.

10   9   8   7   6   5   4   3   2   1
09   08   07   06   05   04   03   02   01   00

Printed and bound in Great Britain by
Antony Rowe Ltd, Chippenham, Wiltshire

Contents

Notes on Contributors

Jenny Edkins is Lecturer in the Department of International Politics at the University of Wales Aberystwyth. She is author of *Poststructuralism and International Relations: Bringing the Political Back In* (Lynne Rienner, 1999) and is completing a book on famines and modernity for the Minnesota University Press Borderlines Series. She is co-convenor of the new masters programme in Postcolonial Politics at Aberystwyth.

Marianne H. Marchand is Senior Lecturer in the Department of Political Science at the University of Amsterdam. Her current research interests focus on the dynamics of global restructuring, in particular the emergence of formal and informal regionalisations/regionalisms, and the responses from civil society to these transformations. She has published widely in these areas, including: *Feminism/Postmodernism/Development* (with Jane L. Parpart), and *Gender and Global Restructuring: Sightings, Sites and Resistances* (with Anne Sisson Runyan). In addition, she is the co-editor of the *RIPE* Series in Global Political Economy (Routledge).

Paul J. Nelson is Assistant Professor in the Graduate School of Public and International Affairs, University of Pittsburgh, where he teaches and conducts research on NGOs, development policy, and international organisations. He is the author of *The World Bank and NGOs: The Limits of Apolitical Development* (Macmillan, 1995) and of recent articles on NGOs and International Organisations in *Non-Profit and Voluntary Sector Quarterly* and *Journal of Peace Research*. He holds a PhD in development studies from the University of Wisconsin-Madison.

Mustapha Kamal Pasha is Associate Professor in the School of International Service, American University. His research interests include comparative and global political economy and culture, Islamic studies, and South Asia. He is the author of several publications including *Colonial Political Economy: State-Building and Underdevelopment in the Punjab* (Oxford, 1998), *Out From Underdevelopment Revisited: Changing Global Structures and the Remaking of the Third World* (with James H. Mittelman; Macmillan, 1997) and has published articles in numerous leading journals, including *Alternatives*, *Millennium*, *The European Journal of Development Research*, and *Studies in Comparative International Development*.

Fiona Robinson is Assistant Professor of Political Science at Carleton University, Ottawa, Canada, where she teaches International Relations. Her publications include articles on human rights, international ethics and feminist theory. She is the author of *Globalizing Care: Ethics, Feminist Theory and International Relations* (Westview, 1999).

Julian Saurin is Lecturer in International Relations in the School of African and Asian Studies, University of Sussex. His research interests include global environmental change, sociology of knowledge, and global agriculture and food security. He is author of several recent articles, including 'Global Environmental Degradation, Ariality and Environmental Knowledge', in *Environmental Politics* (1994); 'Organising Hunger: The Global Organisation of Famines and Feasts' in C. Thomas and P. Wilkins (eds.) *Globalisation and the South* (1996); and 'The State in an Age of Globalisation: The End of International Relations?' in A. Linklater and J. Macmillan (eds.) *Boundaries in Question* (1995).

Jan Aart Scholte is Reader in International Studies at the University of Warwick. Previously he was affiliated to the University of Sussex (1985-96) and the Institute of Social Studies in The Hague (1997-98). His doctorate (1990) examined the Indonesian Revolution of the 1940s from a world-historical-sociological perspective. His publications include *International Relations of Social Change* (Open University Press, 1993), *Globalisation: A Critical Introduction* (Macmillan, forthcoming), and various articles which explore the implications of globalisation for governance, production, and identity.

Sarah Owen Vandersluis is a PhD student in the Department of International Relations at the London School of Economics. She is writing a dissertation on the normative dimensions of cultural issues in international trade agreements. She is former editor of *Millennium: Journal of International Studies*, and is also editor of *The State and Identity Construction in IR* (Macmillan, 1999).

Paris Yeros is a PhD student in the Department of International Relations at the London School of Economics. He is writing a dissertation on citizenship and social movements in Southern Africa. He is former editor of *Millennium: Journal of International Studies*, and is also editor of *Ethnicity and Nationalism in Africa: Constructivist Reflections and Contemporary Politics* (Macmillan, 1999).

Preface

This book project began in 1996 as a Special Issue of *Millennium: Journal of International Studies* (Vol. 25, No. 3). Five of the contributions to this book first appeared in the Special Issue; they include the chapters by Jenny Edkins, Marianne Marchand, Paul Nelson, Mustapha Kamal Pasha, and Julian Saurin. We are grateful to *Millennium* for allowing us to reproduce these works.

In this project, we have sought to focus on various aspects of poverty in the context of a global era. What 'global' means, or what 'globalisation' consists in, are, of course, matters of dispute, and the book does not contain a single position on them. A common motive, however, had been to address poverty in an era in which neoliberal convictions are enjoying an unprecedented preeminence, in which the state has suffered a loss both in legitimacy and capacity, and in which suprastate institutions and non-state actors have assumed the functions that have previously been the responsibility of states.

These are changes of the final two decades of the twentieth century. Alongside these changes, poverty and insecurity have increased dramatically for the bulk of the world's population, with living standards in places falling to the levels of the 1960s. The gap between contemporary ideals and lived realities is repugnant indeed. It is so not only in terms of living standards, but even more fundamentally in terms of political organisation. The idea of democratic participation in political community, the highest moral demand of the contemporary humanist epoch, is becoming ever less tangible. As market-driven globalisation is being hailed in some quarters as the dawn of a bright new era, and as 'third way' ideologues convince themselves that they stand for something 'alternative', democratic participation is being stripped of its meaning and democratic thought is being trivialised by technocrats in the name of 'good governance'.

This book is written in this dissenting spirit. We ask, 'whose global era?', in protest to the assumption that globalisation serves common ends. The book brings together a range of insights from political theory, international relations, international political economy, and development studies to interrogate the exclusionary practices that are constitutive of the contemporary global political economy.

We would like to thank *Millennium* for making this project possible. We also thank the Department of International Relations at the London School of Economics for its institutional support. And most of all, we thank the graduate students of the Department for engendering the lively, critical, and friendly intellectual community that has sustained both this book project and our PhD theses over the several years.

Sarah Owen Vandersluis
Paris Yeros

Part I

Introduction

1. Ethics and Poverty in a Global Era

Sarah Owen Vandersluis and Paris Yeros

In the midst of ongoing globalisations, one cannot fail to question whether the expansion of citizenship, the ideal of the humanist era, is being affirmed or neglected. As globalisations of all sorts continue to deepen, the idea of democratic participation in political community is becoming ever less tangible. One need not reify and romanticise a 'Westphalian' era to note that the democratic *ideals* of the contemporary era, however differently interpreted and underachieved they have been, are becoming more precarious and, for the majority of the world's population, less actual.

Contrary to much contemporary commentary, we claim that a 'global era' cannot exist in a meaningful *moral* sense, unless there is a practical assent to the humanist ideal of citizenship. For an era does not achieve 'globality' merely by the transnationalisation of trade, finance, and production, the revolution in information technology, or the 'deterritorialisation' of identities. If these changes are not also a reflection of social relations of mutual recognition of moral worth and status – the condition of citizenship in any context – globality remains morally deficient. It becomes a trivial globality construed to statistics of economic integration, web links, television antennas, and telephone points. The contemporary era remains highly stratified in the social relations in which it consists; and these relations are easily obscured by the 'unifying' imagery of unqualified and celebratory 'global' language.

It is in this dissenting spirit that we ask, 'Whose Global Era?'. Contemporary writing on globalisation in flourishing, as are *fin de siècle* accounts of the human condition. The present collection of articles is located in these debates. The emphasis, however, is on the failures to realise humanist ideals, evident in the exclusions of a rapidly changing world political economy and the increase in poverty, especially in the closing decades of the century. The dissent of this collection embodies also a 'normative' challenge to prevailing methods of academic theorising that disavow their own normativity and make claims to a scientific knowledge that separates out ethics and politics, theory and praxis. Like the subject of globalisation, poverty is not an empirical problem to be merely measured and explained in nomological terms, which are then to be offered as 'advice to the prince'. Poverty is fundamentally a political and praxiological problem, and theorising about it is too.

Within the contemporary intellectual climate, one noteworthy development has been the transcendence of inherited disciplinary boundaries and the conversion of diverse insights precisely on 'global' questions. Such questions have traditionally been the self-professed preserve of one discipline, International Relations (IR). However, the conceptual tools of IR, deriving from its historic concerns with 'great power politics' and 'politics among nations' in a Westphalian states-system, have been shown by now to have been constituted by an imagination that fell far short of any inclusive globality. For the politics of the 'less powerful' could not be 'factored' into models of systemic order and disruption, nor could norms of 'international society' be about anything other than diplomatic relations among bounded, self-contained, ethically homogeneous, and 'sovereign' states. The critical story in IR has, of course, been told many times over, as new concerns have entered the agenda over the last two decades (such as the environment, gender, ethnicity, race, and social movements); and as new ways of thinking have been brought to bear on world politics (such as the normative approaches of political theory, the Frankfurt school, neo-Gramscian Political Economy, and post-structuralism). Nonetheless, poverty, as a topic, has not entered IR curricula in any significant manner. It seems as though it is not 'global' enough, or 'consequential' enough; it remains a 'Third World' problem, and one which is more suitably investigated as 'Development Studies'.

Development Studies (DS) is indeed where poverty has been compartmentalised. For its own part, however, DS has historically been less inclined towards developing conceptual tools for global questions. While also wedded to the Westphalian ontology at its inception, DS had for long been concerned less with the external affairs of states and more with their internal projects of 'modernisation', consisting in 'economic growth', 'industrialisation', and 'nation-building'. Even transnational issues such as debt or transnational corporations (TNCs) had largely been discussed with state sovereignty and nation-building in mind. And even the bulk of neo-Marxist approaches, the varieties of dependency theory, for example, that addressed the global processes of production, finance, and trade, had been mainly underpinned by the normative ideal of the sovereign state and its national project. Over the last two decades, however, theorising the 'global' in DS has emerged out of the same academy-wide epistemological currents that have swept through IR, along with the interests in the environment, gender, identity more generally, and social movements. The globality of these issues, in empirical subject matter and political implications, have dislodged the state from its privileged ontological and moral status. On these new issues, the two disciplines have converged significantly – and one might even say that disciplinary boundaries have been transcended. Prior to these changes, the only other significant convergence was to be found precisely in neo-

Marxist theorising. This was a convergence not only on matters of method, that of historical materialism, but also on matters of common research focus, that of global capitalist relations. Today, this point of convergence continues, but remains outside the mainstream, for reasons that have to do as much with the challenges that the notion of 'class' has sustained, as with the collapse of Eastern European socialism and the spread of neoliberal convictions.

In this volume we have sought to further past and present initiatives towards the reconciliation of the disciplines, not by any single method, but by a common research focus on poverty in world politics. There are many ways to approach this problem, especially because it requires consideration of a multitude of issues, including those of environment and identity (including class). It seems appropriate to the times, however, to locate the discussion of poverty in relation to, on the one hand, the dilemmas of the 'post-Westphalian' and 'post-national' intellectual contexts, and, on the other, the rapidly changing global political economy. How, then, *should* poverty be theorised after faith in both the capacity and legitimacy of the state has eroded? Or, put differently, if we abandon the *mythical* image of the state as sovereign in its external relations, and as serving the interests of an organic, undifferentiated whole in its international affairs, then to whom should theory be addressed? And whose interests should theory serve?

We suggest that posing these questions – which, in the wake of the 'third debate' in IR and of the 'impasse' in development theory, are all too familiar – requires a two-fold and parallel inquiry (a) in ethics with respect to poverty, and (b) in the exclusionary practices that are constitutive of the contemporary global political economy. The first inquiry requires, at least, a reconsideration of basic questions regarding the nature of political community, rights and obligations, and citizenship. Moreover, it requires that one take seriously approaches to ethics that do not impute ontological primacy to the state/nation, or do not pursue a Kantian-inspired search for universalistic principles of 'right' action that detach ethical discourse from the social context and dichotomise ethics and politics, theory and praxis. The second inquiry requires that one explore the dialogical relations – of which the state itself is one institutional reflection – through which exclusion and poverty are reproduced in the contemporary world. Reflecting these parallel inquiries, the remainder of the book is therefore separated into two sections, the first on ethics and poverty and the second on globalisation poverty.

Finally, there is one further context in which this book is located. Since the early 1990s, the moral grammar of the development dialogue has moved on to such notions as 'participation', 'democratisation', and 'good governance'. In this context, it is important to assess whether or not the contemporary meaning that inheres in these terms lives up to the humanist moral demands that are invoked. For the meaning of such terms is not self-existent and context-free; in the specificity of the contemporary era, the response to humanist moral demands is too often imbued with the particular notions of justice that inhere in the Westphalian, neoliberal, and scientific normative orders. In such a context, the expansion of citizenship falls victim to a plethora of practices that are enabled by the 'legitimacy' of these latter orders.

Humanism and Citizenship in Global Ethical Life

Our first task is to provide an account, as concisely as possible, of the moral constitution of the contemporary epoch.[1] Such a task entails an attempt to articulate the intuitive, 'background' moral languages that constitute contemporary moral consciousness. This is a task that has been championed, among contemporary moral philosophers, by Charles Taylor, and long before him, by G.W.F. Hegel.[2] In the brief account that we provide, we follow certain of Taylor's arguments quite closely, while we diverge significantly on others.

That which is distinct about contemporary ethical life is, first, the humanist moral background languages in which it consists, and, second, their globality. This is a background moral unity which we term the 'humanist order'. It is a background unity that manifests itself *not* in a consensus on moral ends, but in a common moral referent, that of 'human worth', over whose meaning we engage in dialogue and, indeed, struggle. Furthermore, it is a historically peculiar background moral unity that manifests itself in the language of 'rights' and 'citizenship'. When we speak of 'citizenship' as a concept, when we are concerned with it intellectually and politically; indeed, when 'citizenship' and 'rights' are notions that are *intelligible* to us, we are *located* and *founded* in the humanist order.

Put differently still, the humanist order consists in a moral debate over the meaning of the human community, over what it means to be and act 'human'. This is a moral debate that has three features. The first is that it is non-teleological, in the sense that it is neither pre-determined nor does it have an absolute end in sight. Hegel, of course, is the one known to have envisioned the contrary, although even in his case, one may in fact find two Hegels confronting each other. In Robert Solomon's words, one finds 'the more orthodox, academic Hegel, the post-Kantian phenomenologist whose business it is to establish "the Absolute"'; and one also finds the one that is represented here, 'a more radical Hegel, a "historicist" Hegel who sees that the "necessary" movement and transformation of the forms of experience need not be going anywhere in particular and need not have a reachable goal – in order to have a goal'.[3] The second feature of the humanist moral debate is that it is firmly located in communicative relations. Again, Hegel is known to have displaced the primacy of communicative relations by locating moral consciousness in a self-positing Spirit, as well as in the institutional embodiment of the Spirit's reflection, the state. However, there is more than one Hegel on this matter as well. As Axel Honneth has argued, in Hegel's early social philosophy, the relations and movement of recognition were located primarily in the communicative relations of 'a people', not in a monologically defined Spirit. One can retrieve Hegel's concept of recognition from his early social philosophy and re-build a conception of ethical life – and the humanist moral debate – on the basis of communicative relations.[4] The third feature of the humanist moral debate is that, *pace* naturalists, Kantians, and anti-foundationalists, it is inescapable – once in, you cannot opt out. Conceptualising the ethical context as inescapable – or 'ethical nature' as 'inseparable', in Hegel's terms – has been Hegel's fundamental point of departure from naturalist and Kantian moral ontologies, as well as from any moral theory that claims similarly to be able to 'disengage' from the ethical context.[5]

We will clarify the implications of these points in the following discussion of the humanist foundations of citizenship, their historicity and globality. There are three basic claims that we will be making. The first is one already stated earlier, that citizenship requires a humanist background language for its existence. The second follows from the first: citizenship is not a condition that requires a state in the first instance; citizenship is a social status that requires mutual recognition of human moral worth. As such, it is a social status with reference to the human community, not the state. The third claim is that the humanist background language has now attained a global presence, such that it has become a shared and inescapable basis of moral debate in world politics, including the politics of development.

The Humanist Foundations of Citizenship

The first and founding claim in Taylor's thesis is that, beneath any moral reactions and demands that we feel, there lies a particular ontology of the human.[6] Ontologies of the human consist in qualitative distinctions regarding the status and worth of human beings, and they constitute the 'background language' in which all moral obligations that we acknowledge are set. Much like Hegel conceptualised it long ago, such qualitative distinctions are the *inescapable* basis of ethical life. Even if the qualitative distinctions are themselves not articulated explicitly in every-day life (and for this reason are 'background' or 'intuitive'), they are inseparable from the moral obligations that we acknowledge. Taylor's founding claim is exactly opposite to that of 'naturalist' moral philosophers, in Hegel's day as in our own, as well as that of 'anti-foundationalists', who would deny the existence of ontologies in moral thinking entirely, or would otherwise regard them as optional. All moral reactions 'involve claims, whether implicit or explicit, about the nature and status of human beings', about 'what it is that commands our respect'; 'a moral reaction is an assent to, an affirmation of, a given ontology of the human'.[7]

Ontologies of the human, and the moral reactions corresponding to them, have differed widely in human history, and, most significantly, they have differed from the contemporary universalist one – which Taylor confines to a 'modern West'. Taylor argues that, on the one hand, there are a cluster of demands that are acknowledged as moral in all human societies, past and present; he writes, '[p]erhaps the most urgent and powerful cluster of demands that we recognise as moral concern the respect for the life, integrity, and well-being, even flourishing, of others'. On the other hand, however, 'the scope of the demand notoriously varies: earlier societies, and some present ones, restrict the class of beneficiaries to members of the tribe or race and exclude outsiders, who are fair game, or even condemn the evil to a definitive loss of this status'. That which is unique today is that 'for most contemporaries this class is coterminous with the human race'.[8] What this means is that, in the contemporary case, the moral demand to respect the life, integrity, well-being, and flourishing of others applies to *all* human beings. Moreover, in this case it corresponds to a universalist ontology of the human, to an implicit claim that *all* human beings have the same moral status. What this also means is that contemporary moral reactions, or 'gut feelings', such as those to respect 'human rights', are not 'instinctual' in some pre-social sense, but constitute an *affirmation* of a particular ontology of the human, namely, the universalist one.

The second important claim that Taylor makes is that 'moral thinking', far from being conducted by 'disengagement', revolves around three axes. The first axis involves the notion of 'respect' – how to practice it and towards whom, as stated above; the second involves notions of the 'full life' – what kind of life is worthwhile, meaningful, fulfilling; and the third involves the notion of 'dignity' – our sense of ourselves as commanding 'attitudinal' respect.[9] As axes of *moral* thinking, they are, of course, all underpinned by 'background languages'. However, these axes are not always neatly separable. Below, we focus mainly on the first, as it is from this from that the notions of 'rights' and 'citizenship' spring.

Taylor argues that 'modern Western civilisation' is peculiar in that 'its favoured formulation for the principle of respect has come to be in terms of *rights*'.[10] This point is crucial. The moral demand to respect the life, integrity, well-being, and flourishing of others is experienced as a moral demand to respect rights. This is a particular notion of rights: it corresponds to the universalist claim that all human beings have the same moral status, and, as such, it is a notion of rights not as differential privileges, but as equally distributed possessions – as 'human' rights. Moreover, it involves a notion of respect which has three further background languages. First and foremost, '[t]o talk of universal, natural, or human rights', Taylor argues, 'is to connect respect for human life and integrity with the notion of *autonomy*. It is to conceive people as active cooperators in establishing and ensuring the respect which is due to them'.[11] The second background feature of the contemporary notion of respect concerns a unique sensitivity to *suffering*. This connects respect with the sense that human beings should not suffer, and, when further connected with autonomy, it is framed in terms of a right. This, of course, does not mean that practices such as torture have ceased to exist. It means that such practices are regarded as moral violations, that there is no higher moral order within which such practices make sense. The third background feature of the contemporary notion of respect is connected with a unique valuation of *ordinary life*, that is, the life of production and the family, which Taylor traces back to the Reformation and the rejection of elitist moral orders. This feature closely relates to both of the above; it lays stress on human welfare and also implicates the notion of autonomy with the every-day matters of productions and reproduction which are now made relevant to notions of the good life. To affirm ordinary life is to regard productive activity and family life as central to well-being. As Taylor writes,

> I believe that this affirmation of ordinary life, although not uncontested and frequently appearing in secularized form, has become one of the most powerful ideas in modern civilization. It underlies our contemporary 'bourgeois' politics, so much concerned with issues of welfare, and at the same time powers the most influential revolutionary ideology of our century, Marxism, with its apotheosis of man the producer.[12]

Taking together these three background features of the contemporary notion of respect, Taylor concludes that

> [t]his sense of the importance of the everyday in human life, along with its corollary about the importance of suffering, colours our whole understanding of what it is truly to respect human life and integrity. Along with the central place given to autonomy, it defines a version of this demand which is peculiar to our civilization, the modern West.[13]

We wish to go beyond Taylor on this point and argue that this set of qualitative distinctions – or what Taylor himself might call a 'framework'[14] – relating mainly to respect is the shared and inescapable basis of a global moral debate over the meaning of the human community. It is this set of qualitative distinctions that constitutes what we call the 'humanist moral order', and it is this moral order from which demands for 'rights', 'autonomy', and 'participation' spring in every corner of the earth.

In this regard, we profoundly disagree with Taylor's use of the terms 'modern' and 'Western' to designate the contemporary moral consciousness. As any concept, 'the modern' is an ontological and political problem, *not* a mere empirical one. The term 'modern' designates 'civilisational' difference and hierarchy, and, importantly, it designates this in the process of articulating it.[15] Having a sense of moral hierarchy is, of course, unavoidable in any context – to claim that it isn't would be to reject the inescapability of qualitative distinctions in moral thinking. But constructing *civilisational* difference and hierarchy in the way that Taylor wishes to do, involves much more. On the one hand, Taylor wishes to provide a narrative of the cosmological and epistemological changes outlined above – which, as a philosophical project in itself, is fundamental to moral self-understanding. On the other hand, he does so within a Eurocentric narrative which situates 'the modern' within a 'Western' monological historical trajectory.[16] He thus engages in two political projects simultaneously: the articulation the humanist moral consciousness and the construction of a 'Western civilisation'.

The latter political project is not merely and benignly superfluous; it has grave conceptual and political implications. Taylor *constructs* a 'Western' civilisation in the selfsame act of locating the development of the 'self' within a 'West' which, in turn, he posits as bounded, dialogically autonomous, and on a historical journey of its own. Just as nationalist or ethnocentric historiography posits an 'ethnic unit', with an essence, an Archimedean starting-point, a continuity in history, and a destiny, so does a Eurocentric historical imagination posit a 'Western' civilisation, which has an identifiable starting-point, and which is continuous, coherent, never hybrid, and on a historical journey of its own. Otherwise, both 'the West' and its 'modernity' would lose their meaning. The implications of this are that 'the modern' gains meaning through the terms of a monologically understood 'Western' and its 'pre-modernity'; and that it also gains meaning in relation to 'the non-Western' which itself becomes, by definition, 'pre-modern'.

Taylor is, in fact, quite clear on these equations, and goes so far as to create an image of what the 'pre-modern' and 'non-Western' might be. This becomes evident in his discussion of the second axis of moral thinking, the one that involves notions of the 'full life'. 'To understand our moral world', Taylor argues, 'we have to see not only what ideas and pictures underlie our sense of respect for others but also what ideas and pictures underlie our notions of a full life'. This latter has to do with

> questions about how I am going to live my life which touch on the issue of what kind of life is worth living, or what kind of life would fulfill the promise implicit in my particular talents, or the demands incumbent on someone with my endowment, or of what constitutes a

rich, meaningful life – as against one concerned with secondary matters of trivia.[17]

Taylor argues that one of the most important ways in which the 'modern' world differs from others concerns this second axis of moral thinking; and it differs in that the 'moderns' are capable of problematising and questioning notions of the full life, whereas previous 'cultures' were not. In other cultures, Taylor argues,

> some framework stands unquestioned which helps define the demands by which they judge their lives and measure, as it were, their fullness or emptiness: the space of fame in the memory and song of the tribe, or the call of God as made clear in revelation, or, to take another example, the hierarchical order of being in the universe.[18]

By this sleight of hand, Taylor defines a 'pre-modern' and 'non-Western' as morally passive, static, exclusionary, and indeed 'tribal', and counterposes it to a 'modern' which is capable of moral questioning, and is dynamic and inclusionary.[19] Moral difference and hierarchy is thus articulated in very clear 'civilisational' terms: the 'modern West' is the moral antithesis of the 'pre-modern' and 'non-Western'. One is furthermore left with images of a 'West' that is not only in a trajectory of its own, but that its 'modern' phase is also the moral apex of the trajectory of a 'non-West'.

Taylor's account of contemporary moral consciousness inevitably produces these images and associations by *assuming* the existence of a 'West' as an ethical unity which has historically been monologically defined – that it has been in dialogue with itself. By not acknowledging that a 'West' cannot develop in dialogue with itself, Taylor in fact suppresses a whole array of background languages, such as the ones that give rise to notions of 'the tribal', that underlie Eurocentric notions of the full life and that have historically constituted the moral grammar of the relationship of 'the West' to 'the non-West'. Failing to bring these ontologies to light has two consequences. First, Taylor inevitably interprets the 'non-West' on the basis of precisely the 'ideas and pictures' that underlie notions of the full life in the fictionally self-positing 'West'. In this regard, V.Y. Mudimbe's account of the development of a Western identity through images of 'Africa', Edward Said's account of images of the 'Orient', and Tzvetan Todorov's account of the conquest of America offer rich insights and correctives to Taylor's Eurocentric narrative.[20] Similarly, Arturo Escobar's account of the 'modernist' world development project of the post-World War II era brings to light the ignominious practices that have historically been informed and enabled by precisely the Eurocentric images of 'the civilised' and 'the uncivilised', the 'modern' way of being and 'the traditional'.[21] Second, by neglecting to articulate these 'modernist' ontologies, Taylor also fails to acknowledge that the contemporary humanist moral consciousness owes greatly to the 'non-Western' struggles for recognition against images of 'the tribal' and 'traditional', against colonialism and racism. As such, contemporary moral consciousness is not the 'property' of a 'modern West' or any dialogically 'autonomous' civilisational entity. And any account of this moral consciousness must eschew 'civilisational' projects and seek instead the transformation and syncretism of moral languages in their globality.

Before sketching the historical and global dimension of this moral consciousness, it is important to spell out further what it means to say that a humanist order exists. In its most intangible sense, it exists as a set of background languages that, following Taylor, constitute the universalist version of the moral demand to respect the life, integrity, well-being, and flourishing of others. More tangibly, the humanist order exists as a moral framework within which social practices gain meaning as 'acceptable' or 'unacceptable', as 'respecting' or 'denying' rights. This does not mean that the most basic of rights are not violated – that torture and slavery, for example, are not practiced. The humanist order exists as the framework within which such practices gain meaning as 'moral violations', and it is for this reason that they are routinely concealed and denied. In the absence of a humanist order, a claim could be raised as to the virtues of slavery and torture and be redeemed. In a humanist order, such claims are *illegitimate*.

To say that a humanist order exists is not to say that there also exists a consensus over what it is about human beings that is worthy and when this worth is being violated. On the contrary, as already stated, the humanist order exists as a moral debate over the meaning of human worth. This point must be emphasised. A consensus over human worth would imply a homogeneity of moral ends, and, indeed, a 'realised' human community – in the way that Hegel envisioned it. But humanist accounts of the precise nature of the human quality have varied enormously, as have claims about who, when, and where is a 'full' member of the human community, and accordingly, how the human quality should be respected and allowed to flourish. What human worth *is*, is subject to a struggle for recognition. It is not a meaning that exists universally and trans-historically, or outside of the dialogical context. The meaning of human worth develops within a dialogical process of resistance to notions of humanity that are thought to be universal by some, but which are experienced as exclusionary and 'violent' by others. Whether the meaning of humanity is transformed depends, first, on the public condemnation of exclusionary social practices and second on the universal recognition of such practices as morally violent. This would imply the attainment of a higher moral unity – and one which would be subject to further contestation and transformation.

Contemporary struggles over moral meaning are above all struggles for membership in a morally higher *human* community. The diverse and conflictual political projects, moral demands, and obligations that constitute the contemporary humanist dialogical context, whether by workers', women's, or ethnic movements, for example, are animated by the notion of human worth and its non-recognition, regardless of whether this notion remains only implicit in their political claims. Such struggles are most fundamentally staking their claims as *human* subjects whose worth *as such* is being denied and whose rights *as such* ought to be affirmed. In the contemporary humanist dialogical context, a demand for rights is a demand for recognition as a worthy *human* subject.

The contemporary universalist ontology of the human that animates all claims for 'rights' is unique from prior moral orders in that it is driven by egalitarian moral demands, by the negation of hierarchy *tout court*. This egalitarian thrust differs from prior so-called humanisms. Todorov bears out this difference in relation to the violent Christianity practised by the *conquistadores* in their encounter with the Aztecs. He argues that, on the one hand, Christianity has egalitarianism and universalism built into it: 'Christianity's egalitarianism is part of its universalism: since God belongs to all, all belong to God; there is not, in this regard, a difference among peoples nor among individuals'; but, on the other hand, it is also capable of an exclusionary 'egalitarianism': 'Christianity does not combat inequalities (the master will remain a master, the slave a slave, as if this were a difference quite as natural as that between man and woman); but it declares them irrelevant with regard to the unity of all in Christ'.[22] By contrast, the humanist order makes inequality in all its forms and in all spheres of life morally relevant, and in this sense it has revolution built into it.

This finally brings us back to notion of citizenship. Andrew Linklater has recently made the case for 'breaking the nexus between sovereignty [in its statist-absolutist sense, deriving from Thomas Hobbes] territoriality, nationality, and citizenship'.[23] We are thinking along similar lines. Conventionally understood, citizenship refers to two notions simultaneously and conflatingly: (a) the possession of rights, duties, and freedoms, and (b) membership in the community of a state. The latter is often further conflated with membership in a 'nation' – this being one of Hegel's darker legacies. Once conflated, the one notion implies the other: to have rights is to be or become a member of a nation/state. Citizenship here designates a social status, that of a rights-holder, and it designates this with reference to a semiotically demarcated community, that of the 'nation'/'state'. Citizenship is indeed a social status, but not one that presupposes a state in the first instance. Citizenship derives from a humanist moral framework and is a status with reference to the human community, and it is furthermore realised in a moral debate that transcends visions of bounded and dialogically self-contained 'nations' or 'states'.

Citizenship is defined here in different terms which do not derive from theories of contract or conflate community with nationality. Citizenship has five inter-related features. Citizenship is a *social relation* that is meaningful in the specificity of social practices, which themselves derive from our every-day representations of community, of 'who *we* are and are not' and 'what we *do* and don't do'. Second, citizenship is *relative*, as it is contingent on social positionings, such that there may exist, for example, second-class and gendered citizenships. Third, citizenship is a *social status* with reference to the *human* community, even if it is not articulated explicitly. Fourth, citizenship is *dialogical*, in the phenomenological sense that the relation exists in the meaning that is attributed to it and not merely in cognitively unmediated 'social relations' – such as those deriving from a posited 'mode of production'. And fifth, citizenship is *dialectical* in the sense that it is realised by means of a *struggle for recognition* of a person's or group's identity as morally worthy, as a human subject(s), as properly belonging in a (morally higher) human community. States are important, as are international institutions, insofar as they have the wherewithal to enforce a standard of citizenship, or the 'rule of law'. But the state is not ontologically prior in the above conception of citizenship – as it came to be in Hegel's work, for example; nor is it detachable from social relations, such that it can be viewed as an external imposition that is instrumental for the creation of order out of chaos – as it was for Hobbes. Both states and institutions, as well as the 'law' that they enforce, are fully reflective of dialogical relations which, furthermore, transcend the 'enclosed locality' of territorial boundaries as well as nationalities.

Citizenship is the *ideal* of humanism. The meaning of human worth has historically been subject to constant challenge, as 'ordinary' social practices have come to be known as exclusionary and as violative of human worth. It is through this process that hierarchical notions of humanity have been contested and the meaning of humanity itself has been transformed. At every step of the way, the challenge has entailed the negation of one interpretation of 'humanity' and its overcoming by a more inclusive, morally higher humanity. As such, the object of social struggles has been, and will continue to be, the progressive transformation of, and membership in, the human community. Despite the absence of a 'realised' human community (and its conceptual impossibility), membership in it, *the expansion of citizenship*, is the ideal of the humanist epoch.

The Historicity and Globality of Humanism

That which is distinct about the contemporary moral epoch is not only that it is humanist but that it is global. This epoch is a far cry from the one described by Todorov in *The Conquest of America* – an epoch made up of a number of mutually unintelligible dialogical orders. The encounter between Christopher Columbus and the Indians, as Todorov tells of it, is one of mutual incomprehension of each other's signs, misinterpretation of intentions, and, ultimately, the objectification and annihilation of the Aztecs by the Spaniards. It was an encounter in an ethical vacuum. There was no background language common to both Spaniards and Indians on the basis of which to debate moral worth, no common basis to struggle for recognition. Over what moral referents would the struggle have occurred? Was it to be a struggle for recognition as 'Aztec', as 'Indian', as 'Spanish'? But how would these terms have related to each other? What 'kind' was the Indian, or Aztec, or Spanish? There was confusion, wonder, projection of, and scramble for, meaning – all too reminiscent of Hegel's two-person master-slave dialectic.[24] For their part, the Indians thought that the Spaniards might be gods. For his part, Columbus understood them more or less as animals. He failed to recognise such fundamentals (to us, at least) as the diversity of languages – that is, that there was a language that was both different and also qualified as a 'language'. He failed to recognise the existence of customs, rites, and religion among the Indians; what he saw was a cultural void; their practices did not fit his categories of customs, rites, and religion. And, ultimately, Columbus failed to see the Indians themselves as 'different' and 'equal' at the same time. They were either equal and identical to him and, hence, assimilable into *his own* moral order; or they were different and inferior: 'by gradual steps, Columbus will shift from assimilationism, which implied an equality of principle, to an ideology of enslavement, and hence the assertion of the Indian's inferiority'.[25] A master-slave dialectic of global-historic proportions thus unfolds.

The contemporary period is starkly different in its moral background: such encounters, such semiotic voids are a rarity. The dialogical relations that were violently born of the colonial encounter did not somehow cease or whither away; and they were certainly not replaced by another ethical vacuum. An image of such an ethical vacuum has recently been put forth by Linklater, in his assessment of the 'post-Westphalian' era.[26] On the contrary, moral referents have proliferated since the colonial encounter, and moral languages have hybridised to make up a dense and tense web of meanings. The moral languages of religion, race, ethnicity, nation, class, and gender have come to be in wide currency, as has, most importantly, that of humanity. The latter is precisely now the universal background language on the basis of which to make and redeem claims to moral worth. The global pervasiveness of the language of rights is now irrefutable. That which is *not* different between the colonial encounter and the humanist present – and this ought to be equally stressed – is that genocides continue to be perpetrated. They have even gone on to assume 'systemic' varieties which distance perpetrator and victim and which endlessly diffuse responsibility. Such is the case of the 'economic' genocide of the closing decades of the twentieth century, which non-coincidentally has its roots in the master-slave dialectic that was born of the colonial encounter and which now goes under the label of the 'development dialogue'.[27] The humanist present does not make genocide obsolete, but it provides a common moral language on the basis of which to *indict* the objectification and annihilation of human beings. This is a background moral unity that was absent in the colonial encounter and the genocide that ensued.

Any account of the historicity and globality of the moral present cannot overlook the dialogical relations that were inaugurated by the colonial encounter; these have been fundamental to the humanism that we know today. *Pace* Taylor, humanism has not been a 'Western' affair. The contemporary meaning of humanity owes much to the dialogical relations of the coloniser and the colonised, the struggles against slavery, the struggles against a racist colonial regime, and the struggles against a global capitalist dispensation. Within the post-War development dialogue, further transformations to the meaning of humanity owe to struggles against patriarchy, as well as struggles against environmental destruction and the robbing of the well-being of future generations.

These transformations demonstrate the historical contingency of universalist interpretations of humanity. At every historical juncture, a universalist interpretation of humanity has come under attack for the exclusions that are discovered in it. We can trace interpretations of human worth that were once considered secure by some, only to be challenged and transformed. We may recall that interpretations of humanity which were once deemed universal, such as that, for example, that derives from natural law and that conceives of sameness on the basis of an individual faculty of reason, met their opposition by further interpretations, in the form of the Romanticist and Socialist critiques. The latter found the precepts of the first to be false, and criticised them for undermining the expressive and social nature of human beings, and acting as the source of domination rather than self-realisation. We recall also, with the benefit of Todorov's account, that, during the encounter between coloniser and colonised, the humanism that was gaining currency in Europe was in fact constitutive of hierarchies of being which, upon the encounter, manifested themselves in distinctions between the Christian and non-Christian, the more and the less civilised.[28] This interpretation of humanity met its challenge much later, in nationalist anti-colonial movements that were seeking recognition as 'different' from a humanity thus conceived and as 'equal' in a more inclusive human identity. 'Are We Not Also Men?' was the challenge put to colonial interpretations of humanity, as Terence Ranger's recent account of an African nationalist struggle recalls.[29] The historical record is indeed replete with struggles for recognition against secure, universalist interpretations of humanity, which, on the one hand, claim to be inclusive, but on the other, represent humanity in particular terms which distinguish between not only the more and the less 'civilised', but also 'rational', 'knowledgeable', and 'competent'. Today such struggles are ongoing among labour, women's, and environmental movements, as well as within and among identity groups more broadly defined. While we may not know what forms such struggles might take in the future, they are bound to continue, as further 'violations' of human worth and agency come to be known as such.

In this light, 'civilisational' talk such as Taylor's has grave political implications. The construction of a semiotically demarcated entity, like a 'civilisation', is also a claim on an 'essence' – an ethical substance that is self-contained, a particular way of being. This, in turn, risks labelling counter-claims to this posited essence as 'foreign' and 'inauthentic', indeed as 'betrayals' of the community. Such 'civilisational' talk is in poor historical company with the logic that labelled struggles against 'racial superiority' and 'imperial right to rule' as subversive. A 'civilisational' imagination implies also the existence of other demarcated ethical entities – perhaps 'African', 'Asian', or 'Islamic' – with essences of their own; and it is thereby liable to denounce claims for 'rights' within the posited 'non-Wests' also as 'foreign' and as 'betrayals' of their 'own' ethical unities. Contemporary claims by Asian dictators about 'Asian values' serve precisely this purpose. Finally, there is a corollary of the above two implications: since civilisations are semiotically-ethically self-contained, there is no 'cross-civilisational' obligation; within this logic, in other words, one does not 'fail' to ascend to humanist moral demands when, say, workers' rights are eroded elsewhere or when genocide is perpetrated 'outside' one's own 'civilisation'. This, in fact, brings to mind Todorov's observation regarding the 'civilisational boundary' logic of the Spaniards which enabled the massacre of the Aztecs in the 'remote' Americas, and which continues to enable violence 'outside':

> [i]t is as though the conquistadors obeyed the rule of Ivan Karamazov: 'everything is permitted'. Far from central government, far from royal law, all prohibitions give way, the social link, already loosened, snaps....What the Spaniards discover is the contrast between the metropolitan country and the colony, for radically different moral laws regulate conduct in each: massacre requires an appropriate context.[30]

Taylor, of course, does not make these claims. They are the dangerous implications of his historical narrative. In all fairness to Taylor, there are hints in his thesis as to the globality of humanism, though it is not theorised as such. Writing in the context of the 1980s, Taylor comments as follows:

> the moral ontology behind any person's views can remain largely implicit. Indeed it usually does, unless there is some challenge which forces it to the fore. The average person needs to do very little thinking

about the bases of universal respect, for instance, because just about everyone accepts this as an axiom today. The greatest violators hide behind a smoke screen of lies and special pleading. Even racist regimes, like the one in South Africa, present their programmes in the language of separate but equal development; while Soviet dissidents are jailed on various trumped-up charges or hospitalized as 'mentally ill', and the fiction is maintained that the masses elect the regime.[31]

The moral debate over the meaning of human worth is indeed global. Once may certainly despair at the gulf that exists between interpretations of humanity. However, the mere presence of humanist background languages has far-reaching implications for the conduct of politics in every corner of the earth. It is the presence of such notions as human worth and autonomy, the valuation of ordinary life, and the avoidance of suffering, that make *intelligible* all claims for rights – be they claimed as 'natural', 'inherent', 'social', 'national', or 'cultural'. In the absence of a notion of human worth, such claims would sound completely absurd. The claims of the Universal Declaration of Human Rights would fall on puzzled ears. But, they don't and, furthermore, they are intelligible even by those who do not subscribe to them. Similarly, the contemporary demands for more meaningful inclusion in politics world-wide, whether by labour and womens' movements, or by ethnic, racial, and religious groups, are intelligible even by those who deny recognition. It is on the basis of a notion of human worth, and equal membership in morally higher humanity, that demands for recognition and rights are made everywhere.

Citizenship and Development

The 'development dialogue' is itself one context in which the humanist dialectic is being played out. It is a dialogical relation in which claims are made about the meaning of humanity, in which social status inheres, and from which rights and obligations derive on a global scale. States are fully reflective of, and participant in, the relations of this dialogue, as are, of course, international institutions, like the International Monetary Fund (IMF), the World Bank, the United Nations, and the World Trade Organisation (WTO), along with a plethora of other voices that strive to establish the 'truth' of their claims in the consciousnesses of local and global 'masters'. In light of the previous discussion, this era of 'development' has not been a 'historically singular experience', as Escobar understands it, with a 'birth' in the wake of World War II and an envisionable 'post-' era after its 'demise'.[32] The term 'development', indeed, made its debut in international politics in the wake of World War II, and here it came to designate an array of notions, including 'economic growth', 'industrialisation', and 'nation-building'. But this was the 'modernist' interpretation of humanity within an ongoing humanist dialectic. It was also an elitist and violent vision, a *betrayal* of the humanist ideal of citizenship. And it was a vision that came to monopolise the meaning of 'development' for several decades, before giving way to a 'neoliberal', and even more violent, vision of humanity. Such visions, however, do not exhaust the ways of being and acting human; they do not exhaust the humanist dialectic and notions of development. That this is so is in fact demonstrated in Escobar's own account, in which he puts forth a 'development' vision of his own – despite the 'post' prefix that he attaches to it. Escobar's vision is firmly rooted in the humanist order and its revolutionary drive to abolish hierarchy; indeed, he espouses the recognition of ways of 'being human' that *differ* from the modernist one and that are *equal* in a higher moral order. In the contemporary humanist order, struggles for recognition are themselves struggles for the development of humanity. Despite Escobar's claims, given the humanist order in which we are located, 'development' can only be understood as the recognition of human subjectivity within an ongoing humanist dialectic.

In the specificity of the contemporary development dialogue, the expansion of citizenship is conditioned by the particularity of three further normative orders, in addition to the humanist one. We mean 'normative order' in a sense similar to Taylor's 'framework': as a framework consisting in notions of right and wrong, by which political practices in international affairs are enabled, and by reference to which they gain legitimacy. Together with the humanist framework, these orders are constitutive of global ethical life, though in a conflictual manner. The first of these orders is the Westphalian states-system, which is founded on the principle of state sovereignty and which identifies the state as the proper location of citizenship, or the 'full life'.[33] The second is the liberal economic order, which is founded on the idea of the voluntary contract between equal agents and which derives justice from the market.[34] And the third is a scientific epistemology, which relies on a positivist method for the validation of truth claims, and which thereby identifies who is and is not a legitimate knower/agent in politics.[35] All three orders come into conflict with humanist moral demands – by making claims, respectively, as to (a) the 'appropriate' location of political action for the cultivation of the 'full life'; (b) the moral substance itself of the full life; and (c) the proper subjects and objects of political action in its cultivation.

The Westphalian, liberal, and scientific frameworks were fully present in the whole of the post-War era, including the present one of structural adjustment. The post-War dialogue reflected an accommodation between the Westphalian and liberal orders, an accommodation which bestowed legitimacy to statist development practices, within an international trade regime whose objectives were the progressive liberalisation of the trading order.[36] In this era, as Escobar has shown, a body of knowledge emerged about the 'Third World', or 'developing states', it gained the status of an academic discipline, and adopted the scientific methodology and technocratic praxiology that was current among the other disciplines. The development orthodoxy defined the moral ends of development as consisting in the 'modernisation' package of economic growth, industrialisation, and nation-building, and relied on scientific and technocratic means to achieve it. Despite considerable challenges to the orthodoxy over the years, the dialogue reflected only the absence of meaningful membership in the human community.[37]

The structural adjustment phase did not improve the status of citizenship. The crisis in international finance in the 1970s was followed by a transformation in the international politics of development which reshuffled the accommodation between the Westphalian and liberal orders and took the scientism of development theory to new heights. The 1980s saw a shift in the responsibility of structural adjustment onto Third World states, and defined 'adjustment' and 'getting the prices right' as an end in itself.[38] Importantly, the 1980s saw the rise of the IMF and World Bank to unprecedented pre-eminence in the development dialogue, attaining the status of 'global governance agencies' by coordinating bilateral and private lending to indebted states on the condition of policy changes and by taking the leading intellectual role in defining the ends and means of development.[39] The 1980s was eventually acknowledged to be 'the lost decade', and after mounting criticism from diverse circles, the development dialogue moved into the 1990s revived with the new grammar of 'enabling environment', 'sustainable growth', 'participation', and, most notoriously, 'good governance'. This new grammar has consisted in a further and more blatant betrayal of the humanist ideal of citizenship. On the one hand, this new language pretends to be supportive of the broadening of the development dialogue and the abolition of hierarchy by making explicit use of such humanist notions as 'participation' and 'consensus-building'. On the other hand, it interprets and practices these notions within the ever-present Westphalian, liberal, and scientific frameworks.

A series of statements by the Bank have sought especially to define 'good governance'. The need for such a concept arose in the latter part of the 1980s, at the time when the Bank's structural adjustment dream was turning into a nightmare. Based on a decade of 'learning', the official theory of development began to undergo another transformation, consisting in the realisation that the state had a role in development. What was needed was 'not just less government but better government – government that concentrates its effects less on direct interventions and more on enabling others to be productive'.[40] The document that launched the new way of thinking was entitled *Sub-Saharan Africa: From Crisis to Sustainable Growth: A Long-Term Perspective*, and it was followed by the *World Development Report 1990* on poverty, and a booklet specifically on *Governance and*

Development.[41] This new discourse was a result not simply of the failure of adjustment but of a conjuncture of several events in international politics. These included the fall of Eastern European socialism and a new inclination in the West to promote multi-party democracy in 'transitional economies' in general, including the Third World. The new discourse was also a response to adjustment fatigue and a wave of political protests. In the late 1980s and early 1990s, Africa especially experienced an eruption of political protests directed against the continuing collapse of living standards to the levels of the 1960s and erosions of rights to wages, education, and health care. In what appeared to be the 'second liberation', democratic movements gained momentum, demanding the respect of human rights, inclusion in politics, political accountability, constitutional change, and an end to abusive and cleptocratic patrimonial government. This, paradoxically, was also the 'enlightened authoritarian' government on which the Bank had staked its hopes for the implementation of structural adjustment.[42]

The Bank certainly had to redefine itself and make its project somehow relevant to these new realities, lest it would risk losing its leading intellectual role in the definition of development and in the coordination of the world development project. As Peter Gibbon observed early in the decade, '[governance] was part of the assertion of a claim by the World Bank to broader and broader areas of policy expertise, connected to and ideologically justifying expansion in the scope both of the [aid] regime and the World Bank's own role in it'.[43] Thus, at the end of the 1980s, the Bank resolved that the crisis of the 1980s was a crisis of governance – *not of liberalism, scientism, and Westphalianism*; simply put, '[a] root of weak economic performance in the past has been the failure of public institutions'.[44] Furthermore, the Bank rediscovered a fine humanist project, namely, the alleviation of poverty, after having displaced it from its agenda for a decade. The Bank remarks that, despite progress in income and consumption and well-being, 'it is all the more staggering – and all the more shameful – that more than one billion people in the developing world are living in poverty'.[45] Importantly, the moral ends of development did not change. Structural adjustment was to remain an end in itself, while the re-discovered sympathy for the poor was to be integrated into the structural adjustment project and was to find expression in 'targeted transfers' and 'safety nets'.[46]

The means to these ends was to be 'good governance'. Besides 'sound' macroeconomic policy, the Bank now recognised that efficiency in the public service, reliability in the judicial system, and accountability of public administration are fundamental to the process of economic restructuring. In fact, the Bank even spoke of the need for 'political renewal':

> Ultimately, better governance requires political renewal. This means a concerted attack on corruption from the highest to the lowest levels.

This can be done by setting a good example, by strengthening accountability, by encouraging public debate, and by nurturing a free press. It also means empowering women and the poor by fostering grassroots and nongovernmental organizations (NGOs), such as farmers associations, cooperatives, and women's groups.[47]

This is certainly an utterance that makes sense within a humanist order. However, this is not the only order from which it derives its substance. First, despite talk about encouraging 'public debate', this does not also imply the encouragement of debate over the *moral ends* of development. Within a scientific framework, moral ends are assumed to be universal and 'given', not variable and subject to debate. Second, for the Bank, the moral ends of development consist in the implementation of structural adjustment and the cultivation of neoliberal justice. And, finally, the location of 'public debate' and of the cultivation of this 'good life' is assumed to be the state.

It is therefore not odd that the term 'governance' was selected, instead of a term with a more meaningful history in political theory, like 'government' or 'democracy'. The Bank sought to engage in political theory *and* sidestep all the difficult questions. Thus, '[b]y governance is meant the exercise of political power to manage a nation's affairs'.[48] The nation is the state is the nation; its 'affairs' are to be 'managed' – not debated. And, most extraordinarily, the 'political' that is to be 'exercised' is not a conceptual problem. This definition of governance was specified further in *Governance and Development*. Here, the 'affairs' to be managed relate specifically to 'a country's economic and social resources for development'. This is a crucial point. Developmental affairs, according to the Bank, are 'technical' in nature, not political. For this reason, they do not raise the need to engage with the 'political' as a conceptual problem; nor with questions regarding the type of regime that implements development policy – that is, whether it is authoritarian or not; nor does the Bank violate its own 'non-political' mandate when it provides its 'technical' developmental expertise. Thus, we arrive at the definition of 'good' governance:

[g]ood governance, for the Bank, is synonymous with sound development management. The Bank's experience has shown that the programs and projects it helps finance may be technically sound, but fail to deliver anticipated results for reasons connected to the quality of government action....The Bank's concern with sound development management thus extends beyond building the capacity of public sector management to encouraging the formation of the rules and institutions which provide a predictable and transparent framework for the conduct of public and private business and to promoting accountability for economic and financial performance.[49]

Relevant areas of governance are said to include public sector management, accountability, the legal framework for development, and information and transparency.

The theme throughout is consistent with the Bank's understanding of where the full life is located, what it consists in, and how it is to be cultivated. For example, in its discussion of accountability, the problem is presented in technical terms, as one of incongruence of public policy with actual implementation and inefficient allocation of public resources. 'Officials' (*of states*) must thus be held responsible for their actions, and (*neoliberal*) 'policy' must become more responsive. At the 'macro' level, accountability is to be improved by better monitoring, evaluation, and accounting practices. At the 'micro' level, it is to be improved by encouraging competition and participation: competition gives the public an 'exit' option when dissatisfied with a service; participation enables the public to have a 'voice', to articulate preferences and demands.[50] The Bank's rationale for participation is particularly revealing of its understanding of it as a concept: 'The Bank's experience suggests that participation can be important to project success and sustainability....Participatory approaches in Bank projects have been tested successfully in a variety of sectors....The most important lesson has been that participation is a question of efficiency, as well as being desirable in its own right'.[51] 'Participation' as being a good in itself receives feeble and token reference, while the main 'lesson' is that it is instrumental to achieving pre-given ends. As far as the Bank is concerned, participation is not about recognition of human subjectivity, about inclusion in a dialogue over the moral ends of development. The Bank makes a parallel case in its discussion of the legal framework for development and the 'rule of law'.[52] The Bank explicitly opts for a 'formal' concept of law, thereby concerning itself with issues of consistency and transparency in the enforcement of the law, not with the ethical substance itself of the law.[53]

Thus, the thrust of the Bank's 'humanism' is clearly not about a commitment to the recognition of the moral worth of the 'non-experts' that have been excluded from the development dialogue; it is not about recognising that liberalism is a deeply contested moral end, and not a universal and given one; and it is not about recognising that the location of the 'development dialogue' transcends the perimeters of atomised states and encompasses the international financial institutions themselves. In fact, the technical understanding of development that the Bank espouses avoids having to raise such 'political' questions entirely, and, by extension, avoids having to raise the question of the democratisation of the Bank itself. The Bank's new emphasis on 'governance and development' has been a blatant betrayal of the humanist ideal of citizenship.

To say this, finally, is of course not to say that accountability and transparency are not important in any context. It is to say that the 'crisis of governance', in the Bank's terms, is only one of the many crises which the Bank otherwise chooses to overlook. And although many of the contemporary struggles for recognition around the world *do* now employ 'crisis of governance' language and *do* struggle for the establishment of 'the rule of law' and the abolition of patrimonial government, this is by no means a vindication of the Bank's vision. For such struggles adopt a holistic understanding of both governance and law, and are themselves at odds with the liberal, scientific, and Westphalian practices of the Bank. Two cases are worth mentioning by way of example. One is the African Rights report on *Justice in Zimbabwe*. This pays due respect to *both* formal and substantive matters in the delivery of justice. Importantly, furthermore, it criticises the 'foreign donor' version of 'good governance' for undermining the delivery of justice by promoting social and economic conditions which themselves impede egalitarian access to the judicial process.[54] The second example is again drawn from the Zimbabwean context and is that of the Zimbabwe Congress of Trade Unions (ZCTU). Having now become the main opposition force in Zimbabwean politics, the ZCTU has for long been struggling not only against corruption, mismanagement, and the suppression of dialogue. It has also been struggling for 'needs-based' and 'worker-friendly' economic policies, in a country that has been ravaged by both patrimonialism and the liberal logic.[55] Both cases demonstrate that no version of 'governance' is truly committed to the expansion of citizenship as long as it hides behind 'non-political' facades.

The Contributions to the Book

The following chapters in this book address these issues in varying ways. Their common concern is with the theorisation of global poverty in a contemporary context marked by a rapidly changing global political economy and by the erosion of faith in, and indeed the supersession of, the capacity and legitimacy of states. The contributions also converge in their conviction in normative and critical research with respect to global poverty. The book is divided into two parts, the first concerned with ethics with respect to poverty, and the second with the exclusionary practices that are constitutive of the global political economy.

In Part II, Fiona Robinson, Jenny Edkins, and Jan Aart Scholte all employ concepts and methods that stand opposed to the conventional rights-based and Kantian traditions. They draw insights from a broadly defined 'dialogical' tradition, which places ontological primacy on social relations and the phenomenology of the development dialogue. Respectively, the authors draw on feminist ethics of care, post-structuralist ethics, and discourse ethics.

At the outset, Robinson distinguishes her approach to ethics from rights-based and Kantian ethics, which abstract the individual from the social context and which conceptually separate ethics and politics. These two conventional approaches assume a 'generalised' individual, thereby ignoring the social relations in which the problem of poverty is embedded and which themselves require a radical process of transformation if poverty is to be eradicated. Robinson argues that, although rights language has now achieved global significance, and is furthermore useful as a rallying cry for social change, rights-based ethics do not address or capture the scale of activities and the experience that would be required to change social relations and eradicate poverty. Kantian approaches, on the other hand, focus overwhelmingly on the concept of obligation and place emphasis on the search for the justification of moral action. The Kantian strategy is deontological in the sense that it seeks justification for moral actions that are not a reflection of existing behaviour, and it thus falters on the question of motivation. By contrast, Robinson argues that an 'ethics of care', first articulated by Carol Gilligan in her work on 'women's' moral thinking, emphasises the relationships in which persons are located, not abstract logic and systems of rules. Robinson goes further than Gilligan, however, to a 'critical' ethics of care which seeks to avoid the gendered stereotyping of moral thinking, as well as the paternalist forms of 'caring' that may follow from such stereotypes, such as those that hold between North and South and rich and poor. Thus, a critical ethics of care takes as its starting point existing relationships and motivations, but problematises and interrogates these, in order to transform them into relationships that are based on mutual respect. Robinson, finally, refers to the experiences of the Grameen Bank in Bangladesh and the Self Employed Women's Association (SEWA) in India, both of which reject purely economic interpretations of poverty and, instead, value and seek to cultivate the quality of social networks in the eradication of poverty. Robinson argues that it is this form of ethics, which relies on interrogating relationships and building solidarity, that has the potential to transform relationships towards the eradication of poverty.

Edkins evaluates the recent, post-Cold War theorisation of famine as a phenomenon that is linked to war, and that has now come under the label of 'complex emergency'. This new approach interprets famine not as a 'natural' disaster, in the Malthusian sense, nor as an 'economic' problem, in the 'entitlement' terms that Amartya Sen has put forth. 'Complex emergency' theorists understand famines as ruthlessly conflictual socio-political processes, which have 'winners' and 'losers', and which are exacerbated by 'humanitarian' aid. Edkins takes issue with all of the above approaches for their 'technical' understanding of famines, an understanding that forecloses the possibility of ethical judgement and political decision. Edkins argues that Sen, on the one hand, refutes the Malthusian paradigm, by interpreting famines as 'man-made' and, furthermore, as being possible 'within' the law, that is, without involving the violation of property rights. Sen's is an interpretation that is addressed to governments and recommends the development of 'early warning systems', public works programmes, and the provision of 'safety nets'. 'Complex emergency' theorists point out, in turn, that Sen's approach excludes the 'extra-legal' violence inherent in famines, such as intentional starvation, which is perpetrated by the same governments to which Sen is addressed. On the other hand, 'complex emergency' theorists address themselves to 'aid donors', whom they seek to 'educate' in 'conflict analysis' and in more 'sophisticated' technologies of 'relief', while ignoring the violence of the international system and international law. Edkins employs Derridean methods to reveal the ethical dilemmas that are obfuscated by approaches that treat famine relief as a matter of technology and not ethics, and as the province of 'experts', be they located in 'development studies' or 'conflict resolution'.

Scholte, finally, assesses the status of democracy in a 'post-sovereign' era, with a focus on the dialogue between the IMF and civic associations. Scholte argues that, while exchanges between the Fund and civic groups have proliferated in the 1990s, they continue to fall far short of a democratic dialogue. The expansion of global monetary and financial regulation under the supervision of the Fund has gradually transformed the Fund into a supra-state central bank. This supraterritorial development has given rise to the need to a redesign democracy at a global level. The democratisation of global monetary and financial governance should be sought, Scholte argues, via a more open, inclusive, transparent, and critically creative dialogue, with participants that are accountable to, and representative of, constituencies affected. Scholte evaluates the motivations, limitations, and constraints to the democratisation of the dialogue. The motivations of the Fund to enter into dialogue with civic groups have been mixed – partly reactive in the context of increasing public pressure, partly based on self-interest in avoiding the blocking of financial contributions to the Fund, and partly geared towards 'consensus-building' in pursuit of public acceptance of reforms. Civic groups themselves have varied widely in their motivations – between conformists who accept the general principles of the Fund, reformists who accept the need for an IMF-type of institution but with different principles, and radicals who seek the abolition of the Fund. Scholte argues that the limitations of the dialogue have been mainly of three types. First, the Fund is more receptive to conformist organisations and Northern and urban based groups, and less receptive to reformists, radicals, and grassroots organisations. Second, the exchanges in the dialogue have been shallow, as both the Fund and civic groups give low priority to their interaction and as the Fund tends to value 'expert' opinion. And third, the dialogue has been limited due to the existence of entrenched positions on both sides of the debate and a lack of 'two-way' listening. The constrains to the dialogue are equally as significant, and they have been of a resource and structural nature. To date, few resources have been devoted to the strengthening and institutionalisation of the dialogue, there has been lack of staff assigned to this task, and there has been a lack of coordination on both sides, as well as a lack of access to information on the Fund. Furthermore, the Fund maintains a culture of secrecy, while civic groups themselves are often not democratic and transparent. Finally, Scholte argues, North/South, class, and gender biases, along with a persisting emphasis on the principle of sovereignty, all serve to prohibit the democratic expansion of the dialogue.

In Part III of the book, Marianne Marchand, Paul Nelson, Mustapha Kamal Pasha, and Julian Saurin address the contemporary process of global restructuring. The authors provide critiques of the way poverty is being theorised as well as interpretations of the various aspects of globalisation and its exclusions. Taken together, the authors address gender and development, NGO-World Bank politics in the policy domains of environment, poverty, and structural adjustment, the globalisation of the state, the parallel emergence of 'global civil society', and the 'public' and 'hidden' transcripts of globalisation.

Marchand assesses the recent shift within the gender and development field towards a concern with global restructuring, and offers a critique of the limitations of the new debate. Marchand argues that current theorising within the field retains a narrow economistic focus, despite the strides being made to refute neoclassical economic theory. The field continues to interpret dis-empowerment and empowerment in economic, and not socio-political, terms. Furthermore, the economistic focus and the employment of universal gender categories results in the identification of women as a uniform and 'vulnerable group', which obscures the differences among women and which reifies them as passive and as objects. Marchand highlights the shift towards 'global' issues and the new interventions in the debate, and provides a critique and a research agenda for coming to terms with the complexities and contingencies of global restructuring in relation to gender and development. Marchand argues that a fundamental problem continues to be the type of questioning that founds research in the field, which is primarily concerned with refuting neoclassical economics rather than with investigating the different and contradictory experiences of women in trade and global restructuring. The latter starting point would better address the multiple dimensions of empowerment.

Nelson addresses the globalisation of governance with reference to the interaction between the World Bank and three Northern NGO advocacy networks that focus on environment, poverty, and structural adjustment. Like Scholte, Nelson evaluates the exchange between one of the two Bretton Woods institutions and alliances of civic groups, in an era which is marked by the supersession of state-level policy-making. Nelson argues that these issue-specific NGO networks have won important victories on certain matters of public policy, while they have been sidelined on others. The three networks are united in a demand for greater popular participation as the key to just and sustainable political and economic systems. Nelson makes two arguments specifically: that each network has advanced a different version of 'participation' and that, in turn, the Bank has selected, adapted, and adopted the various demands in accordance with its own mandate. In this way, the Bank has presented itself as an ally of the NGOs – even a leader in the promotion of their respective agendas – and has also expanded its influence over governments in response to NGO demands, in a so-called 'boomerang effect'. The most important successes have been achieved in the realm of environmental regulation, in which NGOs have brought national development issues to international policy venues and have taken advantage of international norms. Less successful have been the campaigns for changing the Bank's priorities to become more sensitive to social considerations. In this case, the Bank has been receptive to demands for participation, when 'participation' has been couched in terms of economic effectiveness rather than as a political good in itself. And most unsuccessful has been the campaign to reduce the Bank's influence over national policy. Nelson concludes that the Bank is not a monolithic institution that is insulated from civic actors, but its commitment to 'participation' lags far behind its commitment to the liberal project.

With reference to the context of South Asia, Pasha evaluates the neoliberal restructuring of the state and the parallel promotion of 'global civil society' for the provision of security and the alleviation of poverty. Pasha argues that globalisation raises issues beyond economic restructuring. Globalisation has radically transformed state-society complexes and the role of the state in international relations. At the same time, 'global civil society' is being viewed as the new site for building community and for providing the services that were once the responsibility of the state. However, Pasha argues that without decentralised, participatory structures, and without a state committed to social justice, the gains from globalisation will accrue to those with power and influence, and not those that are least able to join the race to the market. 'Global civil society' is not a homogeneous and undifferentiated entity, as it is portrayed in liberal discourse, nor the aggregate of atomised 'interests'; it is structured by capitalist relations on a global scale. NGOs do not offer an alternative for transformation, as they are either tied to international financial institutions or are engaged in 'philanthropic' pursuits. They thus do not escape the 'public policy' (as opposed to a 'political economy') approach to poverty alleviation. Poverty, in South Asia, as elsewhere, continues to be regarded as an externality of the market-driven order, not an intrinsic part of it; the poor continue to be regarded as objects of policy, not as a class of people in relation to the sources of social wealth.

Finally, in similar light, Saurin evaluates the 'official' transcript of a 'benign' capitalist development in the era of global restructuring, and the neglect of the 'hidden transcript', the lived experiences of working people. Saurin, moreover, indicts the discipline of IR for its focus on 'great powers' and the state as the agents of history, at the expense of the vast majority of the world's population and their social struggles. Saurin makes the case for a holistic social theory that, on the one hand, recognises the structuring forces of a capitalist world economy and the legacy of imperialism, and, on the other hand, examines how people understand and organise the production and reproduction of their own lives. The 'official' story of development has for long centred on the state as the location of development, even measuring development in 'national' league tables within a continuum of the 'developing' and the 'developed', while effacing the global capitalist relations that have given rise to the state as the political form of capitalist accumulation. In the present era, the state itself has not 'eroded', but has been transformed to 'manage' capital, while its responsibility in the formation of public policy has been subverted. Saurin argues that the failure of public policy, then and now, has consisted in the disregard of the 'real' experiences of development and in the non-recognition that poverty is the product of the combined and uneven development of capitalism.

The collection of articles by no means endeavours to cover the full breadth of topics with respect to poverty in a globalising era. Moreover, the collection does not exhaust the numerous approaches to the subject. We do hope, however, that the articles will provoke further debate and, ultimately, contribute to the thinking, writing, and practicing of a 'development' that lives up to humanist moral demands.

NOTES

1. We note that this account is not necessarily shared by the contributors to this volume.
2. Charles Taylor's most comprehensive statement is in his *Sources of the Self: The Making of the Modern Identity* (Cambridge: Cambridge University Press, 1989).
3. Robert C. Solomon, *In the Spirit of Hegel* (Oxford: Oxford University Press, 1983), p. 15. Solomon's interpretation of Hegel differs from Taylor's, the latter tending to read mainly the absolute side of Hegel. See Charles Taylor, *Hegel* (Cambridge: Cambridge University Press, 1975).
4. See Axel Honneth, *The Struggle for Recognition: The Moral Grammar of Social Conflict* (Cambridge: Cambridge University Press, 1995), especially Chapters 2 and 3. For one of Hegel's early statements on ethical life, see G.W.F. Hegel, *Natural Law*, trans. T.M. Knox (Philadelphia, PA: University of Pennsylvania Press, 1975 [1802/03]).

5. See Taylor's discussion of this in Taylor, *op. cit.*, in note 3, Chapters 1–4. Note Taylor's point that the Kantian moral ontology is one which is also shared today by Jürgen Habermas. For Hegel's original statement, see G.W.F. Hegel, 'Reason as Lawgiver' and 'Reason as Testing Laws', in G.W.F. Hegel, *Phenomenology of Spirit*, trans. A.V. Miller (Oxford: Oxford University Press, 1977 [1807]), pp. 252–62.
6. This argument is presented in Taylor, 'Inescapable Frameworks', in Taylor, *op. cit.*, in note 2, Chapter 1.
7. The three previous quotations are from *ibid.*, p. 5.
8. The three previous quotations are from *ibid.*, p. 4.
9. *Ibid.*, pp. 11–16.
10. *Ibid.*, p. 11, emphasis added.
11. *Ibid.*, p. 12, emphasis added.
12. *Ibid.*, p. 14.
13. *Ibid.*
14. *Ibid.*, pp. 19–20.
15. See Jürgen Habermas, 'Modernity – An Incomplete Project', in Paul Rabinow and William M. Sullivan (eds.), *Interpretive Social Science: A Second Look* (Berkeley and Los Angeles, CA: University of California Press, 1979), pp. 141–56. The 'modern' is a term that was first used by the Romans in the fifth century to articulate the difference between 'their' Christian civilisation and their pagan predecessors. As Habermas has argued, '[w]ith varying content, the term "modern" again and again expresses the consciousness of an epoch that relates itself to the past of antiquity, in order to view itself as the result of a transition from the old to the new'. Habermas, 'Modernity', p. 142.
16. Needless to say, this historical imagination is pervasive and deeply entrenched. Hegel himself, for example, understood the demise of the 'classical' *polis* as the beginning of an historic dialectic through which the Spirit would realise itself in a 'modern' *polis*, the state.
17. Taylor, *op. cit.*, in note 2, p. 14.
18. *Ibid.*, p. 16.
19. These images of the 'pre-modern'/'non-Western' have pervaded social and political theory. And 'the tribal' has for long encapsulated the whole array of images of passivity, staticity, and exclusivity that have been understood as 'external' and antithetical to the 'modern Western'. In the last two decades, the notion of 'tribe', and the associated images of moral passivity, staticity, and exclusivity, has been resolutely discredited in anthropology and historiograhy. For a number of statements, see Paris Yeros, 'Towards a Normative Theory of Ethnicity: Reflections on the Politics of Constructivism', in Paris Yeros (ed.), *Ethnicity and Nationalism in Africa: Constructivist Reflections and Contemporary Politics* (Basingstoke: Macmillan Press, 1999), Chapter 6; Terence Ranger, 'Conclusion', in Yeros (ed.), *Ethnicity and Nationalism in Africa*, Chapter 7; Terence Ranger, 'The Invention of Tradition in Colonial Africa', in Eric Hobsbawm and Terence Ranger (eds.), *The Invention of Tradition* (Cambridge: Cambridge University Press, 1983, pp. 211–62; Martin Channock, *Law, Custom and Social Order: The Colonial Experience in Malawi and Zambia* (Cambridge: Cambridge University Press, 1985); John and Jean Comaroff, *Ethnography and the Historical Imagination* (Boulder, CO: Westview Press,

1992); Steven Feierman, *Peasant Intellectuals: Anthropology and History in Tanzania* (Madison, WI: University of Wisconsin Press, 1990); Bruce Berman and John Lonsdale, *Unhappy Valley: Conflict in Kenya and Africa, Book II: Violence and Ethnicity* (London: James Currey; Nairobi: Heinemann Kenya; Athens, OH: Ohio University Press, 1992), especially Chapters 11 and 12; and Frederik Barth, 'Introduction', in Frederik Barth (ed.), *Ethnic Groups and Boundaries: The Social Organisation of Cultural Difference* (Oslo: Scandinavian University Press, 1969), pp. 9–38.

20. V.Y. Mudimbe, *The Idea of Africa* (London: James Currey; Bloomington, IN: Indiana University Press, 1994); Edward Said, *Orientalism* (Harmondsworth: Penguin, 1985); Tzvetan Todorov, *The Conquest of America: The Question of the Other*, trans. R. Howard (New York, NY: Harper and Row Publishers, 1984).

21. Arturo Escobar, *Encountering Development: The Making and Unmaking of the Third World* (Princeton, NJ: Princeton University Press, 1995). See especially Escobar's critique (pp. 77-79) of W. Arthur Lewis's theory of 'modernisation', as articulated in the latter's influential essay, 'Economic Development with Unlimited Supplies of Labor', in Amar Narin Agarwala and S.P. Singh (eds.), *The Economics of Underdevelopment: A Series of Articles and Papers* (Bombay: Oxford University Press, 1958 [1954]), pp. 400–49.

22. Todorov, *op. cit.*, in note 20, pp. 106–7.

23. Andrew Linklater, *The Transformation of Political Community: Ethical Foundations of the Post-Westphalian Era* (Cambridge: Polity Press, 1998), p. 60. See also Friedrich Kratochwil, 'Citizenship: On the Border of Order', *Alternatives* (Vol. 19, No. 4, 1994), pp. 485–506.

24. Hegel, *Phenomenology of Spirit, op. cit.*, in note 5, paragraphs 178–96.

25. Todorov, *op. cit.*, in note 20, p. 46.

26. See Linklater, *op. cit.*, in note 23.

27. The term 'genocide' is hardly ever applied to the 'systemic' variety. A rare exception is Michel Chossudovsky's statement in *The Globalisation of Poverty: Impacts of IMF and World Bank Reforms* (London and New York, NY: Zed Books Ltd.; Halifax: Fernwood Publishing Ltd.; Cape Town: IPSR Books; Sydney: Pluto Press, 1998).

28. See Todorov, *op. cit.*, in note 20, pp. 162–7.

29. Terence Ranger, *Are We Not Also Men? The Samkange Family and African Politics in Zimbabwe, 1920-64* (Harare: Baobab; Cape Town: David Philip; Portsmouth, NH: Heinemann; London: James Currey, 1995).

30. Todorov, *op. cit.*, in note 20, pp. 144–5.

31. Taylor, *op. cit.*, in note 2, p. 9.

32. Escobar, *op. cit.*, in note 21, p. 10.

33. For a classic account of the rise and significance of the Westphalian order, see Hedley Bull, *The Anarchical Society: A Study of Order in World Politics*, Second Edition (Basingstoke: Macmillan Press, 1995). See also Robert Jackson, *Quasi-states: Sovereignty, International Relations, and the Third World* (Cambridge: Cambridge University Press, 1990).

34. For another classic in this context, see Karl Polanyi, *The Great Transformation* (New York, NY: Octagon Books, 1975 [1944]).

35. See Mark Neufeld, *The Restructuring of International Relations* (Cambridge: Cambridge University Press, 1995).

36. See James Mayall, *Nationalism and International Society* (Cambridge: Cambridge University Press, 1990), especially Chapters 4 and 5.

37. See Escobar, *op. cit.*, in note 21. For an account of the rise and fall of collective challenges of Third World states to the international order, see Philippe Braillard and Mohammad-Reza Djalili (eds.), *The Third World and International Relations* (London: Frances Pinter; Boulder, CO: Lynne Rienner, 1986). For an account of the exclusionary nature of states themselves, with reference to Africa, see Jean-François Bayart, *The State in Africa: The Politics of the Belly* (New York, NY: Longman, 1993).

38. The document that set out the agenda of the new order was the 'Berg Report'. World Bank, *Accelerated Development in Sub-Saharan Africa: An Agenda for Action* (Washington, DC: The World Bank, 1981). For a statement regarding specifically the changes in global responsibility, see John Toye, 'Structural Adjustment: Context, Assumptions, Origin and Diversity', in Rolph van der Hoeven and Fred van der Kraaij (eds.), *Structural Adjustment and Beyond in Sub-Saharan Africa: Research and Policy Issues* (The Hague: Ministry of Foreign Affairs (DGIS); London: James Currey; Portsmouth, NH: Heinemann, 1994), pp. 18–35.

39. For various accounts of the rise and significance of the international financial institutions, see Paul Mosley, Jane Harrigan, and John Toye, *Aid and Power: The World Bank and Policy-Based Lending, Volume I: Analysis and Policy Proposals*, Second Edition (London and New York, NY: Routledge, 1995); Tony Killick (ed.), *The Quest for Economic Stabilisation: The IMF and the Third World* (London: Overseas Development Institute, 1984); Bade Onimode (ed.), *The IMF, the World Bank and the African Debt, Volume I: The Economic Impact* (London and Atlantic Highlands, NJ: Zed Books, with the Institute for African Alternatives, 1989); and Peter Gibbon, 'The World Bank and the New Politics of Aid', *European Journal of Development Research* (Vol. 5, No. 1, 1993), pp. 35–62.

40. World Bank, *Sub-Saharan Africa: From Crisis to Sustainable Growth: A Long-Term Perspective* (Washington, DC: The World Bank, 1989), p. 5.

41. *Ibid.*; World Bank, *World Development Report* (Oxford: Oxford University Press for the World Bank, 1990); and World Bank: *Governance and Development* (Washington, DC: The World Bank, 1992).

42. See Peter Gibbon, Yusuf Bangura, and Arve Ofstad (eds.), *Authoritarianism, Democracy, and Adjustment: The Politics of Economic Reform in Africa* (Uppsala: Nordiska Afrikainstitutet, 1992), and Michael Bratton and Nicholas van de Walle, *Democratic Experiments in Africa: Regime Transitions in Comparative Perspective* (Cambridge: Cambridge University Press), 1997.

43. Gibbon, *op. cit.*, in note 39, p. 52.

44. World Bank, *op. cit.*, in note 38, p. xii.

45. It is worth quoting a passage at length from the 1990 Report on poverty: 'During the 1980s many developing countries had to cope with macroeconomic crises. Their experience drew attention to a new concern: the need to frame adjustment policies that give due weight to the needs of the poor. In many developing countries a period of painful macroeconomic adjustment was unavoidable. In the longer term the economic restructuring associated with adjustment is perfectly consistent with the two-part strategy [of emphasis on labour-intensive projects

and on provision of social services]. In the short-term, however, many of the poor can be protected through a judicious mix of macroeconomic policies (for example, pricing policy reforms that benefit poor farmers) and measures to moderate declines in private consumption. Experience also shows that it is possible to shift public spending in favour of the poor, even within an overall framework of fiscal discipline, and to target transfers more accurately. In addition, increased capital inflows can be used to help cushion the impact of adjustment on the poor'. World Bank, *World Development Report, op. cit.*, in note 41, p. 1.

46. *Ibid.*, p. 3.
47. World Bank, *op. cit.*, in note 38, p. 6.
48. *Ibid.*, p. 60.
49. World Bank, *Governance and Development, op. cit.*, in note 41, pp. 1 and 3.
50. *Ibid.*, pp. 22–3.
51. *Ibid.*, pp. 26–7.
52. *Ibid.*, p. 30.
53. For fuller critiques of the Bank's concept of 'good governance', see Gibbon, *op. cit.*, in note 39, pp. 52–6, and Björn Beckman, 'Empowerment or Repression? The World Bank and the Politics of African Adjustment', in Gibbon *et al.* (eds.), *op. cit.*, in note 42, pp. 83–105.
54. African Rights, *Justice in Zimbabwe* (London: African Rights, 1996). The following is instructive: 'In 1990, the Government of Zimbabwe introduced a World Bank-supported structural adjustment programme (the Economic and Social Action Plan, ESAP). Although economic liberalisation has encouraged new investment, especially domestically, health and education services have deteriorated and living standards have declined. Wages have not increased despite high inflation and an 18% devaluation of the Zimbabwe dollar in January 1994. Unemployment is widespread. Retrenchment in the urban areas has significantly reduced many families' cash income and forced people to return to their rural homes. In one rural district, the Department of Social Services reported that it was paying thousands of dollars more in school fees for children since the implementation of ESAP. The effects of the 1995 and 1994 harvests, although not as severe as during the 1992 drought, have brought severe malnutrition to some areas. Because families are hungry, school enrolment is decreasing as children are forced to farm and fish. Given this economic reality, a lawyer, not to mention all the other expenses involved in going to court, is wholly beyond the reach of the majority of the people'. African Rights, *Justice in Zimbabwe*, p. 11.
55. The ZCTU estimates that since the beginning of the liberal reforms in 1991 in Zimbabwe, incomes have been eroded by 60%, real wages have fallen to a quarter of their 1980 value, 700,000 workers have lost their jobs, and the employment rate has dwindled to 0.67%. See the recent interview with Morgan Tsvangirai, Secretary-General of the ZCTU, on the eve of the 1999 May Day celebrations and the pending formation of a labour party in Zimbabwe, entitled 'Impoverished, Morale at Rock Bottom: Workers in No Mood to Celebrate', *Zimbabwe Independent*, 30 April 1999.

Part II

Ethics and Poverty

2. Beyond Rights and Duties: Building Attachments and Focusing Moral Attention on World Poverty

Fiona Robinson

> The agent, thin as a needle, appears in the quick flash of the choosing will.... The agent's freedom, indeed his moral quality, resides in his choices, and yet we are not told what prepares him for the choices.... [i]t ignores what appears at least to be a sort of continuous background with a life of its own; and it is surely in the tissue of that life that the secrets of good and evil are to be found. Here neither the inspiring ideas of freedom...nor the plain wholesome concept of a rational discernment of duty, seems complex enough to do justice to what we really are.[1]

In spite of the immense and undisputed moral significance of the problem of world poverty, the relationship between moral philosophy and economic/development analysis on the subject has always been, at best, an uneasy one. Moral and political philosophers point out that many of the makers of social policy are not trained to think about moral questions of social justice, and are thus encouraged to think in terms of efficiency without heed to moral questions.[2] Economists and development policy-makers accuse moral philosophers of profound ignorance of economic realities, and of wasting time on elaborate, abstract moral justifications which bear little, if any, relationship to the hard facts of a highly-stratified, power-ridden global political economy.

Many philosophers have responded to this challenge. The birth of 'applied ethics' represented an attempt on behalf of certain moral and political philosophers to create a bridge between philosophical thinking and the 'realities' of social crises. In 1974, Peter Singer's article, 'Philosophers are Back on the Job', championed the philosophical turn to applied ethics, employing the ethics of famine relief as a leading example.[3] While this category of applied ethics seems to be more acceptable to certain social scientists, many are still sceptical about the role of moral philosophy and philosophers in International Relations (IR). Robert Jackson, for example, has recently supported Stanley Hoffman's claim that international ethics 'is not

Fiona Robinson

the province of the ethical philosopher', but rather that of the international relations scholar who takes an interest in normative theory.[4]

I would argue, however, that these accusations regarding the nature of moral philosophy – that it is abstract, arcane, and naive – are more relevant to some types of philosophy than others. The dominant approaches in Western ethics – Kantian, neo-Kantian, liberal contractualist, and rights-based theories – all rely on a high level of abstraction in their moral reasoning. These traditions are primarily concerned with arriving at principles or rules of right action – of justifying, for example, aid to distant people, by constructing universal principles which will answer the questions: 'do we have a duty to help?', or 'what rights do human beings have?' Thus, Kantians, for example, focus on the *obligations* of moral agents. They argue that the demands of moral duty are not conditional on particular social structures or practices, but that, rather, they emerge out of a conception of practical reason which insists only that acknowledged others can be given no reasons for acting on principles which it is impossible for them to adopt.[5]

Given their emphasis on abstract principles and justification, it is not surprising that these dominant approaches have been criticised for contributing little towards answering important questions such as, 'how can we act in order to prevent people from suffering and dying as a result of widespread poverty and hunger?' These traditional ethical approaches rely on the separation of ethics and politics; deontological approaches regard moral reasoning as distinct from 'the way things are in the world'. They also rely on a limited number of moral concepts: obligations, rights, fairness, and justice, and on a conception of moral judgement which is characterised by universality, impartiality, and rationality. As such, these approaches to moral reasoning perpetuate the distinction between the realm of our experience and the realm of 'the normative'; morality is seen as an exercise of the will, valorising the freedom of the autonomous agent to make choices when confronted with moral problems. Moreover, it is worth remembering that this sort of ethics has been described as the 'inspiration for political liberalism'.[6] Given its intimate association with the hegemonic global and political economic philosophy, it seems unlikely that an ethics of rights and duties, of formal equality and reciprocity, could significantly disturb existing inequalities in levels of access to power, resources, and well-being at the global level.

If we limit our picture of morality in this way – according to a rigid definition of what 'counts' as an ethical argument – ethics is unlikely to make much progress towards mitigating poverty on a global scale. What we must do, instead, is recognise that not all approaches to ethics are so far removed from the social and political context of the problems they seek to address. Recently, a number of moral philosophers have articulated profound scepticism about the usefulness of that elaborate, thoroughgoing, and ambitious kind of structure known as 'ethical theory', which may be defined as 'a theoretical account of what ethical thought and practice are, which...implies a general test for the correctness of ethical beliefs and principles'.[7] Bernard Williams has made the case for a different kind of moral philosophy:

> [s]uch a philosophy would reflect on what we believe, feel, take for granted; the ways in which we confront obligations and recognise responsibility; the sentiments of guilt and shame. It would involve a phenomenology of the ethical life. This could be a good philosophy, but it would be unlikely to yield an ethical theory.[8]

These suggestions for an alternative way of thinking about morality stem from Williams' deep scepticism about what he calls 'philosophical ethics' and, specifically, about the ability of moral philosophy to provide convincing and useful answers to questions about ethical life in the modern world.

Clearly, moral philosophy has little to recommend it if it bears no relation to the actual context in which moral problems exist. With this in mind, the ethical approach to poverty on a global scale that will be put forward in this chapter will be informed by feminist philosophy which eschews abstract theorising in favour of a contextual, situated ethics which takes as its starting point the personal and social relations among real, concrete, rather than generalised, persons. I will draw on feminist arguments regarding the 'ethics of care' in order to construct a critical, relational ethics that recognises the moral value of sustained, continuous attention, and caring between persons, and regards as a moral priority the maintenance and promotion of good social relations within and among communities. As a critical approach, however, it also recognises the degree to which the causes of poverty are embedded in the structures of global politics and the global political economy, and the extent to which these relationships, like all relationships, contain the potential for exploitation and exclusion. By rejecting the separation of ethics and politics, this approach to ethics takes social relations as its starting point, resisting the claim that a purely economic approach can help us to understand, or to solve, the problem of poverty on a global scale.

It will be argued that a critical ethics of care can take us beyond the leading ethical perspectives towards useful moral thinking about the problem of world poverty. The first part of the chapter will explore two of these leading perspectives: the first is the 'human rights approach', which relies on rights-based ethical reasoning, and focuses specifically on the 'welfare' rights or 'positive' rights of the poor. I will argue that while rights-based ethics may be valuable in terms of its rhetorical appeal and its accessibility as a discourse, it is ultimately flawed, not least in terms of its focus on the rights-holders (the poor) rather than on those agents or institutions which are responsible for ensuring that those entitlements are met. The second perspective derives from Kantian ethics, which focus not on rights, and rights-holders, but on the duties or obligations of moral agents. In spite of the superior rigour of this approach, it offers an unsatisfactory account of moral motivation, and how reason is linked to action. While Kant's ethics may offer a test to determine whether actions, institutions, or policies meet the demands of justice, it says little about the sorts of circumstances under which agents will act in accordance with those demands, or about what moral action which meets these demands would actually look like.

Both of these approaches seek, first and foremost, to provide a justification – moral, legal, and rational – for moral action, rather than seeking to explore what adequate moral action might entail. Moreover, they ignore both the *particularity* and *connectedness* of persons, and focus instead on their moral status as human beings and as autonomous individuals. By understanding persons as abstract and autonomous, rather than concrete and attached, these approaches overlook a crucial facet of moral motivation and an important feature of what adequate moral responsiveness actually means. Indeed, they systematically obfuscate the social and political dimension of poverty; they make little or no reference to the relationships – personal, social, and political – and the structures – economic, social, and political – in which the lives of impoverished individuals, and the moral problem of poverty, are embedded. By contrast, an approach to world poverty which starts from the moral idea of care is one which values the moral efforts of continuous attention, and sees it as a moral good that people should benefit from positive attachments. It argues that in order to tackle poverty effectively, we need a rich understanding of social relations, one which sees each intimate relationship as in turn embedded in ties among neighbours, members of religious and ethnic groups, fellow citizens, all of which are deeply but not entirely determined by the political system and economic circumstances. It recognises that moral responses flow out of human relationships, and focuses on how we can learn the moral qualities of attentiveness, understanding, and responsiveness to others in need. This is not to suggest, however, that this can only ever be a 'micro' approach which focuses only on special relationships and one-to-one caring. On the contrary, it will be argued that an ethics of care can have a broader relevance if we consider how social structures and institutions may lead to marginalisation and exclusion, as well as what social and economic structures are necessary to permit continuous, caring human relationships especially responsive to those most dependent on care.[9] Bringing the ethics of care to the problem of poverty in world politics can help us to see the limitations of a moral approach based on universal human rights and the duties of the 'international community', and to understand how and why only continuous attention and strong social and personal attachments can help to create an environment in which poverty and its effects can begin to be reduced.

Freedom from Poverty? – The Limits of Rights-based Moral Reasoning

Analysis of the ethical dimension of international relations is dominated overwhelmingly by the language of rights.[10] Interestingly, rights-based ethics are pre-eminent not only in the academic research of philosophers and theorists of Politics, IR, and Development Studies, but also in the 'practical' circles of policy-makers and analysts. The remarkable influence of rights language in international politics today can be attributed to a number of factors. Rights language is accessible and, today, is virtually universal. In fact, however, it emerged from within a particular tradition of political and economic organisation which has seen a remarkable rise in the late twentieth century and is increasingly being used as a standard for international legitimacy. This tradition – liberalism – emphasises the primacy of the individual, and specifically, the individual's capacity to make rational decisions. Deontological liberal ethics exalt the moral value of freedom; rights exist in order to protect the individual from the undue interference of others and from the state. Human rights are, moreover, a great leveller – to be a rights-holder is, apparently, to possess the dignity and the formal equality to which all human beings are entitled.

While we most readily associate human rights with those civil and political freedoms first articulated by the early liberals – freedom of speech, thought, conscience, and movement – contemporary advocates of rights are quick to point out that human rights have evolved considerably since the eighteenth and nineteenth centuries. Today, there are two international covenants on rights – one on civil and political rights, and one on economic, social, and cultural rights. The latter covenant details the so-called 'welfare' rights – to food, health care, education, *etc.* Most advocates of rights today will argue that these rights are as important, if not more important, than those which aim to secure people's legal and political freedom. Indeed, much contemporary analysis regards these two sets of rights as indivisible and nonhierarchical. Thus, positive welfare rights are treated as being the same in kind as negative, political rights. But, one might well ask, is such a conflation useful? Is it really practical to rely on the same moral categories when we are seeking fundamentally different ends?

A right is an entitlement; more specifically, however, to have a right is to be accorded the necessary freedom to pursue some chosen end. Interestingly, Article 11 of the International Covenant of Economic, Social and Cultural Rights refers not only to a right to 'adequate food', but also to a 'right of everyone to be free from hunger'. This second right not only places the emphasis on the individual rights-holder as the moral agent, but describes the value of being properly nourished in terms of a negative freedom, rather than a positive good. Rights, in the liberal-democratic tradition, ensure not only negative liberty and formal equality, but also pluralism, embodied in the idea of the separation of the right – which is universal and primary – from the good. As Iris Murdoch has noted,

> [t]he idea of the good remains indefinable and empty so that human choice may fill it. The sovereign moral concept is freedom, or possibly courage in a sense which identifies with freedom, will, power. This concept inhabits a quite separate top level of human activity since it is the guarantor of the secondary values created by choice.[11]

Certainly, poverty is a condition from which we all want to be 'free', but is it not perverse to focus our moral attention on *freedom from* poverty? What seems to take over here, in moral terms, is the fact that poverty acts as a constraint on our freedom, and that this is a bad thing. Even when we try to express the unacceptability of poverty as a right *to* something, the idea of right seems not to capture the scale of the activities and the experience – not only in terms of political and economic decisions and social relations, but in transformations of people's entire modes of life and connections with one another and with the world – that would be required in order to bring groups of people from a state of impoverishment to a state in which they can live healthy lives.

This is not to say that the moral language of rights is not useful. Rights language is, today, almost universally accessible; it has and can continue to act as a rallying cry for social change by providing a vocabulary through which to articulate the values of empowerment and self-esteem. However, we must recognise the limits of rights language, and the extent to which this is a language which coincides with the individualist ontology of liberal political and economic theory. A rights-based ethics is a contractualist ethics which either takes for granted, or proceeds as if, all parties were equal. It is based on the assumption that if moral subjects are given the right – the freedom – to live their 'own lives', they will be able to seek, claim, and enjoy the 'good life'. However, not all goods of moral significance can be *claimed* by those who need or value them; not all those things we need or value make sense in the context of a contractual ethics of rights and correlative obligations. Again, this is not to say that what we clumsily call positive rights are not important; indeed, it is because they are so important that we must find a way of articulating the moral significance of human well-being that actually works towards its achievement.

It is, perhaps, telling that advocates of rights often ultimately resort to an abandonment of rights language in their attempts to defend it. For example,

James W. Nickel argues that the right to food will not be meaningful if it does not yield guidance as to who has the responsibility for ensuring that adequate food is available. He also admits that 'people are often perplexed by the right to adequate food because they are not sure what it means for them. Does it mean that they have an obligation to feed some particular hungry person, or to feed some fair share of the world's hungry?'.[12] Thus, when the need for moral action is considered, we seem to find it necessary to try to make sense of the *obligations* which may correspond to rights, rather than considering the rights themselves. Similarly, Henry Shue argues that seriousness about rights leads to seriousness about duties and, moreover, that seriousness about duties opens up the underlying social character of rights. Ignoring the positive duties correlative to a right, he argues, is like saying that 'we believe people have a "right not to be flooded" but we don't want to talk about dams, which are expensive economic projects' – what would a "right not to be flooded" mean if nothing were done to block the flow of water?.[13] Both writers seem to be suggesting that rights only become meaningful when we turn our attention to the nature of the duties or responsibilities which are necessary to ensure that rights are fulfilled. Moreover, as Shue suggests, once we begin to think about duties and responsibilities, we realise that such duties must, inevitably, reflect social relations – attachments and communities, rather than individuals. I will argue that it is only when we begin from social relations, recognising them as both an ethical and an ontological starting point, that we can begin to think usefully about appropriate moral responses to poverty on a global scale. Before elucidating this argument, however, I will explore the Kantian, obligation-centred approach, in an attempt to uncover whether or not a focus on duties, rather than rights, can overcome the apparent limitations of the rights-based ethics.

Duties Before Rights: Kantian and Neo-Kantian Approaches to Poverty

At first glance, a Kantian approach to the moral question of world poverty appears to have a number of advantages over rights-based approaches. Because it is a theory of human obligations, rather than of human *rights*, it relies on the agency not of those who are impoverished, but of those who are relatively powerful and free from want or hardship. Interestingly, however, despite the fact that Kantian philosophers are at pains to point out the differences between rights-based and duty-based ethics, it is worth remembering that both are examples of deontological, rule-oriented moral theories. Of course, it is important that we recognise Kant's ethical theory for what it is, and avoid what has been described as its frequent and misleading assimilation to theories of human rights.[14] However, as will be argued below, the shortcomings of this approach result not from the way it diverges from rights theory, but rather from the fact that it does not move far enough from the universalism and the abstraction found in rights-based ethics.

In its barest form, Kant's accounts of ethics requires moral agents to act only on principles that can be acted on by all. Justice, then, demands that we neither adopt nor condone institutions or policies which cannot be acted on by all. This is not to say, as Onora O'Neill insists, that justice demands institutions and policies that receive either actual consent from all affected or the hypothetical consent of beings with enhanced, idealised rationality or knowledge. It is simply to claim that, for example, because principles which are committed to injury of others will always represent a commitment that is possible for perpetrators but not for victims, they cannot be enacted by all, and so are unjust. Thus, because poverty is clearly an enormous source of vulnerability and dependence of many sorts, it is unjust to leave in place the institutional structures which produce and perpetuate poverty.[15]

As proponents are quick to admit, Kant's strategy is a minimal one; it represents a certain attitude to *justification* – what types of principles can we demonstrate to be universally just. It represents only a test for principles, rather than a plan of action for implementing them. Moreover, it is an essentially negative strategy; it does not seek to show what constitutes a flourishing life, nor which are the most flourishing lives, but simply to establish constraints that must be observed for any flourishing life. It is concerned, then, with the outline or limits rather than the target.[16] It is also very much concerned with justice and, hence, with the problem of *competing* claims – the fact that people want to act in different ways and simply to be different. It does not, however, like some neo-Kantian liberal theories of justice, confine justice to the availability of sufficient freedom to pursue subjective goods or preferences. Such accounts may be able to give us a reasonable argument about motivation, but, as O'Neill argues, have some difficulty in providing a convincing account of justice.[17] Kant's formula, by contrast, is about laying down a minimal condition for achieving mutual consistency in the action of a plurality of rational beings.[18]

Certainly, a Kantian approach overcomes the problem of indeterminate agency found in rights-based ethics; it pays serious attention not to rights, nor simply to correlative obligations, but also to imperfect duties to act only in ways that are just. However, it still does not offer us a satisfactory ethical approach to the problem of world poverty. As I suggested above, Kantian moral theory is deontological. This means that the claims made about morality and justice are neither a reflection of, nor generated by, people's actual behaviour. It is this facet of the theory which has been at once its strength and its weakness. It has been a strength because it has provided an answer to those critics who ask, 'why tell us that justice demands that no one act with cruelty or deception, when it is evident that people do, and that they will continue to do so?' The Kantian response is that the purpose of moral theory is to offer a moral justification for action, to tell us what the demands of morality are; this is more, rather than less important, Kantians argue, as people continue to act in ways which transgress those demands. To the sceptics, however, these arguments are unconvincing. In spite of the claim that Kant's ethics are primarily concerned to establish a strategy to ensure that rationality ensures the adoption of universal moral principles, critics will claim that the powerful have no need and, probably, no desire to act according to the categorical imperative; thus, a strategy which is built around the notion of universalisability ends up faltering on the question of motivation.

This problem of motivation is linked to the Kantian theory of judgement and the reliance on rule-based forms of ethics. As Roger Spegele argues, Kant's account of judgement proceeds from the dubious assumption that the rules definitive of any concept suffice by themselves to determine whether something falls under that concept. But, he asks, is it always true that judgement has no other task than simply to see that such rules suffice to identify the things on which the concept may be predicated?[19] Indeed, even if all moral responses could be governed by rules (which is certainly doubtful), there is clearly a significant gap between the knowledge of rules and the ability of moral agents to determine, in real contexts, what moral action should be taken.

It could be argued, then, that Kant's ethics leave unanswered large questions about motivation and how acts of pure will can necessarily bring about real social change. These are not the only weaknesses of Kant's ethics. One might also question the overwhelming focus on the concept of *obligation* and the resultant marginalisation of other moral concepts; or the feasibility of constructing universal principles of justice which are both free from cultural and moral imperialism as well as not being so abstract and minimal that they become meaningless. However, these shortcomings are not my concern here. Rather, I am questioning the validity of a system of ethics which is concerned only with asserting that people should act morally, rather than with whether people *will* act morally, how the motivation to act morally will connect with the priorities and circumstances of their own lives, and what, finally, that moral action might look like. Also, I am deeply critical of the view that we, as moral theorists, can be responsible only for providing rule-based justifications regarding moral action, that is, an answer to the question, 'is this act morally justified?', rather than to the questions, 'what will motivate people to act morally?' and 'what form should our moral responses take?', or, quite simply, 'how can we help?' An approach to ethics which is concerned only with the construction of an elegant and rigorous theoretical test for whether principles 'count' as being 'moral' may deserve our intellectual respect, but it does not help us to get any closer to the deeply social and political problems surrounding the human suffering and deprivation brought on by world poverty.

The Permanent Background to Moral Action: Attachments and Attention

In this third section, I would like to suggest an approach to poverty which differs radically from those outlined above. It is one which views the moral problems associated with poverty on a global scale not as abstract problems – regarding whether or not we have a duty to attempt to mitigate or ameliorate poverty – which can be solved with a convincing theoretical argument. Too much of what is widely recognised as work on ethics and international relations is characterised by the separation of ethics from politics. The scope of ethics, especially in its Kantian form, as described above, is to justify whether or not, and in which cases, political action may be regarded as justified or indeed as imperative The role of the moral theorist is to construct principles regarding when and when not, and under what circumstances, to act. The 'practicalities' of that action – of what it actually means to act, for example, only on principles that could be accepted universally – are left to the domain of politics. Certainly, providing justification for moral action is an important part of what ethics is all about. Courses of action – especially those which might affect hundreds of thousands of people, such as those relating to world poverty and violence – require the backing of some kind of moral argument to lend them legitimacy. But the role of moral thinking cannot end there.

The approach that I am advocating here is one which I call a 'critical ethics of care'; it is informed by, but is by no means identical to, the ethics of care first articulated by Carol Gilligan, and later by other 'feminist' moral theorists including Joan Tronto, Virginia Held, Annette Baier, and Margaret Urban Walker, as well as other moral theorists who are critical of the Kantian approach, such as Lawrence Blum.[20] The idea of an approach to morality based on caring first emerged with Gilligan's pathbreaking book, *In a Different Voice*.[21] In the book, Gilligan challenges the basically Kantian model of moral development put forward by Lawrence Kohlberg – a six-stage, three-level progression from an egocentric understanding of fairness based on individual need (stages one and two), to a conception of fairness anchored in the shared conventions of societal agreement (stages three and four), and finally to a principled understanding of fairness that rests on the free-standing logic of equality and reciprocity (stages five and six). Moral maturity, according to Kohlberg, is reached when the subject has arrived at an understanding of morality as a principled conception of justice.[22] Gilligan challenges this model using empirical and interpretative analyses of girls' and women's responses to a series of moral dilemmas. In listening to her subjects speak about themselves, and about morality, she claims to have heard not one but two moral voices, two ways of speaking about moral problems, two modes of describing the relationships between other and self. Gilligan argues that the 'different voice' of girls and women did not signify that women simply stopped at an 'inferior stage' of moral development, but rather that the voices of women represented a different but equal moral orientation which was morally valuable. For example, she describes how 'Amy', a young female subject, saw a particular moral dilemma not as 'a math problem with humans', but as 'a narrative of relationships that extends over time'; she describes how Amy sees 'a world comprised of relationships rather than of people standing alone, a world that coheres through human connection rather than through systems of rules'.[23]

A number of moral theorists have recognised the significance of Gilligan's research. Lawrence Blum has argued that Gilligan's body of work in moral development psychology is of the first importance for moral philosophy in terms of the questions it raises. If there is a 'different voice' – a coherent set of moral concerns distinct both from the objective and the subjective, the impersonal and the purely personal – then moral theory will need to give some place to these concerns.[24] Susan Hekman has suggested that what Gilligan is proposing is an alternative framework in which women's 'stories' are interpreted as genuine moral statements. If we interpret relationship, care, and connection as integral to human life and development, then we will interpret women's stories as genuinely moral narratives, distinct from, but every bit as moral as, those based on abstract principles.[25] Finally, Seyla Benhabib has observed that the widespread recognition and controversy surrounding Gilligan's work arose not only because it reflected the coming of age of women's scholarship within the paradigms of normal science; equally significant was that the kinds of questions which Gilligan was posing to the Kohlbergian paradigm were also being posed to universalist neo-Kantian moral philosophies by a growing and influential number of critics, including communitarians, neo-Aristotelians, and even neo-Hegelians. Thus, she argues that there is a remarkable convergence between the Gilligan-type feminist critique of Kantian universalism and the objections raised by these other thinkers.[26]

Of course, there have also been those who have rejected outright the idea of an ethic of care, arguing that, while feelings of care are certainly something we all possess, they have nothing to do with morality, which is characterised by rationality, universality, and impartiality. However, there are also those more subtle critics, who point out what they see as the dangers of paternalism and dependence inherent in an ethics of care:

> feminist critics of abstract liberalism…can end up endorsing rather than challenging social and economic structures that marginalize women and confine them to a private sphere….A stress on caring and relationships to the exclusion of abstract justice may endorse relegation to the nursery and the kitchen, to purdah and to poverty. In

rejecting 'abstract liberalism' such feminists converge with traditions that have excluded women from economic and public life. An appeal to 'women's experience', 'women's traditions' and 'women's discourse' does not escape but rather echoes ways in which women have been marginalized or oppressed.[27]

Similarly, Susan Moller Okin has argued that, to the extent that findings about women's moral development are interpreted to mean that women are more attached than men to particular others and less able to be impartial or to universalise in their moral thinking, they seem not only to misread the data but to reinforce the negative stereotyping of women that has been employed to exclude them from political rights and positions of authority.[28]

Certainly, these criticisms demand serious attention. However, I would argue that they should encourage us to rethink the scope and applications of care, rather than force us to reject the ethics of care outright. In response to these criticisms. We must resist the idea that the ethics of care is explicitly gendered – that it is naturally a 'women's morality'. Such claims cannot be supported by empirical research, and can potentially lead only to the stereotyping and reinforcement of gender differences feared by the critics cited above. Second, we must resist the temptation to see care as an ethics of the private sphere, while retaining abstract, 'justice' ethics in the public arena. To do so is fundamentally to leave in place the boundaries which have separated public from private life. As Tronto has argued, there is no victory in the admission that 'caring' deserves to be seen as a part of moral theory, as long as it is kept in its place, especially in the household or in 'relationships'.[29] To be both truly radical and morally and politically useful, an ethics of care must serve as a starting point for a wider questioning of the proper role of caring in society. It must begin by broadening our understanding of what caring for others means, both in terms of the moral questions it raises and in terms of the need to restructure social and political institutions if caring for others is to be made a more central part of the everyday lives of everyone is society.[30] An ethics of care focuses not just on the moment of moral decision-making as if morality could be isolated from other aspects of life. Rather, this kind of ethics focuses on what Murdoch has called the 'continuous background' – the whole of our mode of living and the quality of our relations with the world.[31] When morality is seen in this way, addressing moral problems – such as world poverty – cannot be boiled down to decisions and actions about rights and duties; rather, it involves a recognition that addressing poverty is a slow, long process of learning how to focus moral attention and pay attention to the quality of our real attachments to others.

What would it mean, then, to adopt a critical ethic of care in the context of North-South relations and, specifically, in terms of the problem of world poverty? First, perhaps, it should be made clear what it would *not* mean. It would not mean that caring would take the form of the wealthy and the powerful 'caring about' the weak and impoverished in a manner which is both paternalistic and in danger of robbing those moral 'subjects' of their own agency and self-esteem. As I suggested above, this is a potential danger of an ethics of care that must be addressed. Certainly adopting an ethics of care, in a global context, *may* involve the creation of new social and even personal relations between groups and individuals from very different socio-economic levels and territorial locations which may, in turn, motivate moral attention and caring. More importantly, however, it would require that those already in a position to intervene in the South – especially development INGOs – explicitly adopt strategies which take seriously the relationships and attachments, both within existing communities and between their own members and peoples in the South, and explore how the nature of those relations might perpetuate, or might lead to solutions concerning, levels of poverty and well-being. This would be an intensely moral task, but also one which is not separate from, but the very embodiment of, the goal of political and socio-economic change to mitigate poverty.

Furthermore, a relational approach to world poverty based on caring would not advocate only individual to individual 'care', such as might be achieved through sponsoring a child in a developing country, for example. Such an approach is not only limited, as it focuses attention on only a few, rather than on the many who are suffering; it is also misguided, in that it either ignores or misunderstands the wider, structural causes of poverty. Indeed, it could even be argued that such an approach is potentially dangerous, because it is a paternalistic strategy based on charity, which encourages and reproduces existing patterns of inequality and relations of dependence. While the approach suggested here does not advocate this 'one to one' strategy, it does, however, argue that the evident appeal of such an approach may be able to teach us an effective lesson about the nature of moral motivation and responsiveness. Sponsoring a child is 'meaningful' to moral agents because it is directed towards a 'concrete' rather than a 'generalised' other; the child, through photographs and letters, is 'known' by the moral agent as a real human being with a name, a face, and a history.

A critical ethics of care does not mock these feelings as 'sentimental', nor does it brand them as 'personal' or 'particular' and therefore beyond the scope of impartial morality. But once we recognise such connections as truly moral, how and where do we proceed from here? Should we seek to 'translate' these moral impulses into political action? As was argued above, moral and political action aimed at reducing global poverty cannot be confined to one-to-one, personal relationships; such a strategy would be neither realistic nor effective. What is required, instead, is a restructuring of political action in such a way that enduring relationships may develop, which can allow agents to focus their moral attention, and ultimately, to act with the virtues of care – attentiveness, responsiveness, and responsibility. If the methods and activities of organisations involved in development and the eradication of poverty are structured in such a way that the growth of sustained, long-term connections between members from both the North and the South is encouraged – rather than ignored or actively discouraged – the development of genuine moral concern would be more likely to emerge. Thus, instead of seeking to find wealthy and powerful parent-figures to provide material support and 'care about' impoverished children, poverty-eradication projects must pay attention to the ways in which parents themselves may be empowered to care adequately for their own children. Such a strategy of 'empowerment', moreover, need not rely on a ethos of individualism; achieving empowerment must involve not just a declaration of individual rights, or an articulation of 'our' moral obligations, but the creation of projects which help to promote healthy, strengthening social and personal ties within communities, and which are run on the basis of mutual attention and mutual learning between actors.

Jenny Edkins has suggested how such an approach may be useful in the context of famine. She argues that, in our understanding of famine, we should move towards an approach based on an analysis of the relationships of connection between people. This implies a movement from the 'abstract', 'logical', analytical approach implied by the question, 'should we intervene to stop exploitation and domination?', to the more practical, specific question, 'how can we best act to promote good relations?' This approach suggests a different way of looking at, and responding to, famine. In her words,

> [f]amines can be seen…as processes where relationships between people have produced unacceptable results and transgressed limits of inhumanity. The web of relationships is more complex and extensive than the simple separations into 'winners' and 'losers', developed and underdeveloped, rich and poor can account for. Living with the inevitable antagonism – undecidability – at the heart of the social relations is arguably what we must learn to do.[32]

The approach put forward in this chapter does not valorise or romanticise existing and potential social relations. Importantly, it is one which, as Edkins argues, 'recognises the potential for violent domination and inequalities in all social relationships'.[33] An ethics of care in the context of international relations – and specifically, in the context of world poverty – must be a *critical* approach which seeks to demonstrate that overcoming social exclusion demands attention to the nature and functioning of social relations. Such an ethics can be useful in demonstrating that the existence of 'difference' which leads to processes of exclusion is neither natural nor objective, but that the act of naming difference can only be understood in the context of a relationship. Viewed in this way, no individual or group can be seen as objectively 'different' and therefore deserving of social exclusion. Thus, while a critical-relational ethics of care places moral value on the sustained, continuous attention which characterises stable, caring relations, it also seeks to situate social and personal relations in their wider socio-political and structural context of uneven and potentially exploitative social relations. From this perspective, poverty in the South would be regarded, in part, as a breakdown of global social relations, where inequalities in power and influence have resulted in the legitimation of existing patterns of exclusion and domination. Patterns of local relations – familial attachments, gender relations, social hierarchies, *etc.* – would also be explored in order to uncover the extent to which they may also perpetuate the impoverishment of certain groups within societies. An approach to ethics which values caring must interrogate these relations in an effort to create, or restore, a situation in which relations are characterised by mutual and self respect.

Finally, it must be made clear that this approach to ethics is concerned not only with relationships, but with the persons themselves whose lives are caught up in these intricate social and personal webs. An ethics of care takes seriously the identity and particularity of moral agents and subjects; it focuses not on the abstract other – the individual human being, who is thought to have a pre-social identity – but on the concrete other, whose own quality of life can only be made sense of through some basic knowledge of that person's particularity. This is not to suggest that we must gain an intimate understanding of the details of every person's life before we can begin to respond morally to their suffering; it does mean, however, that groups and individuals involved in projects and policy concerning social and economic relations with the South should see it as a priority to gain as much long-term knowledge as possible of the context of particular cases of poverty and suffering in order to respond to them usefully and effectively.

Commitment to relationships and sensitivity to the particularity of persons is also an important aspect of moral motivation which, in an ethics of care, is a crucial part of thinking about morality and moral responses. Dominant rights or duty-based approaches to ethics often tell us very little about motivation, concentrating instead on principles of justice or right action. To the extent that they do address motivation, they focus on the idea of 'shared humanity'. Certainly, this may elicit a rational response, in that we recognise the shared traits of humanity and therefore bestow some special status on all those exhibiting those traits; we may even respond emotionally to the rhetoric that 'no human being should have to suffer in such a way, or be subjected to such treatment'. These, of course, are all valid responses. But as Hugh LaFollette and Larry May argue, moral obligations to 'humanity as such' are viewed by most people as separate from, and indeed competing with, the priorities of their everyday lives:

> moral obligations which require us to abandon what is important to us, especially in the absence of some connection with those in need, will rarely be met by many people – and thus, will make no moral difference. Some might argue, on more abstract philosophical grounds, that we should not need that link. Perhaps that is true. But, whether we should need to feel this connection, the fact is, most people do need it. Thus, we want to know what will *actually* motivate people to act.[34]

An approach to ethics based on the idea of care is committed to the idea that we can, and must, learn to care. To illustrate how this may be possible, Murdoch uses the example of love, and the attention that it consumes. 'Deliberately falling out of love is not a jump of the will', she argues, 'it is the acquiring of new objects of attention and thus new energies as a result of refocusing'.[35] 'Human beings are naturally "attached" and when an attachment seems painful or bad it is most readily displaced by another attachment, which an attempt at attention can encourage'.[36] We need not be physically close to our objects of attachments, nor need we accept the way that social and political structures have determined to whom and what we are 'naturally' attached. A critical ethics of care questions both the nature and quality of apparently natural attachments, and encourages the focusing of moral energy on the creation of new and healthy relations to address moral and social problems.

From the perspective of an ethics of care, it is our personal and social relations – our feelings of connection and responsibility – which motivate us to focus our attention and respond morally to the suffering of others. Thus, the ability to care with commitment about another can only emerge through sustained connections among persons and groups of persons. Of course, there are many people in the wealthy countries of the North for whom no such connections with impoverished communities in the South exist; this is why, at the outset, the focus must be on those members of organisations already involved in project work or in the making of policy concerning poverty/development. The building of long-term relationships must be made an explicit strategy of NGOs, transnational social movements, and governments. The current use of functional, issue-specific, superficial relationships, designed to maintain 'distance', 'impartiality', and 'reciprocity' must give way to a strategy focused on long-term relationships characterised by mutual learning and a sense of attachment, rather than disconnection. Thus, while the question of moral motivation is, indeed, prior to the question of moral action, it need not be prior to the making of connections. After all, it is the business of development agencies to intervene in, and thus to create relationships with, the lives of those who are dogged by poverty. This chapter argues that the nature of those relationships is crucial to the type of moral responses that will emerge from them; relationships must allow participants in these projects to connect, in a sustained and enduring way, with the real circumstances of the lives of others. As transnational social movements, and global civil society in general, continue to expand in both size and importance, more and more people may find themselves involved in such relationships, and the distance, both physical and moral, which exists between North and South, may begin to reduce. That which remains distant to moral agents will never assume moral priority, in spite of what Kantian ethics and theories of justice as impartiality may tell us. Making the suffering of impoverished persons important to those who are in a position to do something about it relies on building enduring connections into their policies and strategies.

Care in Context: New Ethical Strategies for Eradicating Poverty

Certainly, given the embeddedness of the moral language of rights and duties, it is often difficult to imagine how, and in what contexts, the language and strategies of a critical, relational ethics of care would be put into practice. Indeed, as has already been argued, the language of rights and duties does not exist independently; rather, it is intimately linked to the political philosophy of liberalism – a philosophy that currently dominates theory and practice regarding the global political economy, international legitimacy, and development. Thus, as I have suggested, the moral discourse of rights and duties – emphasising the liberal values of individual freedom and autonomy, private property, accumulation, and progress – is unlikely to disturb the existing asymmetries in power and levels of well-being which currently characterise the global order. The separation of the right and the good in neo-Kantian liberal philosophy maintains the sovereignty of the concept of individual autonomy – associated with negative liberty and the notion of the pure moral will – which, in turn, leads to the predominance of the moral notions of individual rights and rational duties in discussions of international ethics.

It is such a contractualist ethics of rights and duties that lies at the base of the apparently progressive discourse of 'partnership' which characterises the strategies of many development NGOs. The term implies the existence of egalitarian relationships between actors from both North and South, as opposed to the paternalism and hierarchy of the past.[37] As Laura Macdonald argues, however, the language of interdependence and partnership conceals the real power relations at work in development policy. She quotes Brian Murphy, of the Canadian NGO Inter-Pares:

[p]artnership is a dichotomy, and implies an objectification of relationships....Partnership implies a division: a division of labour, of reward, of responsibility, of authority, of ownership. Partnership is a limited, negotiated relationship for mutually supportive, but separate action towards limited but (at least on the surface) mutually consistent goals. Partnership does not challenge existing relations or disparities, for example, or power, resources or affluence. Partnership, based within disparity, can only work to maintain and increase the existing disparity and fundamental inequality between and among partners.[38]

As this critique implies, certain members of the NGO community have begun to recognise the inherent limitations in the discourse of partnership, and in the ethics of formal equality which underwrites it. Indeed, there is a growing recognition among members of the NGO community of the need actively to dismantle the prevailing ideology, 'its language, its syntax, its questions and its answers, and the possibilities it predicts, and prevents'.[39]

It is in this spirit that a new model for North-South relations has emerged among some Northern NGOs. Sometimes referred to as 'accompaniment', this model is based on respect for control by the local partner and an attempt to provide non-monetary forms of support for the struggles of local groups and a deeper form of commitment to the processes of social change in the Third World.[40] The accompaniment approach often includes development education and political advocacy work within the home countries of the NGOs, both to support Third World struggles, but also to promote social change within the North.[41] As Macdonald points out,

> [t]his type of work attempts to break down stereotypical images of the South, and to identify shared interests between individuals in both South and North. While this is certainly not the dominant pattern among NGO programs, it is a necessary model for constructing counter-hegemonic global identities.[42]

Certain grassroots strategies to eradicate poverty which target women can also be identified with, and used to illustrate the potential significance of, a critical-relational ethical perspective. What is important about these alternative strategies is that they are 'based on close, face-to-face interaction between organizations and their constituencies so that ideas and policies are shaped in the crucible of everyday practice rather than in the upper echelons of remote and rule-bound bureaucracies'.[43] These are strategies of *closeness* rather than distance or *remoteness,* based on promoting *interaction*, rather than concentrating on following *rules*.

The Grameen Bank in Bangladesh is becoming well-known for its successes in providing credit to the poor and assetless – mainly women –

based on the recognition that the major constraint on their well-being was the lack of access to financial institutions, rather than to the waged labour market. Starting out as a poverty-eradication programme, what was a small credit operation in 1976 became an independent national bank in 1983, with women constituting over 90 per cent of bank borrowers. Similarly, the less well-known Self Employed Women's Association (SEWA) in India also works with poor self-employed women, but primarily in urban areas. This association emerged in response to the expressed needs of women workers in the unorganised sector who had largely been ignored by the male-dominated trade-union movement.[44]

As Naila Kabeer points out, in both the Grameen and the SEWA cases, the initial set of needs identified were economic ones. However, the great strength of these participatory methods is the recognition of other, non-economic needs, and the realisation that categories of needs are not discrete, but interdependent.[45] Most important, however, are the opportunities for women to uncover the socially-constructed and socially-shared basis of apparently individual problems.[46] The Grameen Bank, for example, focuses explicitly on building new collective identities for women through the process of group formation; they also, furthermore, emphasise the interpersonal dynamics involved in the process. It is not only the women themselves who build attachments and solidarities; women borrowers have interacted with bank workers to agree on tangible and intangible aspects of social development.[47]

Group formation is critical to Grameen credit disbursement, insofar as the group is involved in making decisions about lending, and also, significantly, in providing social collateral.[48] SEWA, mentioned above, also has a model of joint action at the heart of its organisational strategy; through co-operatives and more conventional unions, SEWA provides a social connection to a section of the work force whose members are either isolated within the home or in dispersed and shifting work locations. These strategies clearly value the quality of personal attachments for their potential to bring about social change, but they are also critical about the ability of 'normal ties' to act in a counter-hegemonic and progressive manner. As Kabeer argues,

[a]ccess to these new and collective relationships, built around their shared needs and interests as workers and as women, has given SEWA's members an opportunity to think of themselves in terms other than those imposed by their traditional domestic, caste and community roles.[49]

These projects suggest a role for a critical ethics of care in the context of North-South relations and, specifically, in the eradication of poverty. First, they demonstrate quite clearly that a purely economic interpretation of the strategies of states and non-state actors is inadequate to achieve a clear understanding of the motives, assumptions, and goals which inform policies and projects. These approaches are guided explicitly by *an ethics*, which is more than just a recognition of a problem – that 'it is morally wrong that people live in poverty' – a problem about which it is often assumed that we can then go on to address and solve using economic strategies. By contrast, these approaches reject the separation of economics, politics, and morality, by recognising the transformatory potential of so-called 'intangible' resources, such as 'social networks, organizational strength, solidarity and a sense of not being alone'.[50]

The nature of this ethics, however, is significant, insofar as it seeks to promote strong, healthy, caring attachments among members of existing communities, as well as to create new networks across communities, and to build new alliances, which often break down or cross cut traditional personal and social ties. As the rhetoric of 'partnership', which stresses rights and duties, individual autonomy, and formal equality, gives way to the strategy of 'accompaniment', there is a growing recognition of that moral problems, and their economic and political dimensions, must be addressed, and potential solutions found, at the level of social relations. These approaches, moreover, view relationships in a critical light, and with an awareness that all attachments contain the potential for paternalism, dependence, and even violence and exploitation. Thus, the approaches discussed above place an emphasis on learning how to listen and to be attentive to the women themselves, in order to understand which relationships and attachments are most conducive to the fostering of strength and solidarity. This is not to say, however, that such strategies ignore the values of independent selfhood. Indeed, the language of 'empowerment', 'self-esteem', and 'self-determination' is central to these grassroots, participatory approaches. However, there is a recognition that self-esteem and autonomy only exist in the context of relationships, and that the level of our self-esteem, and, indeed, our autonomy, is often dependent on the quality of our personal and social attachments with others.

Conclusion

In this chapter, I have argued that approaches to ethics which focus on rights and duties, individual freedom, and formal equality can do little to alter existing patterns of exclusion in the world today, and thus cannot take us very far towards our goal of eradicating poverty on a global scale. In contrast to these rule-based, legalistic approaches, I have argued in favour of a contextual, situated ethics, which starts from a relational ontology; such an ethics is concerned both to explore critically existing relations and to enhance our capacity to focus attention on the other through the promotion and creation of healthy, strong attachments both within and across existing social groupings. According to this approach, world poverty is not something that can be 'solved' through isolated attention to individual rights, or through rational judgement of our obligations; indeed, to suggest this is to perpetuate the divide between 'ethics' and 'politics', and to fuel the argument that 'ethics' can contribute nothing to the solution of social problems. A critical ethics of care, however, starts from the position that both the causes of poverty and the strategies we use to address it can be found only through attention to relationships, and, specifically, a critical analysis of the ways in which attachments that are exploitative and marginalising can be transformed to create social conditions characterised by interdependence and mutual learning and respect.

An ethics of care is not a theoretical, rule-based ethics that focuses on a moment of pure will or rational moral judgement; rather, it is an ethics which believes that morality is a messy, lengthy process which is part of the fabric of people's everyday lives. It is only once we make poverty in the South a part of the lives of those with the ability to transform it – once there is a commitment to learning how to care both for impoverished peoples and their concerns, and to focus our attention on their suffering – will we start the slow process towards change. This process must almost certainly begin with those members of 'global' civil society who are already 'connected' with impoverished communities; these groups must radically and explicitly alter their strategies for engaging with the poor, by shifting from functional, ostensibly equal, short-term relationships, towards enduring relationships based on mutual learning and guided by an explicit awareness of the inequalities of power which govern their interactions. As global civil society continues to expand, and as the relationships and 'communities' are no longer governed by territory and contiguity, opportunities to build relationships may also increase in scope and number. However, we must put effort into the task of constructing these attachments, and recognise that it will take time to learn how to focus our attention on both the human suffering related to poverty and the causes of that suffering. This will mean 'getting our hands dirty', so to speak, by paying close attention to the daily, habitual misery endured by concrete persons. Only once we get beyond the abstract rhetoric of 'economic rights' and 'duties beyond borders' can we begin our 'poor but epic battle' against global poverty.[51]

NOTES

I am grateful to my colleagues and students at the University of Sussex for listening to, and providing me with helpful comments on, my ideas on ethics in international relations. I would also like to thank Laura Macdonald for her encouragement and her useful ideas about the links between an ethics of care and the new strategies of some development INGOs.

1. Iris Murdoch, *Existentialists and Mystics: Writings on Philosophy and Literature* (London: Chatto and Windus, 1997), pp. 343–4.
2. Radhika Balakrishnan and Uma Narayan, 'Combining Justice with Development: Rethinking Rights and Responsibilities in the Context of World Hunger and Poverty', in William Aiken and Hugh LaFollette (eds.), *World Hunger and Morality*, Second Edition (Upper Saddle River, NJ: Prentice-Hall, 1996), p. 245.
3. David A. Cocker, 'Hunger, Capability and Development', in Aiken and LaFollette (eds.), *op. cit.*, in note 2, p. 212.
4. Robert H. Jackson, 'The Political Theory of International Society', in Ken Booth and Steve Smith (eds.), *International Relations Theory Today* (Cambridge: Polity Press, 1995), pp. 124–5.
5. Onora O'Neill, 'Ending World Hunger', in Aiken and LaFollette (eds.), *op. cit.*, in note 2, p. 210
6. Murdoch, *op. cit.*, in note 1, p. 366.
7. Bernard Williams,, *Ethics and the Limits of Philosophy* (London: Fontana Press, 1985), p. 72.
8. *Ibid.*, p. 93.
9. Martha Minow and Mary Lyndon Shanley, 'Revisioning the Family: Relational Rights and Responsibilities', in Mary Lyndon Shanley and Uma Narayan (eds.), *Reconstructing Political Theory: Feminist Perspectives* (Cambridge: Polity Press, 1997), p. 102.
10. I make this argument in detail in 'The Limits of a Rights-based Approach to International Ethics', in Tony Evans (ed.), *Human Rights Fifty Years On: A Critical Appraisal* (Manchester: Manchester University Press, forthcoming).
11. Murdoch, *op. cit.*, in note 1, p. 366.
12. James W. Nickel, 'A Human Rights Approach to World Hunger', in Aiken and LaFollette (eds.), *op. cit.*, in note 2, p. 176.
13. Henry Shue, 'Solidarity among Strangers and the Right to Food', in Aiken and LaFollette (eds.), *op. cit.*, in note 2, p. 118.
14. O'Neill, *op. cit.*, in note 5, p. 94.
15. O'Neill, *Towards Justice and Virtue: A Constructive Account of Practical Reason* (Cambridge: Cambridge University Press, 1996), pp. 147–148.
16. *Ibid.*, p. 146.
17. *Ibid.*, p. 141.
18. O'Neill, *op. cit.*, in note 5, p. 105.
19. Roger Spegele, *Political Realism in International Relations* (Cambridge: Cambridge University Press, 1996), p. 237.
20. See Joan Tronto, *Moral Boundaries: A Political Argument for an Ethic of Care* (London: Routledge, 1992); Virginia Held (ed.), *Justice and Care: Essential Readings in Feminist Ethics* (Boulder, CO: Westview, 1995); Virginia Held,

Feminist Morality: Transforming Culture, Society and Politics (Chicago, IL: University of Chicago Press, 1993); Annette Baier, *Moral Prejudices: Essays on Ethics* (Cambridge, MA: Harvard University Press, 1992); Margaret Urban Walker, *Moral Understandings: A Feminist Study in Ethics* (New York, NY: Routledge, 1998); and Lawrence Blum, *Moral Perception and Particularity* (Cambridge: Cambridge University Press, 1994). Although she was writing long before Carol Gilligan, there are resonances of Gilligan's ideas in the philosophy of Iris Murdoch. See Murdoch, *op. cit.*, in note 1.

21. Carol Gilligan, *In a Different Voice: Psychological Theory and Women's Development*, Second Edition (Cambridge, MA: Harvard University Press, 1993).

22. *Ibid.*, p. 27; see also Lawrence Kohlberg, *Essays in Moral Development*, 2 Volumes (New York, NY: Harper and Row, 1981 and 1984).

23. Gilligan, *op. cit.*, in note 21, pp. 28–9.

24. Lawrence Blum, *Moral Perception and Particularity* (Cambridge: Cambridge University Press, 1994), pp. 215–16.

25. Susan Hekman, *Moral Voices, Moral Selves: Carol Gilligan and Feminist Moral Theory* (Cambridge: Polity Press, 1995), p. 7.

26. Seyla Benhabib, *Situating the Self: Gender, Community and Postmodernism in Contemporary Ethics* (Cambridge: Polity Press, 1992), pp. 179–80.

27. Onora O'Neill, 'Justice, Gender and International Boundaries', in Robert Attfield and Barry Wilkins (eds.), *International Justice and the Third World* (London: Routledge, 1993), p. 55.

28. Susan Moller Okin refers to this argument in her article 'Reason and Feeling in Thinking About Justice', in Cass R. Sunstein (ed.), *Feminism and Political Theory* (Chicago, IL: University of Chicago Press, 1990), p. 34. See also Susan Moller Okin, 'Thinking Like a Woman', in Deborah Rhode (ed.), *Theoretical Perspectives on Sexual Difference* (New Haven, CT: Yale University Press, 1990), pp. 145–59.

29. Joan Tronto, *Moral Boundaries: A Political Argument for an Ethic of Care* (London: Routledge, 1992), p. 91.

30. *Ibid.*

31. Murdoch, *op. cit.*, in note 1, pp. 343 and 380.

32. Jenny Edkins, 'Legality with a Vengeance: Famines and Humanitarian Relief in "Complex Emergencies"', *Millennium: Journal of International Studies* (Vol. 25, No. 3, 1996), p. 573, reprinted in this volume.

33. *Ibid.*, p. 563.

34. Hugh LaFollette and Larry May, 'Suffer the Little Children', in Aiken and LaFollette (eds.), *op. cit.*, in note 2, p. 81.

35. Murdoch, *op. cit.*, in note 1, p. 345.

36. *Ibid.*

37. Laura Macdonald, 'Unequal Partnerships: The Politics of Canada's Relations with the Third World', *Studies in Political Economy* (Vol. 47, 1995), pp. 130–1.

38. *Ibid.*, pp. 134–5.

39. *Ibid.*, p. 135.

40. I am very grateful to Laura Macdonald for bringing to my attention the links between a critical ethics of care and the NGO strategy of 'accompaniment'.

41. Laura Macdonald, 'Globalising Civil Society: Interpreting International NGOs in Central America', *Millennium* (Vol. 23, No. 2, 1994), p. 284.

42. *Ibid.*
43. Naila Kabeer, *Reversed Realities: Gender Hierarchies in Development Thought* (London: Verso, 1994), p. 223.
44. *Ibid.*, p. 231.
45. *Ibid.*, pp. 232 and 234.
46. *Ibid.*, p. 245.
47. *Ibid.*, pp. 247–8.
48. *Ibid.*, p. 254.
49. *Ibid.*, pp. 254–5.
50. Kabeer, *op. cit.*, in note 43, p. 246.
51. The phrase 'poor but epic battle' is borrowed from Judith Shklar. See Judith Shklar, *Ordinary Vices* (Cambridge, MA: Harvard University Press, 1984), p. 235.

3. Legality with a Vengeance: Famines and Humanitarian Relief in 'Complex Emergencies'

Jenny Edkins

The law stands between food availability and food entitlement. Starvation deaths can reflect legality with a vengeance.[1]

Current academic studies emphasise the link between hunger and war or conflict. Famines are regarded as being part of a new, post-Cold War phenomenon, 'complex emergencies'.[2] This new conceptualisation challenges previous theories that saw famine as an economic problem and proposed remedies based on development, as well as the widespread view of famines as a scarcity of food.[3] It has implications for international politics and, especially, current debates around issues of humanitarianism, relief, and intervention. The argument of complex emergency theories is that starvation and famines should be seen neither as natural disasters nor as evidence of economic failure, but as complex socio-political crises. In this view, famines should be linked with wars, rather than with economic breakdown.

The roots of the 'complex emergency' approach lie in its opposition to 'entitlements' theories of famine. This article will examine Amartya Sen's entitlement theory from a Derridean perspective.[4] It will argue that 'force' was already implicated in Sen's notion of entitlements, even in the absence of military conflict. Sen's analysis leads to a practice of relief that relies on technical and managerial solutions. Despite their radical contention that relief can be a cause of famine, there is a risk that 'complex emergency' theories too will retain a reliance on 'experts'; this time, experts in conflict prevention and resolution.

This article argues that we should take a much broader view of the role of force and violence, eschewing easy dichotomies between peace and conflict, or famine and plenty, in favour of a questioning of connections and relationships. This would lead to a more critical approach to specific international situations in which decisions must be, and are, made. Rather than seeing famines, conflicts, and poverty as problems that call for technical solutions from 'experts', what is needed is political and ethical engagement, where responsibility for decisions about intervention is inescapable.

The struggles to articulate and re-articulate theories of famine can themselves be seen as continuing attempts to 're-inscribe' the political – attempts to re-write what counts as needing ethical or political decisions – and, hence, situate the boundaries of what will be accepted as the terrain of the 'expert', the 'professional'. In part, the current theoretical debates reflect struggles between different disciplines for the ear of policy-makers and the funding that goes with such status. Is famine a question of food supply, to be tackled by greater agricultural production, new varieties of seed, and advanced farming methods, in which case it is the province of the development expert? Or is it a matter of poverty and vulnerability, to be tackled by a welfare safety net, public works programmes, and early warning systems? Or is it a question of an emergency situation calling for action by the relevant non-governmental organisations? Further, if it is an emergency, is it a question of humanitarian relief, military intervention, or conflict resolution? In what is seen by some writers on complex emergencies as a new (dis)order emerging in a post-Cold War world,[5] the old disciplinary boundaries are being renegotiated. The debate over whether resources should be concentrated on 'relief' efforts or on longer term 'development' projects, and the so-called 'relief-development' continuum, has been revived by some[6] and proclaimed irrelevant by others.[7] Development specialists who saw their assumptions challenged in Cold War crises,[8] and who witnessed the balance swing in financial terms to massive funding for high-profile relief operations, are now taking the role of critics of the new humanitarianism.[9]

Food Scarcity

Offering food aid to suffering victims of famine is widely regarded by the 'international community', donor states, and nongovernmental organisations (NGOs) as an uncontentious example of humanitarianism. A starving population is assumed to be in need of relief in the form of food supplies, and this is duly, although often belatedly, offered. This seemingly straightforward response in fact invokes a specifically Malthusian notion of what 'famines' are. Thomas Malthus held famine to be Nature's 'last, most dreadful resource'[10] in the face of an inexorably expanding human population. His argument was that 'the power of population is so superior to the power in the earth to produce subsistence for man that premature death must in some shape or other visit the human race'.[11] If other instruments of depopulation fail, then famine is inevitable.

This view has been widely contested. For example, there are those who point to the fact that population has, so far at least, failed to outstrip food supplies in general, and that, after a famine, it is only a relatively short time before population returns to levels it would have reached had there been no famine.[12] There are also those who contend that the Malthusian picture relies on the separation of Man and Nature, and a particular, gendered view of nature as the site of competition over scarce resources.[13] Despite these challenges, Malthus' view is still a powerful component of images of apocalypse and disaster associated with media coverage of famines, and the Malthusian picture remains prominent in policy-making and public debate.[14] For example, the 1996 World Food Summit in Rome, organised by the Food and Agriculture Organization of the United Nations (FAO), draws on understandings that link famine with agriculture, food supply, and population.[15]

Entitled to Starve

The view that famines involve mass starvation due to a general shortage of food has been challenged by Sen. Sen's approach, first propounded in the late 1970s and early 1980s, claims that contrary to Malthusian assumptions, famine is not caused by food shortages or a failure of food availability.[16] In this view, famine is ultimately caused by a breakdown in food entitlements. This fall in entitlements, which would typically affect only certain small sections of a population, could be triggered by a shortage of food in general, but this shortage is only one of the factors that could give rise to a fall in entitlements. A fall in entitlements to food could equally be caused by unemployment, a rise in prices not itself indicative of shortage, or a number of other factors.[17] This would leave the affected groups vulnerable to starvation, and extensive starvation would lead to famines, defined by Sen as 'involving fairly widespread acute starvation'.[18] Famine is seen as an extension of starvation, which itself is an acute manifestation of poverty.

Although a powerful denunciation of the picture of famine as a natural disaster, attributable to causes, such as 'drought' or pestilence, beyond the control of states or governments, Sen's approach retains the notion of famine as a sudden economic collapse, a failure, but this time in the economic system. The remedies advocated include the establishment of early warning systems to detect signs of entitlement collapse, as well as systems of public welfare to provide replacements for those entitlements through public works or, if the process has gone too far, free distribution of food.[19] Through the play of market forces, food would be attracted to food shortage areas as soon as the affected groups have re-established their exchange entitlements. This approach has been widely welcomed as a major advance, enabling detailed attention to be focused on the specifics of the entitlements of particular groups in historical cases, rather than on broad-brush statistics of quantities of food per head.[20] It stresses two crucial points: first, in any population it is only certain vulnerable groups that are affected by starvation; and second, famines are 'man-made', they are not the equivalent of earthquakes, or hurricanes, or floods. As such, the remedy is to be sought in the economic system, by government intervention to replace lost entitlements through public welfare programmes.

The entitlements approach has been roundly criticised on a number of counts, and it is widely accepted that in a large number of contemporary cases of famine, particularly in Africa, its account is unsatisfactory. The most fundamental and earliest criticism has arisen from two issues raised by Amrita Rangasami in 1985.[21] First, entitlement theory treats famine as a 'biological' process, a process which essentially leads to starvation. For Rangasami, famine is much more than this. It is a 'politico-socio-economic process', and what is more, Rangasami claims that mortality is not a necessary condition of famine. Famine as a process goes through several stages – of dearth, famishment, and morbidity – and 'the culmination of the process comes well before the slide into disease and death'.[22] Second, entitlement theory considers only the victims of starvation. As Rangasami puts it, famine 'is a process in which benefits accrue to one section of the community while losses flow to the other'.[23] It is a process with 'winners' and 'losers', and in order to determine what famine is – which, for Rangasami, is the same as determining its causes – we must look at 'the adaptations, manoeuvres and strategies utilised by both victim and beneficiary [which] can be economic, social or psychological or partake of all three'.[24]

Rangasami offers a definition of famine as a 'pressing down', or oppression: 'a process during which pressure or force (economic, military, political, social, psychological) is exerted upon the victim community, gradually increasing in intensity until the stricken are deprived of all assets including the ability to labour'.[25] She claims that accounts of famine focus on the last phase of this long process, the phase of morbidity: '[t]he state as well as the do-gooders, the voluntary agencies, do not enter the arena, until the process is resolved against the victims. The famine accounts we have today, begin even with the moment of state intervention'.[26] So-called 'early warning systems' only pick up these final stages, where dislocation and movement of people is already apparent. Assistance, when it comes, may be sufficient to save lives, but it does not replace lost assets.

Complex Emergencies

While Sen examines how legal structures can prevent access to food by those without legitimate 'entitlements', current theoretical approaches developed in response to famines in the Horn of Africa emphasise the role of the 'extra-legal', namely war and conflict. This has led to a situation in which debates about 'complex emergencies' and the 'humanitarian intervention' that claims to respond to them are replacing talk of 'famines' and 'famine relief'. According to this view, not only may relief food aid not solve the problem, as it may never reach those it is intended to help, but, in addition, it may actually produce or exacerbate famine.[27] Famine is seen as a product of conflict, and donations of food in this context can increase the benefits to those who are 'winning' anyway. Famine is a political issue: it is the result of what is seen to be internal war produced to a large extent by conflicts over resources.[28]

The 'complex emergency' theorists – Alex de Waal, David Keen, and Mark Duffield – all distinguish their work from Sen's entitlement theory of famine.[29] As witnesses and analysts of relief operations in conflict zones, in the Horn of Africa in particular, they have developed an alternative analysis described as a 'novel paradigm',[30] which draws heavily on the work of Rangasami. Initially, this paradigm was focused on loosening famine theory from its links with 'entitlements' and 'vulnerability', to stress instead the active response of 'victim' communities and the view of famine as a process over time. De Waal, in an analysis of famine in the Sudan, argued that relief operations do not take into account or support the coping strategies of victims, who see famines not as disastrous events but as processes.[31] The outcome most feared was not death by starvation, but destitution, a total deprivation of assets.[32] This was then combined with a call for more attention to be paid to the existence of both 'winners' and 'losers' in famines, and more care to be taken over the distribution of relief to prevent it from being appropriated by the powerful.[33] In other words, there are beneficiaries as well as victims of famines. Keen has analysed the way famines are not prevented, and indeed are often actually promoted, by those who stand to gain, either from the famines themselves or from the relief operations. These 'winners' can include the governments of countries where famines occur, local economic interests or warring factions, *and* international agencies or donor governments.[34] This approach has moved on to propose that what we now have is an entirely novel post-Cold War situation; a situation of more or less permanent 'complex emergency'.[35] Famine is re-articulated with 'counter-insurgency' and 'conflict'. Those specialists who initially saw themselves as responding to economic oppression and underdevelopment are increasingly adopting a position of 'human rights advocacy'.[36]

The term 'complex emergency' originated in the late 1980s,[37] in relation initially to conflicts in Africa and the Gulf, where for the United Nations it meant 'a major humanitarian crisis of a multi-causal nature...a long-term combination of political, conflict and peacekeeping factors'.[38] For Joanna Macrae and Anthony Zwi,[39] complex emergencies are 'intentionally created and...sustained in order to achieve their objectives of cultural genocide and political and economic power...a potent combination of political and economic factors driving and maintaining disaster-producing conflicts'.[40] Duffield attempts to distinguish 'complex emergencies' from 'natural disasters':

[s]o-called complex emergencies are essentially political in nature: they are protracted political crises resulting from sectarian or predatory indigenous responses to socioeconomic stress and marginalisation. Unlike natural disasters, complex emergencies have a singular ability to erode or destroy the cultural, civil, political and economic integrity of established societies.... Humanitarian assistance itself can become a target of violence and appropriation by political actors who are organic parts of the crisis. Complex emergencies are internal to political and economic structures. They are different from natural disasters and deserve to be understood and responded to as such.[41]

Despite this attempt, the notion of 'complex emergencies' still draws on notions of food shortage or 'stress'.[42] In that sense, its repudiation of the image of a 'natural disaster' is unsuccessful.[43] The danger of this, first, is that the political or military conflict that characterises such emergencies is seen as secondary, and also that it is seen only as complicating efforts to provide relief. Assistance itself is assumed to be 'well intended' and politically neutral. Complex emergencies are still seen as a natural 'kind' and hence as a failure of an otherwise benign social and political system. Viewing them in this way has important implications for policy, and can still lead, I will argue, to solutions of a technical or managerial nature.

Force of Law

The 'complex emergencies' theorists draw on Rangasami; the chief criticism that they level at Sen is that as a theory of famine, 'entitlement theory has no place for violence'.[44] I want to explore this claim by looking in some detail at Sen's work, as presented in *Poverty and Famines*.[45] I shall take a deconstructive approach which looks for the marginal, the deferred, and the excluded in Sen's account. What is put to one side as irrelevant to the matter under examination can turn out to be more instructive than it might appear. The separations that are made, and the oppositions and hierarchies that form the often unspoken basis of the argument, can help in the analysis. I will look first at two exclusions: the exclusion of 'non-entitlement transfers' and the exclusion of deliberate starvation. I will argue that these exclusions can be seen as central to an understanding of what Sen is doing. This will be discussed in relation to Jacques Derrida's work on the 'Force of Law'.[46] Sen uses the exclusion of 'non-entitlement transfers' to define the existence of 'entitlement' and 'legality'.[47] His argument also relies on separating the economic and the political and placing them in a hierarchical opposition.[48]

For Derrida, the drawing of boundaries by a process of exclusion, which places something 'outside' and thus 'defines' an essence, or an inside, is a process that is typical of logocentric analysis, the form of analysis that is familiar in methaphysics, and Western thought more generally.[49] In this mode of analysis, the process of differentiation is one in which the 'risk' of an 'accident' or failure is placed outside.

However, Derrida argues that it is exactly through this act of displacing or deferring that the 'inside', or what is called the 'essence', is produced.[50] If this is the case, then that which is deferred or excluded can be called a 'constitutive outside',[51] an outside that is *necessary* in order to constitute or form the inside. Derrida asks, '[i]s that outside its inside, the very force and law of its emergence?'[52] In other words, does what has been excluded constitute the essence? Is what is excluded effectively essential? As soon as logocentric analysis recognises this possibility, it denies it. In Derrida's words, logocentric analysis

> consists in recognising that the possibility of the negative…is in fact a structural possibility, that failure is an essential risk of the operations under consideration; then, in a move which is almost *immediately simultaneous*, in the name of a kind of ideal regulation, it excludes that risk as accidental, exterior, one which teaches us nothing about the…phenomenon being considered.[53]

If this is what logocentric analysis does, then what Derrida suggests is another mode of analysis: deconstruction. According to Derrida, in carrying out a deconstructive analysis we need to ponder what follows if

> a possibility – a possible risk – is *always* possible, and is in some sense a necessary possibility. [And] whether – once such a necessary possibility of infelicity is recognised – infelicity still constitutes an accident. What is success when the possibility of infelicity continues to constitute its structure?[54]

Thus, we need to take seriously the role of what is excluded when something is constituted by the process of drawing boundaries. A deconstructive analysis does just this, looking for precisely that which is excluded or regarded as accidental by the account that is being studied.

Returning to Sen, we see that, from something he is going to call 'entitlements', he wants to exclude two things: first, instances when a person starves deliberately (or is deliberately starved) and, second, instances where extra-legal means are used to obtain food. These are regarded by Sen as parasitic, as abnormal, and can be excluded from a theory of starvation and famine:

> [t]he entitlement approach to starvation and famines concentrates on the ability of people to command food through the legal means

available in the society, including the use of production possibilities, trade opportunities, entitlements *vis-à-vis* the state, and other methods of acquiring food. A person starves *either* because he does not have the ability to command enough food *or* because he does not use this ability to avoid starvation. The entitlement approach concentrates on the former, ignoring the latter possibility. Furthermore, it concentrates on those means of commanding food that are legitimised by the legal system in operation in that society. While it is an approach of some generality, it makes no attempt to include all possible influences that can in principle cause starvation, for example illegal transfers (e.g. looting), and choice failures (e.g. owing to inflexible food habits).

Ownership of food is one of the most primitive property rights, and in each society there are rules governing this right. The entitlement approach concentrates on each person's entitlements to commodity bundles including food, and views starvation as resulting from a failure to be entitled to a bundle with enough food.[55]

In his first deferral, Sen sets aside instances of starvation as an intentional act. This includes both cases in which a person starves himself or herself deliberately, and those in which a person is deliberately starved by someone else. Here, I will discuss the first case, where Sen proposes '[l]eaving out cases in which a person may deliberately starve'.[56] Later, I will return to consider how Sen also sets to one side the notion that starving may be an act of 'deliberate harming'.[57] De Waal challenges him on the former deferral, arguing that, in famines, people often choose to go without food rather than sell assets.[58] However, Sen argues, this can be accounted for by a straightforward extension of the theory. It is a rational decision to choose to safeguard entitlements in order to avoid starvation in the future, as against avoiding hunger now: 'people sometimes choose to starve rather than sell their productive assets, and this issue can be accommodated [by] taking note of future entitlements'.[59]

However, choosing to starve has more significant ramifications than this. It can, on occasions, be a political act, even part of a violent struggle. Starvation has been used as a weapon by those who have no other weapon available to them; Irish prisoners in the 1980s are one example. Bobby Sands was the first of 10 Republican prisoners who 'deliberately' starved themselves to death in a campaign for political status in British prisons.[60] These actions were 'following an international political legacy that had gained moral legitimacy since the time of Ghandi [and] reinterpreting and enacting the cultural model of the Christian sacrifice'.[61] In these cases, then, the act of fasting can be a political act that influences relationships of power. Sen's omission of deliberate starvation omits a relation which demonstrates the entanglement of hunger and the political. Fasting also has other implications, particularly in its connection with the sacred and the emotive; for Sen, however, understanding these instances is not necessary 'in order to understand starvation'.[62] They can readily be put to one side.

Sen also sets to one side the notion that the starving of people may be a deliberate act. He makes a distinction between starvation and famine, but he wants to make this without 'attribut[ing] a sense of deliberate harming to the first absent from the second'.[63] This ascription is commonly made, as Sen acknowledges. He quotes a passage from Bernard Shaw's play *Man and Superman* about the Irish famine that draws attention to the 'deliberate harming' implicit in the word 'starvation': '[w]hen a country is full of food and exporting it, there can be no "famine" only deliberate starvation'.[64] Sen concedes that the word 'starvation' still carries the meaning of causing death through lack of food, and that '[t]he history of famines as well as of regular hunger is full of blood-boiling tales of callousness and malevolence'.[65] However, he then proceeds to set aside any notion of intentionality behind famines and to strip 'starvation' of its transitive quality. For the purposes of Sen's analysis, '[s]tarvation is used...in the wider sense of people going without adequate food, while famine is a particularly virulent manifestation of its causing widespread death'.[66]

This setting aside of the intentionality behind starving and being starved enables famines to be regarded as an 'accident' – a failure of the natural or economic system – and is what 'complex emergency' theorists are contesting.[67] Famines, they contend, have 'winners' and 'losers'.

Sen's second deferral is the exclusion of 'non-entitlement transfers'. As far as entitlements theory is concerned, transfers that are extra-legal – looting and raiding, for example – do not count. They are seen as quite distinct from activities that involve the upholding of legal rights in the face of starvation.[68] Sen does see this exclusion as representing one of the 'limitations' of the entitlement approach:

> while entitlement relations concentrate on rights within the given legal structure in that society, some transfers involve violation of these rights, such as looting or brigandage. When such extra-entitlement transfers are important, the entitlement approach to famines will be defective. On the other hand, most recent famines seem to have taken place in societies with 'law and order', without anything 'illegal' about the processes leading to starvation. In fact, in guarding ownership rights against the demands of the hungry, the legal forces uphold entitlements; for example, in the Bengal famine of 1943 the people who died in front of well-stocked food shops protected by the state were denied food because of *lack* of legal entitlement, and not because their entitlements were violated.[69]

Clearly, the notion of 'entitlements', in Sen's use of the word, does not reflect in any sense a concept of the right to food, or a concept of what people might be entitled to as a human right or as a question of justice. The legitimate violence of the state can be employed to uphold the ownership rights of one section of the community against the demands of another. This is seen by Sen, in this section of the book, as unproblematic. However, in the final sentence of the book, which provided the epigraph and title for this paper[70], he returns to the central conundrum produced by this entire approach: '[t]he law stands between food availability and food entitlement. Starvation deaths can reflect legality with a vengeance'.[71] The fact that Sen's theory, which purports to provide a framework for understanding starvation and famines, excludes any adequate understanding of precisely those conditions that obtain *whenever there is a famine* – the denial of access to food *by force* employed on behalf of those who possess food – is a clear cause for concern. Further, I would argue, this exclusion indicates more than that the theory is 'defective' in certain cases. It returns our attention to the role of the 'force of law' in relation to justice.

For Derrida, law itself is inextricably bound in a complex, internal relationship with force, power, or violence in two ways. The first is related to that which is entailed by the phrase 'to enforce the law', when an existing system of law or a legal code is enforced. In Derrida's words,

> law is always an authorised force, a force that justifies itself or is justified in applying itself, even if this justification may be judged from elsewhere to be unjust or unjustifiable…. The word 'enforceability' reminds us that there is no such thing as law [a legal code] that doesn't imply *in itself, a priori, in the analytic structure of its concept,* the possibility of being 'enforced', applied by force. There…is no law without enforceability, and no applicability or enforceability of the law without force, whether this force be direct or indirect, physical or symbolic, exterior or interior, brutal or subtly discursive and hermeneutic, coercive or regulative, and so forth.[72]

The second way in which law is related to force, power, or violence involves the state and state formation, and invokes the performative violence of the founding moment of the law. This founding moment, '[t]he very emergence of justice and law, the founding and justifying moment that institutes law implies a performative force'.[73] As we have seen, law has to be 'enforced'. It does not have any effect without 'enforcement'. This second notion claims something more. It claims that in the very founding moment of law itself there is a performative force, a 'violence without ground': '[v]iolence is at the origin of law'.[74]

This founding violence is closely linked with the state. The foundation of a state takes place alongside the institution of a new law, and 'it always does so in violence. Always, which is to say even when there haven't been those spectacular genocides, expulsions or deportations that so often accompany the foundation of states'.[75] However, this founding moment is outside time: '[it] always takes place and never takes place in a presence'.[76] In the foundation of the state, discourse will 'justify the recourse to violence by alleging the founding, in progress or to come, of a new law. As this law to come will in return legitimate, retrospectively, the violence that may offend the sense of justice, its future anterior already justifies it'.[77] The founding moment of the state is outside time, in that, until the state has already been founded, its foundation is in question, and, as a state, it does not exist. In retrospect, it will seem as if a certain act constituted the moment of foundation; at the time when that act takes place (could such a time exist), the violence that accompanies it cannot be legitimised. These moments are terrifying – they involve suffering, crimes, tortures – and they are also 'in their very violence, uninterpretable or indecipherable'.[78] The terror arises in part because the founding moment is one in which the social and symbolic order no longer holds sway.[79] These moments are the unspeakable, that of which we cannot speak, that which is outside all language and all discourse.

Here we can return to famine, and that which is the 'unspeakable' of famine; that which does not get any acknowledgment from 'theories' of famine causation, or from discourses of relief and intervention. The link between famines and complete social catastrophe is not often made. In first-hand accounts, the horror of the absence of social ties, the degradation and inhumanity of starvation deaths, and the 'madness of hunger'[80] occasionally appear. More often, eyewitnesses and survivors are silent in the face of the unspeakable trauma they encounter. It is perhaps this which impels theorists to 'tame' famine, to refer to its harshest aspects only in non-emotive terms and to confine themselves to 'hard facts'.[81]

Such approaches confine themselves to a technologised view.[82] This is limiting, as Derrida points out, and denies engagement with justice.[83] He distinguishes between law and justice:

> [l]aw is the element of calculation…but justice is incalculable, it requires us to calculate with the incalculable; and aporetic experiences are the experiences, as improbable as they are necessary, of justice, that is to say of moments in which the decision between just and unjust is never insured by a rule.[84]

This is so because '[e]ach case is other, each decision is different and requires an absolutely unique interpretation, which no existing, coded rule can or ought to guarantee absolutely'.[85] A decision in a singular, particular case has to go through what Derrida calls the 'undecidable'.[86] At the point when the decision is made, it is not a question of the straightforward application of a code of law. There is something more involved in each particular instance, and this, for Derrida, is where the notion of justice can arise. Before the decision has been made, there can be no claim that justice has been achieved. After the decision has been taken, it is seen to have followed a rule, whether that rule is one produced by the decision or not. So, justice is impossible: 'there is apparently no moment in which a decision can be called presently and fully just'.[87] Although the ordeal of the undecidable must be gone through, it cannot be overcome, and '[t]he undecidable remains caught, lodged, at least as a ghost – but an essential ghost – in every decision, in every event of decision. Its ghostliness deconstructs from within any assurance of presence, any certitude or any supposed criteriology that would assure us of the justice of a decision'.[88] We cannot even know that a decision has taken place, and we cannot say whether it was 'just'. I return to the notion of undecidability and justice later.

Does this leave us with an acknowledgment of the violence inherent in all attempts at a legal system, but with no 'ethical' message, no way of distinguishing different kinds of violent acts? Drucilla Cornell raises the question of whether the intervention of deconstruction comes to an end with its exposure of 'the nakedness of power struggles and, indeed, of violence masquerading as the rule of law'.[89] She claims that, on the contrary,

> the undecidability which can be used to expose any legal system's process of the self-legitimisation of authority as myth, leaves us – the us here being specifically those who enact and enforce the law – with an *inescapable responsibility* for violence, precisely because violence cannot be fully rationalised and therefore justified in advance.[90]

What Cornell is arguing here is that Derrida's notion of undecidability and the process of decisioning inevitably leads us back to the notion of individual (ethical) responsibility. The process of decision, as we have discussed, cannot follow a code of law, and is not calculable. As such, it entails responsibility. This responsibility cannot be evaded by an appeal to the law. What this means, to return to Sen, is that the actions of agents of the state in 'forcing' people to starve by protecting food stocks in shops cannot be 'justified' by referents to 'the law' or 'legitimacy', as Sen comes close to claiming.[91] The law itself is produced and reproduced in particular decisions. What happens cannot be 'legislated' in advance – it has to be the subject of a decision – and enforcement of the law in any case contains within itself the violence of the law. Sen attempts to exclude from his account instances of violence outside of the law. The exclusion of the violence of the extra-legal in Sen's constitution of 'entitlements' returns to haunt his account in the violence of the law itself, both its foundation, in the state, and its enforcement.

Enough Food

Finally, and briefly, in the last part of my examination of Sen's work, I will look at two other exclusions, distinctions, or deferrals which he makes: first, Sen's exclusion of food supply, by considering food as a commodity (where *having* is opposed to *being*), and second, the exclusion of the prescriptive. The latter leads to a discussion of how Sen nevertheless shares with Malthus a view of famine as having a cause, and a 'scientific' or managerial solution; this discussion returns to the question of the technologisation of famine and relief.

In the opening sentences of *Poverty and Famines*, Sen makes a distinction between the existence and the possession of food:

> [s]tarvation is the characteristic of some people not *having* enough food to eat. It is not the characteristic of there *being* not enough food to eat. While the latter can be a cause of the former, it is but one of many *possible* causes. Whether and how starvation relates to food supply is a matter for factual investigation.[92]

As we see here, Sen's argument begins by setting aside the Malthusian assumption that formed the foundation for much theorising about famines prior to his work. This is the assumption that famine is caused by, indeed is characterised by – in other words, famine *is* – a lack of food. Right at the start, Sen proceeds by distinguishing a particular notion of what starvation is. It is 'the characteristic of some people not *having* enough food to eat'; it is not 'the characteristic of there *being* not enough food to eat'. The contrast that Sen makes is between 'there *being* not enough' and 'some people not *having* enough', which he proposes later is the contrast between statements about a commodity 'on its own' – there being not enough food – and statements about the *'relationship* of persons' to a commodity.

Sen argues that this is a contrast between 'the [Malthusian] tradition of thinking in terms of what *exists* rather than in terms of who can *command* what'.[93] Yet, in what sense does 'food' exist? This may seem an absurd point – surely we all know what food is, and clearly food, essential to maintain physical existence, the difference between life and death for millions of people in famines throughout the world over the centuries, obviously has to be something that 'exists'. And yet, is it? Is not 'food' something which, of all things, is socially defined? It is not possible to read accounts of famines and the hardships and inhumanities to which people are driven during such periods without coming across accounts where things are eaten which under 'normal' circumstances would in no sense count as 'food'.[94] During famines, people search the land for wild fruits, such as berries, which serve as 'famine foods'. If circumstances become more extreme, bark is stripped from the trees, grass is eaten, even the dirt is consumed, and finally, people may resort to eating each other's children, or even their own children. Such practices of cannibalism are well documented.[95] They appal the imagination, and make one wonder precisely in what sense 'food' *exists*.

Sen contrasts not *having* enough to eat with there *being* not enough to eat: who can *command* what with what *exists*. He regards the former as having to do with relations – relations between people and a commodity – whereas the latter, food supply, is 'merely' statements about a commodity. For Sen, ownership is privileged over existence: in the hierarchy of having/being, having is the more valued. Questions of existence are deferred. However, what *counts as food* in any given situation is socially constituted, in much the same way as is ownership, or 'having'.[96] Moreover, it is only if one disregards those very circumstances Sen claims to be considering – circumstances where people facing starvation consume 'foods' that are unimaginable – that one can accept Sen's version of starvation. In this precise sense, *having* food and there *being* food are both statements to do with relations between people.[97]

We have in Sen's work an attempt to bring into economic considerations questions of relations between people; but such discussions in the economic realm arguably must, by definition, exclude consideration of social relations. As Karl Marx showed, in capitalism, social relations become relations between commodities.[98] To adopt a position where economics is seen as quantifiable and 'scientific' and separate from values and politics is to adopt a discursive stance that *cannot see* relations between people as such – these are fetishised as relations between things (commodities).[99] Thus, although Sen's work advocates a 'relationship-based' approach, I would argue that this does not translate into any meaningful consideration of the *social* nature of relations, since these are deferred at each step of the way. The entitlement relations at the heart of his approach are relations of people to food, and the dependence of this on relations between people is deferred as secondary.

The final point I want to consider is Sen's deferral of the prescriptive. For Sen, as we have seen, a number of things – rising prices, loss of employment, or food supply problems – can lead to a 'decline in exchange entitlements', and it is this that counts as a 'cause' of starvation. Which of these triggers applies in a particular case of starvation is 'a matter for factual investigation'. This emphasis on 'factual investigation' and 'cause' puts the study of 'starvation' firmly in the realm of economics and social *science*: the answers to be sought are not in the form of *reasons* for actions (why one group of people allowed another group to starve to death; or perhaps why they killed them), but the form of *causal explanations*. Answers do not lie in the realm of the study of *relationships between people*, but in the *relationship of people to commodities*. There is to be no history or narrative of famine, no account of what happened in a particular case in terms of who did what. Instead, there is an account in terms of cause and result, an account that is quantifiable.

This point is closely linked to the fact/value distinction that Sen makes when he introduces entitlement relations: his 'interpretation of entitlement relations…is descriptive rather than prescriptive'.[100] He is concerned not with who *should be* entitled to own what, but who *is* entitled to own what. The word 'entitlement', which carries overtones of human rights (food for the starving, for example), turns out to be solely concerned with buying and selling, ownership and legality, under a market economy. It is through the exclusions which Sen makes that we begin to grasp what his argument might be.

In Sen's work, famines are treated as a particular case of starvation, which itself is a particular instance of the more general phenomenon of poverty. He does not look at the role of political struggle or conflict, but, like Malthus, sees famines as an instance of a 'disastrous phenomenon'.[101] The distinction between Sen's work and the Malthusian view of famines as a failure of food supply, Nature's 'last, most dreadful resource'[102] in the face of an inexorably expanding human population, is that, as Sen says, 'the entitlement approach views famines as economic disasters, not just as food crises'.[103] This approach means that famine is still a problem to be solved by technology and management (as is development itself). What has happened, in Derridean terms, is that famine itself has been 'excluded'. The risk (of famine) has, in effect, been set to one side as something accidental, something which teaches us nothing about the economic, social, or political system being studied, even though, as we know, the competitive market economic system itself relies on the concept of a certain scarcity.[104] To see famine as either a natural disaster, as in the work of Malthus, or as an economic disaster, as in the work of Sen, ignores the way some people benefit from famine: there are what the new 'complex emergency' paradigm calls 'winners' as well as 'losers'.

What has happened, in effect, is what Michel Foucault describes as the reduction of the problem to one of theory.[105] Famine is seen as a breakdown of liberal economic theory, which leads to the question: 'How can we have such a thing as famine in the 'modern' world?' An alternative would be to ask what is it in the texts of 'economics' that could have made 'famine' possible, and even now continues to justify it. There is also a historical reductionism, which sees the problem of famines as one of causes, as some sort of 'a residue or a sequel of the past'.[106] Seeking a cause makes the problem seem like a sort of *disease* which we can either prevent (by development) or cure (by relief).[107] If we see famine negatively, as a disease, an *accident* – what in deconstruction has been called the constitutive outside – this enables us to retain the pre-existing categories of 'economic' thought. We see famines as obstacles on the road to modernisation: Africa's lack of development, or specific economic difficulties are to blame. The solution is technical or managerial.

What we should be considering, according to Foucault, is not how to solve the problem or cure the 'disease', but 'what use is [it], what functions does it assure, in what strategies is it integrated?'[108] We should treat famine as a 'positive present'.[109] What matters is not the search for the origins of famine, but understanding its function in the here and now, in a particular narrative of power and conflict.

Implications for the Analysis of 'Complex Emergencies'

By taking a deconstructive approach to Sen's work, I have shown that he excludes, sets to one side, or defers aspects of famine which the new paradigm of 'complex emergencies' regards as central. These are the questions of deliberate acts of starvation and extra-legal transfers of entitlements, both of which involve force and violence. I have also shown, through an analysis which employed Derrida's examination of the 'force of law', that these aspects can be seen as central to Sen's notion of 'entitlements' and 'famine', in that the law itself is based on a founding violence and depends on the threat of violence for its enforcement. This violence is seen when famines occur in states under the rule of law – in China, for example, in the Great Leap Forward of the early 1960s, where there were some 30 million deaths.[110] It is also seen when famines occur in states under the 'democratic' rule of law – in Britain, for example, during the Irish Potato famine in the 1840s,[111] or in Bengal, again under British rule, in the 1940s, where around 3 million died.[112]

I have also argued that Sen's analysis can lead to a particular practice of famine relief, one that technologises suffering. Although Sen distinguishes his approach strongly from that of Malthus, in this important respect it remains similar. Both lead to a view of famine as a failure, a disease, that can be 'cured' or 'prevented' by 'intervention' by the state or the international community.

We now have a third form of disaster: 'complex emergencies'. The new approaches to war and hunger are attempting to overcome the limitations of earlier work. The linkages between famine and conflict are explored, the limitations of existing modes of humanitarian intervention exposed, and 'features of contemporary conflict which promote hunger'[113] analysed. These contemporary conflicts or 'complex emergencies', which are a feature of Africa in particular, are seen as being generated by a shortage of resources – already limited by economic pressures from without. The so-called 'new paradigm', which appears, as we have seen, in the work of Duffield, Keen, and de Waal, is shifting 'away from an emphasis on the external causes of conflict in favour of attempting to analyse the internal factors that shape the nature and form of conflict…as the outcome of competing strategies between rulers and ruled, the powerful and the weak, the winners and losers'.[114]

Despite this shift, I would argue that in three ways 'complex emergency' theorists have not moved as far from earlier approaches as might appear. First, they are still operating within a Malthusian framework. They regard subsistence crises as a basic cause of conflict. Their work is based on an analysis of African famines of the 1980s and 1990s, and views 'conflict-famine' as very much an African problem.[115] Food insecurity is seen as endemic, exacerbated by conflict. However, it is lack of food (or other resources necessary to produce food) that leads to conflict, which then leads to famine.

Second, in terms of policy recommendations, the 'complex emergency' approach still produces a series of propositions that rely on quantification, but, in this case, something different is to be counted. That which is to be measured is not nutritional status but violence. According to Keen and Ken Wilson,

> [w]hat is urgently required is for aid donors to give greater attention to protecting the human rights and economic strategies of the most vulnerable groups…. [One] key starting point in any attempt to improve the effectiveness of international aid [includes]…changing what is counted and measured – moving away from a concentration on measuring nutritional status and towards assessing levels and types of violence.[116]

In Derridean terms, this can be seen as an attempt to 're-centre' famine theory *as a structure* on conflict analysis, trying to erase the excess (the violence of the extra-legal) by re-centring around it. One centre is substituted for another.[117] However, 'the force of *différance* prevents any system…from encompassing its other or its excess…. Derrida's project is not only to show us why and how there is always the Other to the system; it is also to indicate the ethical aspiration behind that demonstration'.[118] To attempt to form another system, one that can be closed and can produce 'technical' answers, solutions that operate according to a 'rule' that can be applied by 'experts', risks repeating the previous error. It leads to a denial of the need for, or the possibility of, political or ethical choice; since the answers are provided by an analysis that claims to be closed and complete ('scientific'), there is no opening for a decision or a judgement. If 'complex emergency' theory calls for a rejection of the analysis of food supply or entitlements in favour of a study of levels and types of conflict, it may provide an alternative theoretical system, but it still endorses the possibility of closure. This endorsement sidelines the political and the ethical, and defers to 'experts'. The alternative is to accept the impossibility of closure, 'the limit of any system of meaning'.[119] The impossibility of knowing positively, once accepted, opens the possibility of the ethical relationship. In Cornell's words, '[f]or Derrida, the excess to the system cannot be known positively; hence there is no beyond to what he would call the undecidable. We must try, if we are to remain faithful to the ethical relationship, to heed its otherness to any system of conventional definition'.[120]

Third, and most significantly, the 'complex emergency' approach leads to the conclusion that aid should not be seen as a *remedy* for famine, but as a *cause*. Duffield and other theorists of the 'complex emergency' school have argued that famine relief and humanitarian aid strengthen the disaster situation and produce a structure of 'permanent emergency'.[121] The argument is that the discourse of famine as disaster has led to forms of international action – through NGOs, food aid, and development projects – that have institutionalised famine as one of several forms of disaster and emergency. This approach has been objectified in institutional arrangements. These are now an integral part of a social system in which forms of oppression that produce and reproduce inequality, injustice, and disregard of human rights are perpetuated. The conclusion is that not only do international emergency intervention and aid not *solve the problem of* famine; aid, through the mechanisms of power and control which it enables, *produces* famine.

In Derridean terms, we have a situation of inversion, where aid is no longer the *remedy*; aid is the *cause*. However, Derrida argues against any simple opposition of symptom and cause; one is always haunted by the other: '[t]he pharmakon will always be apprehended as both antidote and poison...along with that supplementary discomfort stemming from the indecidability between the two'.[122] Viewed in this way, famine relief is the supplement, the undecidable. However, the new paradigm, crucially, does not admit to its own conclusion about relief. Despite arguing that aid causes, or renders possible, famine and human rights abuses, it is nevertheless *almost immediately* suggested that the solutions could be found if 'aid donors' approached the situation in a different way.[123] This move is characteristic of logocentric analysis, as Derrida sees it: the possibility of the negative is recognised (aid does indeed cause famine), but then, in a move which is almost simultaneous, this possibility is discounted, and rendered accidental; thus, the problem with aid can be overcome through educating donors.

Following through the deconstructive analysis, we could perhaps argue that, on the contrary, famine relief as supplement is *undecidable*: whether it solves or exacerbates the famine is undecidable, and hence political. We have here an example of what Derrida calls the 'double contradictory imperative'.[124] On the one hand, famine relief must be given, since food cannot be withheld from the starving. On the other hand, famine relief must be withheld, since it is the relief aid that is causing the famine.[125] This leads to what Derrida calls an 'aporia', which takes the form of a contradiction; but, for Derrida, 'ethics, politics and responsibility, *if there are any*, will only ever have begun with the experience and experiment of the aporia'.[126] In other words, it is only through the 'logic' of the aporia, where a decision has to be made, that we will arrive at something that can be called 'political'. Without this, what we are doing is following a programme, claiming a priority for knowledge, and an epistemological certainty: 'when a path is clear and given, when a certain knowledge opens up the way in advance, the decision is already made, it might as well be said that there is none to make: irresponsibly, and in good conscience, one simply applies or implements a programme'.[127] It may not be possible to escape 'the programme', but if this is what is happening, then moral or political responsibility does not come into it. For Derrida, '[t]he condition of possibility of this thing called responsibility is a certain *experience and experiment of the possibility of the impossible: the testing of the aporia* from which one may invent the only *possible invention, the impossible invention'*.[128] It is through the experience of this contradiction or aporia, to which no answer can be found, that ethical responsibility becomes possible. By accepting the question of famine relief as 'undecidable', in the sense that an answer cannot be found through knowledge, the way is opened to the process of ethico-political decision.

Thus, while the Sen/Malthus approach to famines presents 'relief' as unproblematically the solution, and Duffield or Keen's view sees relief as (more or less unproblematically) the problem, a Derridean approach supposes that relief is the undecidable: it is not a question of formulating a more adequate theory of famine, or a more sophisticated technology of relief, it is a question of politics and decision.

This emphatically *does not* mean that we do nothing. Indeed, as we have seen, it is only in these situations that we can *act* responsibly. It brings us back to Derrida's comment:

> [t]hat justice exceeds law and calculation, that the unpresentable exceeds the determinable cannot and should not serve as an alibi for staying out of juridico-political battles, within an institution or a state or between institutions or states and others.... Not only *must* we...negotiate the relation between the calculable and the incalculable...but we *must* take it as far as possible, beyond the place we find ourselves and beyond the already identifiable zones of morality or politics or law, beyond the distinction between national and international, public and private, and so on....[129]

David Campbell emphasises this point, namely that it is the presence of the undecidable that leads to politics rather than technology: '[w]ere everything to be within the purview of the decidable, and devoid of the undecidable, then – as Derrida constantly reminds us – there would be no ethics, politics, or responsibility, only a program, technology, and its irresponsible application'.[130] The terrain of the undecidable is the 'impossible' terrain. However, this *does not* mean that taking responsibility limits one to 'impossible, impractical and inapplicable decisions'.[131] One must rather 'assume a responsibility that announces itself as contradictory because it inscribes us from the very beginning of the game into a kind of necessary double obligation, a *double bind'*.[132] It is impossible at one and the same time to both give and withhold relief, but this is what we must take responsibility for. What this might imply is a responsibility for finding a way to contain, in each decision, the principle with the specificity of its application. In other words, in applying any 'principle', such as the need to give aid, divergences between the principle and 'the concrete conditions of [its] implementation, the determined limits of [its] representation, the abuses of or inequalities in [its] application as a result of certain interests, monopolies, or existing hegemonies'[133] need to be denounced. In the case of famine relief, these divergences might arise, for example, through the offering of aid that is inappropriate to the particular situation, through the misuse of aid by powerful groups within the relief administration, or through the appropriation of aid for military purposes. Resolving this, in any one of a number of possible 'impossible' ways 'is what politics is all about'.[134]

Conclusion

The new approaches to theories of famine that link it with conflict claim to represent a break with those theories that take a purely economistic or naturalistic approach to famine and poverty. This article has sought to demonstrate that the economistic theories, exemplary here being Sen, are equally based on a view of famine as violence, except that, in this case, the violence concerned is the 'legitimate' violence of the force of law. Current theories can best be seen as a special case of the economistic approach which itself implicates famine as the unacceptable face of the law. They make the link between poverty and powerlessness, between exploitation and violence, but they do not go far enough, in that they neglect to see the violence inherent in 'peacetime' state and international structures that equally represent a structure of domination and oppression. Moreover, not only do they neglect this, but in ideological terms, they provide a way of diverting attention from it. What has happened can be seen as an overturning of the hierarchy between normality and disaster represented by prosperity/famine, without a corresponding displacement. This can be politically destructive. It runs the risk of arguing that the type of poverty represented by famine (that which is involved in situations of conflict) is totally separate from, and has nothing to do with, poverty that exists in states under the rule of law. The role of the 'international community' in relation to famine and starvation is then a straightforward one of intervening to restore a situation of peace and 'normality', in the sense of democratic government.

This article has argued that, on the contrary, the law and the legal system can better be seen, following Derrida, as only one form of violence and domination. International law, intervention and humanitarianism are *part of this system*; they are not exempt from violence and oppression. Denying this, and seeking to analyse and ameliorate famine as a 'disaster' requiring 'intervention', is to concede the main object, that of seeking an approach to society and the social that *recognises* the potential for violent domination and inequalities in *all* social relationships.

If the separations assumed by both theories of entitlement failure and those of 'conflict-famines' are accepted, the question becomes one of what duties or obligations there are on states to intervene to prevent human rights abuses and suffering. Much of the literature on food aid and famine takes this approach, as do debates on humanitarianism more generally. However, we do not have to start from here. If we contest the dichotomies on which this thought is based, and which sustain a view of the political as separate, we can perhaps move towards an approach based on an analysis of the relationships of *connection between* people. We then move from the 'abstract', 'logical', analytical approach implied by the question, 'should we *intervene* to stop exploitation and domination?', to the more practical, specific, question, '*how* can we best act to promote good relations?'[135] Famines can be seen not so much as the outcome of processes with 'winners and losers', though they are that, but as processes where relationships between people have produced unacceptable results and transgressed limits of inhumanity. The web of these relationships is more complex and extensive than the simple separations into 'winners' and 'losers', developed and underdeveloped, rich and poor can account for. Living with the inevitable antagonism – undecidability – at the heart of the social relation is arguably what we must learn to do. In this context, famine 'theory' becomes irrelevant. We do not need to ask 'what caused the famine?', if famine is not seen as a natural or economic 'event' or disaster.

It cannot be assumed, as is commonly done, that 'famine' (any more than 'conflict') is an ill that the entire 'international community' will fight against. This is a position reinforced by ideologies of famine as disaster. It is reinforced by ignoring that, as Rangasami reminds us, we all benefit in one way or another from famine. It is reinforced by positions that see the rule of law as unproblematically non-violent. The work of Keen, de Waal, and Duffield has shown that an analysis of 'complex emergencies' in the Horn of Africa can reveal numerous beneficiaries of famines. Although Keen pointed out that international donors also have much to gain from famine, the more comfortable assumption has been that the 'complexities' or 'political difficulties' of the situation have occasionally meant that donor governments have inadvertently prolonged or worsened the famine situation. I would argue that we need to look dispassionately at the way donor governments themselves profit from famine. In order to do this, we need to differentiate between the governments and NGOs in donor countries, and the motivation of people in those countries who, perhaps recognising or 'remembering' the ghosts of famines past, may wish to alleviate the suffering of fellow human beings elsewhere in the world. Occasionally, the latter can provoke useful action by donor governments. More frequently, this motivation is appropriated by those development professionals and NGOs who claim the expertise to translate these desires into practice. Their claim to neutrality and humanitarianism must be continually questioned. Their 'decisions' are just that, and their expertise is no more than a *claim* to knowledge. We need to enquire on whose behalf the agencies are acting, rather than assume that their own account can be accepted uncritically. Such assumptions can lead to episodes like that in Ethiopia where 'famine assistance, provided primarily by Western governments and non-governmental organisations, reinforced the policies and programs that produced the 1984–85 famine'.[136] Such examples are not exceptional; indeed, they may be widespread. However, they are not confined to cases where famine is linked with military conflict. There are many instances where states under the rule of law have caused, condoned, or turned a blind eye to famines in their jurisdiction, as we have seen in the examples of China, Bengal, and Britain. Nor is the discussion confined to the extremes of famine. The implication of the argument put forward in this article is that it applies equally to decisions about development and the alleviation of poverty more broadly.

The answer is not to provide no famine 'relief', development assistance, or humanitarian aid. It is crucial to stress again that, although I have claimed that famine relief can be regarded as *undecidable*, this does not mean that no decision can or should be taken. It merely implies that such a decision is just that: a political or ethical decision. It cannot be left to 'experts' or the 'international community'. It is not a technological or managerial matter that can be resolved by better theories or techniques. Whether any particular decision is just or not will remain unknown. However, although 'justice' itself is impossible, we have a 'duty' to act with responsibility in addressing what Derrida calls the 'double contradictory imperative'. This process – an interminable process of decision-taking and questioning – *is* politics. The problem exceeds 'the order of theoretical determination, of knowledge, certainty, judgement, and of statements in the form of "this is that"'.[137] Or, as Amy said: 'you've got to decide, but you'll never know'.[138]

NOTES

The research on which this article is based was funded by the Economic and Social Research Council (ESRC) at the Department of International Politics, University of Wales, Aberystwyth. I would like to thank David Campbell, Mark Duffield, Véronique Pin-Fat, Steve Smith, and Cynthia Weber for their helpful comments.

1. Amartya Sen, *Poverty and Famines: An Essay on Entitlements and Deprivation* (Oxford: Clarendon Press, 1981), p. 166.

2. This term is used by Mark Duffield, for example. See Duffield, 'Complex Emergencies and the Crisis of Developmentalism', *IDS Bulletin* (Vol. 25, No. 4, 1994), pp. 37–45. I discuss the term in more detail below.

3. For a recent review of theories of famine, see Stephen Devereux, *Theories of Famine* (Hemel Hempstead: Harvester Wheatsheaf, 1993). The view of famine as scarcity is found in many press reports and articles. See, for example, Debora MacKenzie, 'The People Problem: Will Tomorrow's Children Starve?', *New Scientist* (Vol. 143, No. 1941, 3 September 1994), pp. 24–9, and the discussions in the issue of *New Internationalist* entitled 'Hunger in a World of Plenty', (No. 267, May 1995). The World Food Summit organised by the UN Food and Agriculture Organisation in November 1996 was concerned, as was the UN World Food Conference in 1974, with increasing production and improving agricultural methods, an approach that seeks to remedy scarcity. See also FAO, 'Towards Universal Food Security: Draft of a Policy Statement and Plan of Action', Document No. WFS 96/3, FAO World Food Summit, Rome, 13–17 November 1996.

4. For Sen's entitlement theory, see Sen, *op. cit.*, in note 1.

5. See, for example, Rakiya Omaar and Alex de Waal, 'Humanitarianism Unbound? Current Dilemmas facing Multi-Mandate Relief Operations in Political Emergencies', *Discussion Paper No. 5* (African Rights, 1994), and Joanna Macrae and Anthony Zwi, *War and Hunger: Rethinking International Responses to Complex Emergencies* (London: Zed Books, in association with Save the Children Fund, UK, 1994).

6. Simon Maxwell and Margaret Buchanan-Smith (eds.), *Linking Relief and Development, IDS Bulletin* (Vol. 25, No. 4, 1994).

7. Duffield, *op. cit.*, in note 2.

8. In Ethiopia, for example, aid was appropriated by the government and used allegedly to enforce genocidal resettlement policies, while in Eritrea, relief supplies sustained the eventually victorious rebel fronts in the liberation war. See Jason W. Clay, Sandra Steingraber, and Peter Niggli, *The Spoils of Famine: Ethiopian Famine Policy and Peasant Agriculture* (Cambridge, MA: Cultural Survival, 1988); Mark Duffield and John Prendergast, *Without Troops and Tanks: The Emergency Relief Desk and the Cross Border Operation into Eritrea and Tigray* (Lawrenceville, NJ: Red Sea Press, 1994); and John Sorenson, *Imagining Ethiopia: Struggles for History and Identity in the Horn of Africa* (New Brunswick, NJ: Rutgers University Press, 1993).

9. These include Alex de Waal, Mark Duffield, and David Keen; their work is discussed below. See, for example, Alex de Waal, *Famine That Kills: Darfur, Sudan, 1984–1985* (Oxford: Clarendon Press, 1989); Duffield and Prendergast,

op. cit., in note 8; and David Keen, *The Benefits of Famine: A Political Economy of Famine and Relief in Southwestern Sudan, 1983–1989* (Princeton, NJ: Princeton University Press, 1994).

10. Thomas Malthus, *An Essay on the Principle of Population* (Oxford: Oxford University Press, 1993 [1798]), p. 61.

11. *Ibid.*

12. See Amartya Sen, 'Population: Delusion and Reality', *New York Review of Books* (Vol. 15, No. 15, 1994), pp. 62–71, for a discussion of some of these issues.

13. Michael Gross and Mary Beth Averill, 'Evolution and Patriarchal Myths of Scarcity and Competition', in Sandra Harding and Merrill B. Hintikka (eds.), *Discovering Reality* (Dordrecht: D. Reidel, 1983), pp. 71–95. For other critiques of Malthus, see Nicole Ball, 'The Myth of the Natural Disaster', *The Ecologist* (Vol. 5, No. 10, 1975), pp. 368–71; Ester Boserup, *The Conditions of Agricultural Growth: Economics of Agrarian Change under Population Pressure* (London: Earthscan, 1965; reissued 1993); and Marshall Sahlins, *Stone Age Economics* (London: Tavistock Publications, 1974).

14. For an influential recent exposition of a Malthusian approach, see Lester R. Brown, *State of the World 1996: A Worldwatch Institute Report on Progress Towards a Sustainable Society* (London: Earthscan Publications, 1996).

15. See, for example, Food and Agriculture Organisation, 'Towards Universal Food Security: Draft of a Policy Statement and Plan of Action' (Document No. WFS 96/3), FAO World Food Summit, Rome, 13–17 November 1996.

16. Sen, *op. cit.*, in note 1, and Sen, 'The Food Problem: Theory and Policy' *Third World Quarterly* (Vol. 4, No. 3, 1982), pp. 447–59.

17. Sen, *op. cit.*, in note 1, p. 4.

18. Sen, *op. cit.*, in note 1, p. 43.

19. For a full discussion of the policy implications of entitlements approaches, see Jean Drèze and Amartya Sen, *Hunger and Public Action* (Oxford: Oxford University Press, 1993).

20. Despite this, entitlement theory has by no means replaced the emphasis on food shortages that characterised food availability approaches, as emphasised above.

21. Amrita Rangasami, 'Failure of Exchange Entitlements Theory of Famine', *Economic and Political Weekly* (Vol. 20, No. 41, 1985), pp. 1747–52, and (Vol. 20, No. 42, 1985), pp. 1797–1801. Rangasami also challenges the novelty of Sen's approach. She claims that the provincial Famine Codes of India and other official documents show that those administering relief in the period from 1880 to 1905 treated unemployment and decline in real wages as critical factors, alongside food shortage; see *ibid.*, p. 1789. In addition, the notion of entitlement had been previously articulated; see *ibid.*, p. 1799. Other examples of critical discussions of the entitlements approach, and rebuttals, include Peter Bowbrick, 'The Causes of Famine – a Refutation of Sen Theory', *Food Policy* (Vol. 11, No. 2, 1986), pp. 105–24; Amartya Sen, 'The Causes of Famine – a Reply', *Food Policy* (Vol. 11, No. 2, 1986), pp. 125–32; George Allen, 'Famines – the Bowbrick-Sen Dispute and Some Related Issues', *Food Policy* (Vol. 11, No. 3, 1986), pp. 259–63; Amartya Sen, 'Rejoinder: An Untenable Hypothesis on the Causes of Famine – Reply', *Food Policy* (Vol. 12, No. 1, 1987), pp. 10–14; Alex de Waal, 'A Reassessment of Entitlement Theory in the Light of Recent Famines

in Africa', *Development and Change* (Vol. 21, No. 3, 1990), pp. 469–90; S.R. Osmani, 'Comments on Alex de Waal's "Reassessment of Entitlement Theory in the Light of Recent Famines in Africa"', *Development and Change* (Vol. 22, No. 3, 1991), pp. 587–96; Alex de Waal, 'Logic and Application: A Reply to S.R. Osmani', *Development and Change* (Vol. 22, No. 3, 1991), pp. 597–608; Peter Nolan, 'The Causation and Prevention of Famines: A Critique of A.K. Sen', *Journal of Peasant Studies* (Vol. 21, No. 1, 1993), pp. 1–28; Amartya Sen, 'The Causation and Prevention of Famines – A Reply' *Journal of Peasant Studies* (Vol. 21, No. 1, 1993), pp. 29–40; and Charles Gore, 'Entitlement Relations and "Unruly" Social Practices: A Comment on the Work of Amartya Sen', *Journal of Development Studies* (Vol. 29, No. 3, 1993), pp. 429–60.

22. Rangasami, *op. cit.*, in note 21, p. 1748.
23. *Ibid.*
24. *Ibid.*, p. 1749.
25. *Ibid.*
26. *Ibid.*, p. 1750. Accounts of famines as 'complex emergencies' still do this.
27. See, for example, Keen, *op. cit.*, in note 9, p. 235, and Mark Duffield, 'NGOs, Disaster Relief and Asset Transfer in the Horn: Political Survival in a Permanent Emergency', *Development and Change* (Vol. 24, No. 1, 1993), p. 148.
28. Keen, *op. cit.*, in note 9, and Mark Duffield, 'Famine, Conflict and the Internationalisation of Public Welfare', in Martin Doornbos, Lionel Cliffe, Abdel Ghaffar M. Ahmed, and John Markakis (ed.), *Beyond Conflict in the Horn: Prospects for Peace, Recovery and Development in Ethiopia and the Sudan* (The Hague: Institute of Social Studies, in association with James Currey, 1992), pp. 49–62.
29. All three draw on their work in the Horn of Africa in relation to famines of the 1980s. See de Waal, *op. cit.*, in note 9; Duffield and Prendergast, *op. cit.*, in note 8; and Keen, *op. cit.*, in note 9. For an account of the impact of more recent humanitarian emergencies in Africa on this thinking, see Alex de Waal, 'African Encounters', *Index on Censorship* (Vol. 23, No. 6, 1994), pp. 14–31.
30. William DeMars, 'Mercy Without Illusion: Humanitarian Action in Conflict', *Mershon International Studies Review: Supplement to the International Studies Quarterly* (Vol. 40, No. S1, 1996), pp. 81–9. For a discussion of the 'new orthodoxy' that they represent, see the contributions to the volume edited by Macrae and Zwi, *op. cit.*, in note 5. Although described as a new paradigm, the 'complex emergency' theorists are still a minority view, as developmental approaches arguably continue to predominate. In a paper published while the present article was in press, Duffield draws some useful distinctions between his position and the 'aid agency view', which he calls 'developmentalism'. See Duffield, 'The Symphony of the Damned: Racial Discourse, Complex Political Emergencies and Humanitarian Aid', *Disasters* (Vol. 20, No. 3, 1996), pp. 173–93. By implication, this distinction extends to the other 'complex emergency' theorists. In summary, his argument is that developmentalism is a mirror image of 'New Barbarism' – the view of the post-Cold War world as a new world (dis)order. This relationship in the 'external', or international, realm is paralleled by that in the 'internal', or domestic, realm between multiculturalism and 'new racism'. Duffield claims that these two also mirror each other. Both pairs of apparent opposites – developmentalism/New Barbarism

and multiculturalism/new racism – have a large area of shared terrain. Both lack a concern with power, and both see ethnic identities as natural and rooted in history. Both share a functional approach that leads, in the case of developmentalism, to aid technocracy. 'Complex emergency' theorists, in contrast, contest this accommodation on the part of aid agencies and argue, as the present paper does, for politico-ethical involvement.

31. De Waal, *op. cit.*, in note 9.
32. *Ibid.*
33. Keen, *op. cit.*, in note 9.
34. *Ibid.*
35. Duffield, *op. cit.*, in note 2.
36. The work of de Waal with African Rights is notable here. See, for example, Omaar and de Waal, *op. cit.*, in note 5.
37. It is a contentious term. Omaar and de Waal have proposed the alternative phrase, 'political emergencies'; see Omaar and de Waal, *op. cit.*, in note 5, p. 2. Earlier, Duffield had used the term 'permanent emergency'; see Duffield, *op. cit.*, in note 27. The widespread use of the term in describing conflicts may be due to the way it diverts attention from any possible political connotations, blaming instead the 'complexity' of the causal picture, and excuses the absence of solutions. See, for example, the discussion of the use of the term in the Sudan, in Ataul Karim, Mark Duffield, Susan Jaspars, Aldo Benini, Joanna Macrae, Mark Bradbury, Douglas Johnson, George Larbi, and Barbara Hendrie, *OLS Operation Lifeline Sudan: A Review* (Unpublished Independent Report With Administrative Support From the UN Department of Humanitarian Affairs, July 1996) p. 43.
38. Duffield, *op. cit.*, in note 2, p. 38.
39. Joanna Macrae and Anthony Zwi, 'Famine, Complex Emergencies and International Policy in Africa: An Overview', in Macrae and Zwi (eds.), *op. cit.*, in note 5, pp. 6–36.
40. *Ibid.*, p. 21.
41. Duffield, *op. cit.*, in note 2, p. 38.
42. *Ibid.*
43. For other writers, like Larry Minear and Thomas G. Weiss, 'complex emergency' refers to 'situations that may be triggered by natural disasters such as droughts or floods, by intercommunal violence with roots in ethnic or religious tensions or exclusionary politics, by economic or environmental stress, or by some combination of these factors'. Larry Minear and Thomas G. Weiss, *Mercy Under Fire: War and the Global Humanitarian Community* (Boulder, CO: Westview Press, 1995), p. 17.
44. De Waal, 'A Reassessment of Entitlement Theory', *op. cit.*, in note 21.
45. Sen, *op. cit.*, in note 1.
46. Jacques Derrida, 'Force of Law: The "Mystical Foundation of Authority"', in David Gray Carlson, Drucilla Cornell, and Michel Rosenfeld (eds.), *Deconstruction and the Possibility of Justice* (New York, NY: Routledge, 1992), pp. 3–67.
47. Sen, *op. cit.*, in note 1.

48. In his examination of the speech act theory of J.L. Austin, Derrida uses an approach of the type I will draw on here. He questions the way Austin uses processes of exclusion to produce the 'essence' of the matter under discussion – the 'performative' speech act – by placing the 'risk' outside, as the excluded failure – the failed performative. Jacques Derrida, 'Signature Event Context', in Derrida (ed.), *Limited Inc* (Evanston, IL: Northwestern University Press, 1988), pp. 1–23.

49. For Derrida's discussions of logocentrism see, for example, Jacques Derrida, *Of Grammatology*, trans. G.C. Spivak (Baltimore, MD: John Hopkins University Press, 1976), and *Writing and Difference*, trans. A. Bass (London: Routledge, 1978).

50. For the process of differentiation, see, for example, Jacques Derrida, *Positions*, trans. A. Bass (London: Athlone Press, 1987), pp. 8–9 and 28–9.

51. Henry Staten, *Wittgenstein and Derrida* (Oxford: Basil Blackwell, 1984).

52. Derrida, *op. cit.*, in note 46, p. 17.

53. *Ibid.*, p. 15.

54. *Ibid.*, emphasis in original.

55. Sen, *op. cit.*, in note 1, p. 45, emphasis in original.

56. *Ibid.*, p. 1.

57. *Ibid.*, p. 40.

58. De Waal, 'A Reassessment of Entitlement Theory', *op. cit.*, in note 21, pp. 474–8.

59. Sen, *op. cit.*, in note 1, p. 50, fn 11.

60. Begoña Aretxaga, 'Striking with Hunger: Cultural Meanings of Political Violence in Northern Ireland', in Kay B. Warren (ed.), *The Violence Within: Cultural and Political Opposition in Divided Nations* (Boulder, CO: Westview Press, 1993), pp. 217–53.

61. *Ibid.*, p. 223. Begoña Aretxaga does not make a distinction here between pacifist hunger strikes and those that are part of armed conflict. She makes a link with famines, noting that 'the 1981 fast had deep historical resonances; many people in Ireland, although disagreeing with the hunger strikers, thought the English were again starving Irish people', as in the Great Hunger, the 'potato famine' of the 1840s. *Ibid.*, p. 250. See also Allen Feldman, *Formations of Violence: The Narrative of the Body and Political Terror in Northern Ireland* (Chicago, IL: University of Chicago Press, 1991), Chapter 6.

62. Sen, *op. cit.*, in note 1, p. 1.

63. *Ibid.*, p. 40.

64. Bernard Shaw, *Man and Superman* (Harmondsworth: Penguin, 1946), p. 196, quoted in *ibid.*

65. Sen, *op. cit.*, in note 1, p. 40.

66. *Ibid.*

67. Setting aside intentionality is also part of structuralist approaches that would argue that famines are not a failure but a product of the capitalist economic system. See, for example, Susan George, *How the Other Half Dies: The Real Reasons for World Hunger* (Harmondsworth: Penguin, 1986).

68. This distinction is necessary to uphold 'a concept of law which allows the invalidity of law to be distinguished from its immorality'. Herbert Hart, quoted by Sen, *op. cit.*, in note 1, p. 49.

69. Sen, *op. cit.*, in note 1, p. 49, emphasis in original.
70. There is, of course, a certain irony in the way I use, as part of the title, a phrase that I am 'critiquing'. This has to do with the difference between a deconstruction and a 'critique'. In the last sentence of his book, Sen seems to recognise the problem with his own argument (or, as Derrida might say, deconstruction happens). I interpret the phrase he uses here, 'legality with a vengeance', as meaning legality gone beyond itself, legality which has got out of hand. In Lacanian terms, the phrase evokes that which is in legality more than legality itself. For a discussion of how naming produces this surplus, see Slavoj Žižek, *The Sublime Object of Ideology* (London: Verso, 1989), p. 97. What this article is arguing is that law is *always already* like this (out of hand), in the sense that it always already involves a founding and an enforcing violence. Derrida's point is that law is not, as might be expected, a non-violent, consensual, ordering mechanism. On the contrary, it always embodies violence. Thus, it should be no surprise that 'starvation deaths can reflect legality', since, I argue, legality is always 'legality with a vengeance'.
71. *Ibid.*, p. 166.
72. Derrida, *op. cit.*, in note 46, pp. 5–6, emphasis in original.
73. *Ibid.*, p. 13.
74. *Ibid.*, p. 40. This brings us back to the notion of 'limit'; as Derrida says, '[h]ere the discourse comes up against its limit: in itself, in its performative power itself. It is what...I call the mystical. Here a silence is walled up in the violent structure of the founding act. Walled up, walled in because silence is not exterior to language'. *Ibid.*, pp. 13–14.
75. *Ibid.*, p. 36.
76. *Ibid.*
77. *Ibid.*, p. 35. Jacques Lacan's notion of time sees it as acting retroactively in a similar way: '[w]hat is realised in my history is not the past definite of what was, since it is no more, or even the present perfect of what has been in what I am, but the future anterior of what I shall have been for what I am in the process of becoming'. Lacan, *Écrits: A Selection*, trans. A. Sheridan (London: Routledge, 1977), p. 86. Here, fascinatingly, Derrida then makes the link between this undecidable moment of foundation and the mystical, or what Lacan might call the 'Real'.
78. Derrida, *op. cit.*, in note 46, p. 35.
79. For a discussion of the relation of the subject and the symbolic order in Lacanian terms, see, for example, Žižek, *op. cit.*, in note 70. The Lacanian approach that Žižek presents argues that what we call social reality is only constituted by excluding the real. The real is that which cannot be symbolised or spoken of; it is in moments of terror and violence that we confront the real.
80. Nancy Scheper-Hughes, 'The Madness of Hunger: Sickness, Delirium and Human Needs', *Culture, Medicine and Psychiatry* (Vol. 12, No. 4, 1988), pp. 429–58.
81. Kirsten Hastrup, 'Hunger and the Hardness of Facts', *Man* (Vol. N.S. 28, No. 4, 1993), pp. 727–39.
82. I am using the term 'technologised' in this paper to mean calculable and quantifiable, part of a system of 'techniques' or a programme of rules that, it is claimed, can be applied unproblematically in different practical cases. What we

call 'reality' is broken down and studied by specialists in narrow areas using 'scientific' methods. This produces a claim to expert knowledge that directs action, without allowing any room for responsibility.

83. Derrida, *op. cit.*, in note 46. For Derrida, justice is incalculable.

84. Derrida, *op. cit.*, in note 46, p. 16.

85. *Ibid.*, p. 23.

86. *Ibid.*, p. 24.

87. *Ibid.*

88. *Ibid.*

89. Drucilla Cornell, *The Philosophy of the Limit* (London: Routledge, 1992), p. 155.

90. *Ibid.*, p. 157, emphasis in original.

91. Sen, *op. cit.*, in note 1, p. 49.

92. Sen, *op. cit.*, in note 1, p. 1, emphasis in original.

93. *Ibid.*, p. 8.

94. Examples of first-hand accounts of famines can be found in Paul Richard Bohr, *Famine in China and the Missionary: Timothy Richard as Relief Administrator and Advocate of National Reform, 1876–1884* (Cambridge, MA: East Asian Research Centre, Harvard University, 1972); Peter Garnsey, *Famine and Food Supply in the Graeco-Roman World* (Cambridge: Cambridge University Press, 1988); Roger J. Hugh, 'The Famine in Irish Oral Tradition', in R. Dudley Edwards and T. Desmond Williams (eds.), *The Great Famine: Studies in Irish History, 1845–1852* (Dublin: Browne and Nolan, for the Irish Committee of Historical Sciences, 1956), pp. 391–436; Nancy Scheper-Hughes, *Death Without Weeping: The Violence of Everyday Life in Brazil* (Berkeley, CA: University of California Press, 1992); and Patrick Webb and Joachim von Braun, *Famine and Food Security in Ethiopia: Lessons for Africa* (Chichester: John Wiley, for the International Food Policy Research Institute, 1994). Accounts of war and famine can be found in Africa Watch, *Evil Days: Thirty Years of War and Famine in Ethiopia* (New York, NY: Human Rights Watch, 1991); Jason W. Clay and Bonnie K. Holcomb, *Politics and the Ethiopian Famine, 1984–1985* (Cambridge, MA: Cultural Survival, 1986); and Jason W. Clay, Sandra Steingraber, and Peter Niggli, *The Spoils of Famine: Ethiopian Famine Policy and Peasant Agriculture* (Cambridge, MA: Cultural Survival, 1988).

95. In famines in China, for example, exchanging children between families is reported. For an extended discussion of cannibalism during the famines of the 1960s, see Jasper Becker, *Hungry Ghosts: China's Secret Famine* (London: John Murray, 1996).

96. Other horrors of famines stretch the imagination in this area. Are we to regard people as searching for 'ownerships' to add to what Sen might term their 'entitlement bundles' when they consider options such as prostitution, conversion to other religions, selling their children into slavery and the like?

97. This setting to one side of food supply leaves Sen with a problem when he attempts to 'define' famines. He has to end up by saying that we can recognise one when we see one. Sen, *op. cit.*, in note 1, pp. 39–40.

98. David McLellan (ed.), *Karl Marx: Selected Writings* (Oxford: Oxford University Press, 1977), p. 436.

99. Food is, anyhow, a very particular type of commodity. Charles Gore points out that the socially accepted moral rules which regulate food and provisioning change at times when people suffer from hunger and famine. They are historically specific, ranging, for example, from norms of reciprocity and sharing among peasant communities, in one case, to a morality of distress, where the normal obligations to children and dependents are replaced by the primacy of the survival of particular groups, such as parents, in another. They are also the subject of negotiation and struggle. See Gore, *op. cit.*, in note 21, pp. 445–50. See also Marshall Sahlins' discussion of food as a gift, in Sahlins, *op. cit.*, in note 13, pp. 215–19.
100. Sen, *op. cit.*, in note 1, p. 2, note 3.
101. *Ibid.*, p. 39.
102. Malthus, *op. cit.*, in note 10, p. 61.
103. Sen, *op. cit.*, in note 1, p. 162.
104. See, for example, Michel Foucault, *The Order of Things: An Archaeology of the Human Sciences* (London: Tavistock/Routledge, 1970), pp. 256–8. See also Pieter Tijmes and Reginald Luijf, 'The Sustainability of Our Common Future: An Inquiry into the Foundations of an Ideology', *Technology in Society* (Vol. 17, No. 3, 1995), pp. 327–36. For a discussion that views Sen's work as challenging the reliance of classical economics on scarcity, see Meghnad Desai, 'Story-telling and Formalism in Economics: The Instance of Famine', *International Social Science Journal* (Vol. 39, No. 3, 1987), pp. 387–400.
105. Michel Foucault, *Power/Knowledge: Selected Interviews and Other Writings 1972–1977*, trans. C. Gordon (Brighton: Harvester Press, 1980), pp. 134–8. For an interesting parallel discussion of too rapid universalisation and too rapid historicisation, see Slavoj Žižek's reflections on the ideological, in Žižek, *op. cit.*, in note 70, pp. 49–50. From the Marxist point of view, Žižek argues, the ideological move is to make that which is particular and historical appear universal, so famines appear as a consequence of the failure of the economic system. This is over rapid universalisation. In Lacanian terms, the very opposite – over rapid historicisation – is also ideological. This would occur when famines are seen as nothing more than particular breakdowns that appear in specific places at distinct historical conjunctures.
106. *Ibid.*, p. 136.
107. Keen follows this argument, taking his lead from Foucault. Keen, *op. cit.*, in note 9.
108. Foucault, *op. cit.*, in note 105, p. 136.
109. This is Žižek's phrase. See Slavoj Žižek, *The Indivisible Remainder: An Essay on Schelling and Related Matters* (London: Verso, 1996), pp. 214–15 and p. 234, fn 26, for another discussion of universalism and historicism.
110. Basil Ashton, Kenneth Hill, Alan Piazza, and Robin Zeitz, 'Famine in China, 1958–1961', *Population and Development Review* (Vol. 10, No. 4, 1984), pp. 613–45. See also Becker, *op. cit.*, in note 95.
111. For accounts of the Great Hunger, see, for example, Edwards and Williams (eds.), *op. cit.*, in note 94.
112. Sen, *op. cit.*, in note 1, pp. 52–85.
113. Macrae and Zwi, *op. cit.*, in note 5, p. 223.
114. *Ibid.*, 224.

115. See, for example, Duffield, *op. cit.*, in note 28, p. 49. This approach is also seen in de Waal, *op. cit.*, in note 9, pp. 9–32, when he talks about the African definition of famine as opposed to the English definition. This view is not shared by some African commentators. Solomon Inquai argues that famines are more a result of autocratic regimes that deny freedom and political rights, and interference by foreign powers acting in their own interests. In other words, Inquai claims that conflicts have specifically political (not economic) motives. Africa is not inherently a 'food deficit' continent, and we should not forget the famines in Europe, China, India, *etc.*: 'there is nothing unique or peculiar about famine in Africa'. Comment by Inquai, in Doornbos *et al.* (eds.), *op. cit.*, in note 28, p. 63.

116. David Keen and Ken Wilson, 'Engaging with Violence: A Reassessment of Relief in Wartime', in Macrae and Zwi (eds.), *op. cit.*, in note 5, pp. 209–21. Other 'complex emergency' theorists repudiate this. See Duffield, *op. cit.*, in note 30, p. 185.

117. Derrida, *Writing and Difference*, *op. cit.*, in note 49, pp. 278–9.

118. Cornell, *op. cit.*, in note 89, p. 2.

119. *Ibid.*, p. 1

120. *Ibid.*

121. Duffield, *op. cit.*, in note 27.

122. Jacques Derrida, *Points... Interviews, 1974–1994*, ed. E. Weber, trans. P. Kamuf *et al.* (Stanford, CA: Stanford University Press, 1992), p. 235.

123. See, for example, Keen, *op. cit.*, in note 9, p. 235; Duffield, *op. cit.*, in note 2, p. 43; and Omaar and de Waal, *op. cit.*, in note 5, pp. 2–3.

124. Jacques Derrida, *The Other Heading: Reflections on Today's Europe*, trans. P. Brault and M. Naas (Bloomington, IN: Indiana University Press, 1992), p. 79.

125. This draws on the discussion in *ibid.*, pp. 38–9.

126. *Ibid.*, p. 41, emphasis in original.

127. *Ibid.*

128. *Ibid.*, emphasis in original.

129. Derrida, *op. cit.*, in note 46, p. 28.

130. David Campbell, 'The Deterritorialization of Responsibility: Levinas, Derrida, and Ethics After the End of Philosophy', *Alternatives* (Vol. 19, No. 4, 1994), pp. 455–84. See also Simon Critchley, *The Ethics of Deconstruction: Derrida and Levinas* (Oxford: Blackwell, 1992), p. 199.

131. Derrida, *op. cit.*, in note 124, pp. 45–6.

132. *Ibid.*, p. 29.

133. *Ibid.*, p. 52.

134. *Ibid.*

135. This draws on the work of Carol Gilligan which examines the different 'moral' voices of men and women. See Carol Gilligan, *In a Different Voice: Psychological Theory and Women's Development* (Cambridge, MA: Harvard University Press, 1982). The first question – in the masculine mode – takes the manner of action for granted, presuming it to be a matter of fact; the latter assumes the necessity for action and considers what form it should take. The first sees a conflict between life and property (state sovereignty) that can be resolved by logical deduction, while the second sees the fracture of a human relationship that must be mended with its own thread. Rather than looking at the problem as

one of understanding the logic of justification, what the 'different voice' does is to pose it as a question of the nature of choice. Gilligan quotes the account given by Amy, an eleven-year-old girl in her study, as follows: '[t]here's really no way around it because there's no way you can do both at once, so you've got to decide, but you'll never know' (p. 32). This, of course, is very close to Derrida's notion of the undecidable.

136. Clay, Steingraber, and Niggli, *op. cit.*, in note 8, p. 3.
137. Derrida, *op. cit.*, in note 124, p. 81.
138. Gilligan, *op. cit.*, in note 135, p. 32.

4. Civil Society and a Democratisation of the International Monetary Fund

Jan Aart Scholte

The International Monetary Fund (IMF, or 'the Fund') is an institution of global economic governance with a current membership of 182 states. It emerged from the United Nations Monetary and Financial Conference, held at Bretton Woods in July 1944. According to its Articles of Agreement, the Fund exists to promote international monetary cooperation, to facilitate the expansion of international trade, to secure foreign exchange stability, and to assist in the correction of balance of payments problems.[1]

Although these official purposes have remained the same during the half-century of IMF operations, the institutional arrangements and policy instruments of the organisation have substantially changed over time. In the process, the Washington-based Fund has become deeply involved in questions of economic and social development (particularly since the late 1970s) and in matters of financial market regulation (especially since the mid-1990s). Both of these trends indicate that, in the globalising world of the late-twentieth century, balance of payments must be regulated in the context of macroeconomic policy as a whole.

Officially, by its Articles of Agreement, the IMF deals only with governments. In practice, it is indeed the case that the institution conducts the great majority of its relations with member states. However, the Fund's contacts are not limited to exchanges with states and intergovernmental bodies. The IMF also maintains a dialogue with civil society.

In the present context, 'civil society' refers to a broad collectivity of nongovernmental, non-commercial, more or less formal organisations. Civil society constitutes a 'third sector' next to public institutions and market actors. It encompasses all those groups that, from outside official circles and firms, pursue objectives that relate explicitly to reinforcing or altering existent rules, norms, and/or deeper social structures. The scope of civil society extends wider than that of another catchword of contemporary politics with which it is often linked, namely nongovernmental organisations (NGOs). The range of civic associations includes not only development NGOs, environmentalist associations, women's movements, and so on, but also business lobbies, labour unions, *etc.*

Since its creation in the 1940s, the IMF has maintained at least sporadic contacts with certain parts of civil society (for example, academic associations). However, a greatly accelerated expansion of Fund connections with civil society has occurred since the late 1980s. Not until the 1990s can we speak of relatively more wide-ranging, systematic, and substantial relationships between the IMF and civic groups.

These contacts merit close scrutiny. For one thing, the exchanges have on various occasions influenced the course of IMF policies. In addition, an analysis of relationships between civic associations and the Fund may yield important insights regarding the potentials for increasing efficacy and democracy in global economic governance.

In this chapter it is argued that exchanges between the IMF and civil society have to date remained underdeveloped. Although there has been notable growth in the interchanges between civic groups and the Fund, especially over the past decade, the dialogue has much additional potential that is as yet unrealised. Relations between civil society and the IMF have in some ways contributed valuable inputs to global monetary and financial regulation, but in other significant respects they have fallen considerably short in terms of enhancing both policy effectiveness and democratic governance.

A fully effective and democratic dialogue between the Fund and civic associations would need to meet several broad criteria which are currently at best only partially fulfilled. First, the dialogue would have open access. All stakeholders would have an effective equal opportunity to participate. Second, voices in the dialogue would be representative of, and accountable to, the range of affected constituencies. Third, all parties to the dialogue would make their best efforts to understand the issues under discussion. Fourth, the dialogue would be critically creative, aiming not only to reinforce what was already good, but also to generate new and improved possibilities. Fifth, interchange in the dialogue would be reciprocal, with each party ready to recognise, respect, listen to, learn from, and be changed by the others – even when their respective starting points were radically contradictory. Sixth, participants in the dialogue – and especially the dominant parties – would openly acknowledge any inequalities of power that structure their discussions and would not allow arbitrary impositions of such hierarchies to determine outcomes.[2] Current IMF-civil society exchanges are to some degree – and sometimes severely – wanting on each of these six counts.

To elaborate this argument, the rest of this chapter first discusses the context of post-Westphalian governance in which contacts between civic groups and the IMF have proliferated. The second section reviews the principal motivations which have spurred the Fund and civil society to pursue a dialogue. The third section describes the major current limitations to this dialogue, while the fourth section explains this underdevelopment in terms of various resource and deeper structural constraints.

Post-Westphalian Governance

With the accelerated globalisation of recent decades, significant elements of social relations have become substantially detached from territorial space. In other words, their geography involves more than – and to an important degree transcends – territorial locations, distances, and borders. In contrast to earlier times, contemporary social geography includes a major *supraterritorial* dimension, seen for example in telecommunications, transborder production, electronic finance, global environmental change, and so on.[3]

This historically unprecedented degree of globalisation has had far-reaching implications for governance. That cornerstone of the Westphalian world order, sovereign statehood, persists in name, but in practice a *territorial* state cannot by itself effectively govern *supraterritorial* flows. Not surprisingly, various alternative sites of norm construction, standards monitoring, and rule enforcement have emerged in areas where state sovereignty has become impracticable.

The rise of supraterritoriality has thus encouraged a decentralisation of governance. Regulatory authority has become more dispersed across a host of substate, suprastate, and private agencies as well as national governments. To be sure, states retain a central place in governance and show no sign of making an exit from history. Yet in the 1990s even the best-resourced state is unable to exercise absolute, all-encompassing, unshared authority over a territorially defined jurisdiction in the way that sovereignty has traditionally implied. World governance is therefore no longer reducible, on the neat Westphalian formula, to the states-system.[4]

Accordingly, in many areas public policy cannot today be successfully pursued through the state alone. A key challenge of contemporary history is to effect a constructive shift from state-centric governance to regulation by an interplay of local, national, and global authorities. Among other things, this transition requires a redesign of democracy, that is, new mechanisms through which people can secure participation, consultation, open debate, representation, transparency, and accountability in governance.

Growth of the IMF

Since a great deal of contemporary globalisation has transpired in monetary and financial realms, it is not surprising to observe a concurrent expansion of global monetary and financial regulation. Much of this growth of supraterritorial governance has occurred through the IMF. Increased globalisation has propelled the Fund into many new areas, of which four warrant particular mention.[5]

First, the IMF has since the 1970s undertaken comprehensive and detailed surveillance, both of the economic performance of individual member-states and of the world economy as a whole. Today the Fund conducts so-called 'Article IV consultations' with 150 governments per year. In this process the IMF has promoted important reorientations of macroeconomic policies, partly with a view to accommodating the ongoing globalisation of production and finance.

Second, the Fund has since the 1970s intervened more intensely in many countries by designing structural adjustment programmes for them. The organisation has come to extend loans to many more states (up to sixty per year). The conditionalities attached to these credit lines have often involved major policy changes, including liberalisation, privatisation, fiscal reform, and (most recently) so-called 'good governance'. Contemporary IMF programmes have often required large credits (sometimes running into billions of dollars) and long implementation periods (up to fifteen years in consecutive loans).

Third, the Fund has undertaken major training and technical assistance activities, largely in order to provide poorly equipped states with staff and tools that can better handle the policy challenges of contemporary globalisation. The IMF Institute has since its establishment in 1964 trained more than 10,000 officials in macroeconomic issues.[6] The Fund's technical assistance missions to governments also started in 1964, sharply increased in number from the 1980s, and now total around 600 per annum.[7]

Fourth, the IMF has pursued various initiatives to restore stability to global financial markets. For example, in the 1980s the organisation played a pivotal role in averting defaults on the large transborder debts of many governments in the South and East. More recently, the Fund has coordinated large-scale rescue operations ('bailouts') in financial crises of so-called 'emerging markets': in Mexico in 1994–5 and in Thailand/Korea/Indonesia in 1997–8. In the hope of better anticipating and perhaps preventing such emergencies, the IMF has since 1996 promoted global norms for government publication of economic and financial data (the so-called Special Data Dissemination Standard).[8] To the extent that the Fund has acted as a lender of last resort and addressed questions concerning the supervision of global capital markets, it has moved towards becoming something of a suprastate central bank.

To handle the enlarged agenda just described, the IMF has undergone substantial institutional growth. Staff numbers have more than tripled between 1966 and 1996, to about 2600.[9] Over recent decades the Fund has developed its own 'diplomatic service' of sorts, with Resident Representatives stationed in 64 countries by 1997.[10] Since 1970 the Fund has had its own money form, the Special Drawing Right (SDR). IMF quota subscriptions have grown from the equivalent of 21 billion SDRs in 1965 to 145 billion SDRs in 1995.[11] The supplementary General Arrangements to Borrow (GAB) have almost tripled from the original 6 billion SDRs (in lenders' currencies) in 1962 to 17 billion SDRs since 1983.[12] It was proposed in 1997 to make up to 34 billion additional SDRs available to the Fund through the so-called New Arrangements to Borrow (NAB).[13]

To be sure, it would be mistaken to depict the IMF as an omnipotent ruler of the contemporary globalising world economy. The organisation remains under the strong influence of states, especially its larger members. At the same time, however, the Fund has clearly experienced a major growth in responsibilities and authority over the past several decades. The IMF is not only influenced by its members, but also exerts considerable influence over them, weaker states in particular.

Civil Society and Global Governance

Not surprisingly, given the far-reaching significance of IMF activities for much contemporary public policy, numerous civil society organisations across the world have in recent years sought contact with the Fund. Concerned citizens have wanted to understand and interrogate this new major player in governance. Interest groups have wanted to lobby and perhaps extract advantage from this new locus of policy-making.

This increase in approaches from civic associations to the IMF reflects in part the recent enormous growth in civil society across most of the world. One leading researcher of the phenomenon has spoken of 'a global "associational revolution" that may prove to be as significant to the latter twentieth century as the rise of the nation-state was to the latter nineteenth'.[14] With this expansion of civil society, multiple networks of communication, cooperation, and conflict over regulatory issues have come to bypass states.

For one thing, significant parts of contemporary civil society have involved transborder affiliations, for example, of managers, workers, religious believers, women, and environmentalists. By the count of the Union of International Associations, the number of active transborder civic groups has increased more than tenfold since 1960, to a total of 16,000 in 1997.[15] Arguably, the interests of such associations are not always adequately – or indeed appropriately – pursued through territorial states alone. Concurrently, much other civil society organising has expanded at local and national levels. For example, by the 1990s Kenya has counted some 23,000 registered women's groups, and more than 25,000 registered grassroots organisations have operated in the state of Tamil Nadu in India.[16] Many local and national associations, too, have incorporated global networking into their activities.

Since the 1970s most of the main public global governance agencies have experienced a major growth of exchanges (both formal and informal) with local, national, and transborder civic associations.[17] Almost all organs of the United Nations system have acquired expanded external relations departments, and many agencies have instituted liaison committees with participants from civil society. Furthermore, proposals have circulated for the creation of a permanent UN People's Assembly composed of civil society representatives next to the General Assembly of state delegates. Already civic groups have in the 1990s convened global meetings with fair regularity, for example, alongside the Group of Seven summits, the IMF/World Bank Annual Meetings, and *ad hoc* UN conferences.

The development of direct links between civil society and global regulatory agencies might be welcomed. After all, if governance is no longer reducible to the state, then citizens should probably seek to influence policy and to exercise democratic rights and responsibilities through more channels than national governments. Global governance organisations should be in close touch with the people whom their policies affect. Civic associations can perhaps forge the necessary global-local connections – indeed, they might sometimes (or even usually) do so better than states. The question to assess in the present context is the extent to which relations between civil society and the IMF have fulfilled this potential for improving policy efficacy and increasing democracy.

Motivations for Dialogue

In relation to such an assessment it is helpful to note the parties' intentions in engaging with each other. What has prompted civil society and the IMF increasingly to seek contact with one another over the past fifteen years? As might be expected, the goals have been varied.

On the part of the IMF, one important motivation has been reactive: that is, the organisation has been pulled along in the general contemporary trend towards increased involvement of civil society in global governance. Even a less easily accessible multilateral institution like the Fund has been unable to evade approaches from civil society. Citizens have hammered insistently at the door, and the Fund has not wished to appear retrograde by refusing to answer.

A second key motivation for the IMF to develop dialogue with civil society has lain in financial self-interest. On several occasions since the late 1970s the organisation has discovered that opposition from civil society can complicate or even block the allocation of monies by states to the Fund. Lobbyists on Capitol Hill have constituted a particular thorn for the IMF, as they have repeatedly threatened US congressional appropriations for quota increases and other financing of the Fund. It was largely to combat opposition from Washington-based civic groups that the IMF first embarked on concerted public relations activities in the 1980s.

The Fund's third major reason to develop dialogue with civil society – namely, consensus-building – is a more positive objective and has mainly come to the fore in the 1990s. Common wisdom in today's IMF holds that its prescriptions will have greater chances of success if people in the affected countries understand and support that advice. Contacts with civil society, it is believed, can contribute substantially to the construction of a (possibly indispensable) popular base for economic restructuring.

Within civil society, motivations for dialogue with the IMF have varied widely but can be broadly grouped under three headings: conformist, reformist, and radical agendas. This division is of course rather simplistic; however, it remains analytically useful to distinguish the three streams.

For their part, conformers have broadly endorsed the IMF's aims and activities. True, these circles in civil society have sometimes expressed doubts concerning one or the other measure recommended by the Fund (for example, a particular tax rate). In addition, conformers can be sharply critical of the IMF when they feel it has performed poorly (for example, in failing to anticipate a financial crisis). However, conformist civic groups have had no significant quarrel with the general principles that have informed Fund policies. Most business associations and many economic research institutes have taken a conformist position *vis-à-vis* the IMF. Prominent examples include the Bretton Woods Committee (a group of some 600 prominent American businesspeople, academics, and former government officials) and the Institute for International Economics.

Whereas conformers accept the IMF broadly in its existing shape, reformers wish to reconstruct the organisation. These circles in civil society accept the need for an IMF-type agency, but they criticise its current operating procedures and/or policy directions. For example, many reformers have argued for reformulation of Fund conditionalities to take more account of employment issues, ecological sustainability, and so forth. Reformists have also often urged the IMF to help reduce the external debt burdens of poor countries. In the 1990s various reformers have in addition called for democratisation of the Fund with, for example, more consultation of citizens, greater transparency, and increased accountability. Some reformist voices have furthermore advocated closer cooperation between the IMF and other global governance agencies. Reformist agendas have mainly been espoused by labour unions, church organisations, a host of NGOs, and various academic institutes. Leading IMF campaigners in the reformist stream have included the International Confederation of Free Trade Unions (ICFTU), the Vatican, the Swiss Coalition of Development Organisations, the World Wide Fund for Nature, and the Overseas Development Institute.

Radicals in civil society have sought not alterations in the IMF so much as its contraction or even abolition. For example, some radicals have argued that the Fund should return to its narrow original mandate of the Bretton Woods period. Thus the organisation would withdraw from surveillance activities, structural adjustment programmes, technical assistance, and rescue operations in financial crises. Certain radicals have gone still further to advocate a dissolution of the IMF altogether. Radical voices have risen among ultra-liberal free-marketeers, certain traditionalists and nationalists, and an assortment of radical socialists, environmentalists, and feminists. Prominent proponents of a radical stance towards the Fund have included the Cato Institute and the Fifty Years Is Enough coalition.

The preceding paragraphs have reviewed a wide range of motivations that have spurred the expansion of contacts between civil society and the IMF since the 1980s. From this survey it may already be inferred that dialogue between these two parties can often be troubled. Although the IMF and conformers have pursued broadly complementary aims, the Fund's objectives have found only limited echoes in reformist circles and none whatsoever among radicals.

Limitations to Dialogue

Contacts between the IMF and civic associations are greater than most persons concerned with global economic governance appreciate. Space limitations do not permit a full account here of the proliferation of these interchanges, especially since the late 1980s.[18] Suffice it to say that the IMF has undertaken multiple outreach initiatives in the 1990s. These activities have involved the Managing Directors, the Executive Directors, the External Relations Department, various operational departments, and missions and Resident Representatives in the field. Likewise, the 1990s have witnessed major growth in the number, range, and sophistication of civil society activities *vis-à-vis* the Fund. The IMF has encountered many more civic groups, many of which have had more specific objectives, a tighter organisation, and greater political skill than campaigners of previous generations.

However, in spite of this significant expansion of exchanges, relations between civil society and the IMF remain in important respects underdeveloped. Three main limitations have prevented the dialogue from achieving its full potential for increasing efficacy and democracy in Fund policy. First, many parts of civil society remain marginalised in or altogether excluded from conversations with the IMF. Second, both the Fund and civic groups have often left their reciprocal contacts at a superficial level. Third, the parties to IMF-civil society exchanges have frequently neglected to nurture a genuine 'dialogue': that is, the contacts have to date generally lacked the kind of open, two-way, critical mutual engagement that would be most constructive for policy. As the fourth section of this chapter will emphasise, these shortcomings have resulted chiefly from a range of resource and structural constraints.

Biased Participation

Relations between the Fund and civic groups have not involved equal access. The various types of associations have had differential opportunities to engage the IMF, and many potential exchanges between the Fund and civil society have not developed at all. Moreover, IMF contacts with civic organisations have disproportionately involved groups in the North and persons from middle-class professional circles. As a result of such biases, the Fund's dialogue with civil society has generally been limited to but a small portion of its client populations.

In terms of types of organisations, business associations and economic research institutes have on the whole had easiest entry to the IMF. Broadly fitting the category of 'conformers', these bodies have fairly readily obtained audiences with Fund staff. Most of the Managing Director's speeches to non-official audiences have been made to business conferences and academic gatherings. At the IMF/World Bank Annual Meetings, corporate representatives have carried badges as 'visitors' or 'special guests'. In contrast, representatives of other advocacy organisations have worn 'NGO' labels and have not appeared in the published list of participants. True, certain business lobbies have sometimes complained that the IMF does not adequately consult with them; however, compared to others in civil society, they have generally had privileged contacts.

Second in this rough ranking of access by civic groups to the IMF have been trade unions. The Fund has taken numerous initiatives in the 1990s to, in the words of one official, 'groom' labour.[19] From various previous experiences, the IMF has learned that opposition from organised labour can substantially frustrate the implementation of stabilisation measures or structural adjustment policies. In addition, Fund officials have tended to perceive trade unions as 'representative' bodies in a way that they have presumed NGOs not to be. Among the IMF's noteworthy initiatives *vis-à-vis* labour, management in 1995 issued special instructions that Resident Representatives should, in collaboration with the International Labour Organisation, nurture contacts with local trade unions. Four times since 1992 the IMF has co-sponsored major seminars for labour leaders. In 1996–7, the Managing Director addressed congresses of the ICFTU and the World Confederation of Labour.

Third in line, in terms of access to the IMF, have been various other advocacy groups who demand the Fund's attention: mainly church agencies, development NGOs, environmental lobbies, and, to a lesser extent, certain human rights associations. In contrast to business, academe, and labour, these organisations have tended to be 'uninvited guests' at the Fund. The institution has usually responded to overtures from such groups with reluctance. Occasionally – and with increased frequency in recent years – more experienced NGO lobbyists have obtained interviews with the operational departments of the IMF. Nevertheless, on the whole these advocates have remained 'second-class citizens' in civil society contacts with the Fund.

Fourth in this admittedly crude but broadly viable ranking have been the many completely excluded civic groups, that is, associations that have neither actively sought contact with the IMF nor have been actively sought out by the institution. For example, no women's associations have engaged the Fund in any sustained manner, and the Fund has taken little initiative to reach them. Other sectors of civil society that have been excluded and excluded themselves from contacts with the Fund include non-Christian religious organisations, peace movements, consumer rights advocates, youth associations, grassroots community improvement agencies, indigenous peoples groups, and ethnic lobbies. The most surprising omission in IMF contacts with civil society has been peasant associations. Large-scale commercial farmers have lobbied the Fund (for example, in Zimbabwe), but organisations of smallholders – who constitute a substantial proportion of the population in many programme countries – have stayed outside the dialogue.

So far this discussion of biased participation has focused on types of organisations, but dialogue between civil society and the IMF has also been skewed in other ways. For example, the Fund has generally developed more numerous and more substantive contacts with civic groups in the North relative to those in the South and the East. Of course distinctions between 'North', 'South', and 'East' are to some extent artificial and simplistic; nevertheless, an overall bias has prevailed towards what may loosely be called the North. Fund information pamphlets have appeared in at most five languages – all European – and have had minimal circulation in the East and South. Given the expenses involved, most activists in the South have also had limited if any access to fax and Internet connections. A huge majority of 'visitors', 'special guests', and 'NGOs' at the IMF/World Bank Annual Meetings have come from the North. Even on the ground in programme countries, the IMF Resident Representative has often met more with staff from North-based organisations (for example, development aid agencies or associations of foreign investors) than with indigenous groups (especially NGOs). Indeed, in certain countries local civic groups have complained that they can only access the Res Rep through the mediation of North-based organisations.

Some civic groups have begun in the 1990s to address these inequalities between North and South/East by emphasising the need for dialogue across these divides within civil society. For example, the Development GAP, a Washington-based NGO, has declared as its central objective 'to ensure that the knowledge, priorities and efforts of the women and men of the South inform decisions made in the North about their economies and the environments in which they live.'[20] Several North-based NGOs have taken persons from the South onto their staff. In a similar spirit, a number of North-based associations have in recent years hosted delegations from the South for discussions of debt problems and structural adjustment.

Nevertheless, these consultations between North and South/East could be taken much further. Many North-based activists have conceded that they have not worked out timely and effective ways to communicate with South-based organisations. Indeed, one leading campaigner in Washington for IMF reform has declared dismissively that 'there is so much lipservice about consulting the South – it's a figleaf'.[21] Moreover, most South-based civic groups who communicate with North-based associations have done so in circumstances of substantial dependency, financial and otherwise. The representatives of the South have thereby easily been inhibited from speaking fully and frankly to their own agenda.

In addition to – and intersecting with – unequal access by type of organisation and North/South/East position, a further significant bias in the dialogue between civil society and the IMF has related to class. Civil society contacts with the Fund have almost invariably involved urban-based, university-educated, computer-literate, (relatively) high-earning English speakers. No civic mobilisation concerning the IMF has developed between grassroot groups in the South and underclasses in the North. For its part, the Fund has rarely sought direct contacts with rural groups, the urban poor, and so on. Nor have most elite-based civic associations (whether from North, South, or East) used their connections with the Fund to put carefully gathered views of marginalised groups on the table. A few church groups and development NGOs have stood out as exceptions with their efforts to incorporate 'voices from the base' into their advocacy work, but for the rest underclasses have been locked out of indirect as well as direct dialogue with the IMF.

A gender bias has also limited the scope of relations between the Fund and civil society. Although IMF personnel policy has of late become more gender sensitive, the staff remains overwhelmingly male. The top management of the organisation has never included a woman, no more than three women have served concurrently among the 24 Executive Directors, and only two women have become head of an IMF department. On the whole, women have had notably greater access to NGOs. Indeed, a fair gender balance has developed amongst campaigners for reform of the Fund. However, women have remained severely underrepresented in the sectors of civil society with relatively greater access to the IMF, namely, business lobbies, research institutes, and organised labour.

In sum, then, one major restriction of the contacts that have grown over the past 15 years between the IMF and civil society has been their fairly narrow base. The exchanges have shown strong biases towards certain kinds of organisations, certain countries, and certain social circles. The resultant exclusion of large numbers of stakeholders has, of course, hardly been unique to civic contacts with the IMF; arguably such limited representation has marked the entire dialogue to date between civil society and global governance agencies.

Shallowness of Relationships

A second major limitation in the links that have developed between civic groups and the IMF concerns the general superficiality of the dialogue. There are important exceptions, but most parties to the encounter – both in the Fund and in civil society – have accorded a fairly low priority to these relationships. As a result, the exchanges have on the whole been only weakly institutionalised and in most cases only haphazardly sustained.

Although the IMF has given contacts with civic associations a certain prominence, on the whole the dialogue has remained relatively low on the agenda. For example, whereas the President of the World Bank has repeatedly and specifically affirmed a need for his organisation to develop partnerships with civil society, the Managing Director of the Fund has referred only loosely to a need to build national consensus behind stabilisation and structural reform programmes. Also unlike the World Bank, the IMF has not contributed to – and has only once used – the UN Non-Governmental Liaison Service (NGLS), an agency that provides 16 other global governance agencies with information and advice about NGOs. As one IMF department director has readily conceded, 'I would lie if I said that [contacts with civic groups] were a daily, foremost activity'.[22] Most staff have taken the view that 'I came to the Fund to be a macroeconomist' and have regarded the 'political' aspects of the job as a secondary concern. In the field, some IMF missions and Resident Representatives have undertaken outreach activities *vis-à-vis* civil society with enthusiasm, but many others have made at best perfunctory gestures.

Beyond the creation in 1989 of a Public Affairs Division in the External Relations Department, the Fund has done little to institutionalise its relationships with civic associations. The Articles of Agreement have not been amended to accommodate these links, nor has the Executive Board issued any guiding directives. Almost all IMF contacts with civil society have occurred on an *ad hoc* basis. Head office in Washington has established no liaison committee with civil society, as has been created in the World Bank and other UN agencies. No consultation of civic groups has been formally built into the preparation, implementation, and assessment of IMF stabilisation and structural reform packages. Only in Switzerland have civic associations taken formal part in Article IV consultations. No job description for staff in the operational departments of the IMF has mentioned contacts with civic groups.

In sum, much IMF policy regarding civil society has consisted of improvisation. From the start of contacts in the early 1980s, the Fund has mainly developed relations with civic associations in an incremental and reactive manner. The Board and management have not formulated an overall strategy with precise goals and carefully designed institutional mechanisms.

Approaches in civil society towards the IMF have generally been equally *ad hoc*. Most civic organisations have accorded only relatively low (if any) priority to dialogue with the Fund. Only a few associations, like the Institute of International Finance (IIF), the ICFTU, and Friends of the Earth-US, have pursued sustained, focused, carefully researched campaigns to influence Fund policies. Even fewer agencies, like the Bretton Woods Committee, have been created specifically to engage the IMF. Meanwhile the majority of advocacy groups have treated the Fund with only passing curiosity, if they have given the institution any attention at all. Most activists with an interest in changing global economic governance have preferred to concentrate on more 'tangible' issues related to multilateral trade agreements or World Bank projects. Thanks in good part to the obscurantism of economistic jargon – much of it arguably unnecessary – questions of IMF conditionality and surveillance have caused many a civic organiser's eyes to glaze over. Few civil society associations have shown interest in obtaining – on the Swiss model – direct participation in Article IV consultations. Nor have civic organisations (other than certain research institutes, the IIF, and, more hesitantly, an occasional NGO) given much attention to the Fund's growing role in monitoring global financial markets.[23]

Civic activists who have tried to generate interest in the Fund among the wider public have faced a difficult task. Business associations have been able to energise their constituents by pointing to the commercial interests that various IMF policies can advance or harm. However, reform campaigners have usually faced uphill struggles to secure the support of subscribers and the attention of the general public. In spite of increased NGO efforts at civic education on the IMF, questions of policy surveillance, structural adjustment, debt relief, and foreign exchange crises have rarely grabbed the popular imagination. In the same vein, advocacy NGOs have also had limited success in drawing press attention to campaigns for IMF reform. The South-centric Inter Press Service and local journalists in many programme countries have been fairly receptive to covering the issues, but the principal world press agencies, major newspapers, and global broadcasters have – except in a major crisis – given little space to a debate of Fund policies.

All in all, then, contacts between the IMF and civil society have remained pretty haphazard and shallow. Only a few operational staff at the Fund have developed more sustained relations with outside fora. Resident Representatives usually spend only two years in a country, and many do not establish contacts with civic groups outside of the capital. Conversely, too, only a small number of persons in civil society organisations have maintained regular contacts with the IMF. At most a few lobbyists in each programme country have sustained substantive relationships with the Fund over a longer period.

Many participants on each side of IMF-civil society exchanges have expressed unhappiness about the general shallowness of these relationships. In civic groups, for example, many campaigners have doubted whether the Fund has been taking them seriously. Various lobbyists have also objected that the information which they desire from the IMF is not readily available. (Here the complaints concern the content rather than the – now very large – quantity of Fund publications.) More frustrated civic activists have decided that there is 'not much point' in pursuing relations with the Fund and have instead diverted most of their energies to the seemingly 'more receptive' World Bank.

For their part, IMF staff have often become frustrated with what they regard as unproductive discussions with many civil society representatives. A number of officials have regularly described these exchanges with 'simple hearts and simple minds' as 'fruitless' and 'a waste of time'.[24] Fund staff have commonly objected that, aside from business lobbies and academic researchers, many civic organisations come with only general criticisms and no practicable suggestions for alternatives. Officials have complained, too, that campaigners in civil society have rarely done their homework. In this vein Executive Directors have remarked that 'NGOs are too willing to offer opinions on macro issues they know next to nothing about'.[25]

More positively, it should be noted that the disenchantment just described has by no means reigned continuously or universally in relations between the IMF and civil society. Even some of the most critical opponents of the Fund acknowledge that the institution has taken steps to open up in the 1990s, and optimistic civic organisers believe that many recent outreach initiatives by the IMF have entailed more than public relations exercises. On the side of the Fund, few officials today remain completely dismissive of contacts with civil society, and many acknowledge that some of these exchanges have influenced their thinking on various policy issues. All of this said, however, when compared with most other interchanges between global governance agencies and civic associations, and when measured against what could be possible, the overall relationship between the IMF and civil society has lacked depth.

Limited 'Dialogue'

One key obstacle that has kept this greater depth from emerging is at the same time a third major shortcoming in relations between civil society and the IMF, namely, the underdevelopment of a veritable 'dialogue'. This problem has arisen especially in contacts between the Fund on the one hand and its reformist and radical critics on the other. In general, these exchanges have not been exercises in two-way listening and learning.

To a large extent reformers and radicals have clashed with the IMF because their aims have had little overlap with those of the multilateral institution. IMF staff have on the whole been sceptical about the kinds, degrees, and speeds of change being advocated in reformist circles of civil society. Not surprisingly, Fund officials have shown no sympathy whatsoever with radical proposals to shrink or dissolve their institution. In any case, many radicals have refused to seek dialogue with Fund personnel, regarding any engagement as cooptation. In general, then, it has been difficult for the IMF and many civic groups to find common ground on which to talk.

Given these divergent perspectives, some degree of conflict between the parties has no doubt been unavoidable; however, the tensions have heightened and become less productive insofar as the participants have often not been willing seriously to examine positions other than their own. On the part of the IMF, many officials have simply dismissed alternative views expressed in civil society as 'wrong'. Typically, Fund staff have seen meetings with civic organisers as occasions to 'correct' and 'educate' the misguided; officials have rarely pursued contacts with these advocates out of interest to hear and respond to alternative perspectives on IMF programmes. It does seem that, for the Fund, achieving 'consensus' has not meant building new understandings out of different points of view, but bringing civil society round to an unaltered IMF position. Commenting on one encounter with Fund officials, an experienced campaigner has said with a certain resignation, 'they talked about what they wanted to talk about and talked about it in the way they always do'.[26] Many reformist and radical campaigners have felt that 'the IMF won't have a frank discussion about the problems of its policies' and that 'if you're too insistent in expressing a different point of view, IMF people tell you to keep quiet'.[27] With gentler phraseology, a published IMF account of its relations with NGOs has stated that 'the Fund's strategy...has been selective, and continued efforts at engagement have depended on whether the ensuing dialogue was constructive'.[28]

That said, in adopting this defensive approach, Fund personnel have often been responding to intransigence on the part of many reformers and radicals in civil society. These lobbyists' arguments, too, have been well populated with entrenched positions, unquestioned preconceptions, easy slogans, and self-righteous posturing. Many civic campaigners have been no more prepared to give an open hearing to the IMF than vice-versa. In meetings with Fund staff, many NGO and labour activists have given the organisation little credit for good intentions or at least some policy successes. In response, IMF officials have frequently complained that '[NGOs] spend the whole time telling us we're wrong' and that 'it's hard to get a dialogue going [with such people]'.[29]

To be sure, the intensity of the confrontations just described has varied between individuals and between situations. The hostility has tended to be greatest in Washington and in certain programme countries. Dialogues have generally been more cordial in Europe and in other programme countries. Some of the polarisation has been unnecessary, insofar as many IMF officials have conceded in private that the organisation has made mistakes. Likewise, most reformers and even several self-proclaimed radicals have accepted in private that many Fund interventions may be necessary and can have positive effects.[30]

Hence potential exists for greater mutual trust and, consequently, a more open, two-way, critical, creative dialogue. Optimistic assessments might suggest that some first, rather hesitant steps in this direction have already taken place since the mid-1990s. Perhaps the dialogue of the deaf has transformed into an exchange between the hard of hearing; however, a conversation with open ears has so far remained elusive.

Constraints on Dialogue

Underdevelopment of the dialogue between civil society and the IMF has usually not resulted in the first place from the personalities and attitudes of individuals, although such factors have no doubt played a secondary role in particular situations. If 'blame' is to be allocated, then it lies principally with (a) the limited resources that the parties have had to hand and (b) certain deeper structures (for example, related to institutional culture and the organisation of the world system) that the parties in dialogue have inherited.

Resource Constraints

In order to conduct a dialogue that involves all interested parties in an open, searching discussion of policy, both the IMF and civil society groups would need to devote substantially more resources to their mutual contacts than have been allocated to date. Neither the Fund nor civic associations have had sufficient staff, budgets, information, and coordination capacities to realise the full potential of their relationships with each other.

With regard to inadequate staffing, as of 1997 only the eleven officials of the Public Affairs Division had a specific responsibility for relations with civic groups among other jobs. So small a contingent can hardly be expected adequately to coordinate contacts with civil society bodies worldwide. Nor can an IMF Resident Representative office be expected to achieve much in this regard so long as all but two of these posts have only one professional staffer. For their part, other Fund employees have usually been overstretched with other responsibilities. Often sheer workload has frustrated the good intentions of those operational personnel who might otherwise have liked to develop public outreach initiatives.

As for civil society, most organisations that engage with the IMF have lacked personnel with expertise regarding the institution. The several dozen exceptions worldwide have usually had only one or two specialists each. To this day, a number of programme countries lack any local civic campaigner with extensive experience of dealing directly with the IMF. Most civil society activists have been overextended with other responsibilities that have kept them from becoming adequately educated about the Fund.

Intertwined with and exacerbating personnel problems, financial constraints have also contributed significantly to the underdevelopment of contacts between civil society and the IMF. At the Fund, external relations activities have in the late-1990s commanded less than $20 million annually, or just 3.6 per cent of the IMF's modest operating budget.[31] The Fund has been run under very tight budgetary controls, with both member states and management keeping a sharp eye on administrative outlays. In these circumstances IMF officials have declared that 'any thought of specifically designating one official in each Resident Representative office to pursue contacts with civic bodies would be quite unrealistic'.[32]

Financial constraints in civil society organisations have been even more severe than in the IMF. Although business lobbies have generally not suffered unduly from lack of monies, most labour organisations and churches with an interest in the Fund have struggled on small budgets. As for development and environmental NGOs, their work on the IMF has mainly depended on grants from a few bilateral aid agencies and a handful of private foundations. Moreover, it has been difficult for NGOs to develop connections with the Fund when their grants have usually been small (almost never over $100,000) and short-term (lasting at most two or three years). Many campaigners in NGOs have complained about the amount of time 'lost' on fundraising.

Lack of staff and funds have contributed significantly to a third resource constraint on the development of relations between the IMF and civil society, namely, shortages of information. The Fund has accumulated but a meagre store of data concerning civic organisations. IMF officials thus have little information with which to distinguish those civil society groups that represent substantial constituencies from the many 'briefcase NGOs' that consist of one person and a bundle of grant proposals. Indeed, IMF staff – including Resident Representatives – are usually unaware of the existence of many civic groups. It does seem paradoxical that, whereas the IMF has set such great store by data collection and analysis in its macroeconomic work, it has given so little attention to information gathering and assessment in its public affairs activities.

Concurrently, civic lobbying of the IMF has suffered from major shortages of information in regard to the Fund. For example, many groups with concerns to put to the IMF have not known where to call. Even a bare outline of the Fund's departmental structure was not readily available to the public until the 1996 *Annual Report* included a basic organigram (now also incorporated into the IMF website).[33] Only since 1997 has a visitor to IMF headquarters been allowed to consult a staff list. More positively, the Fund has in recent years published increasing numbers of policy documents. Civil society activists can now access far more information than many of them realise. That said, however, the Fund has not to date released most key programme documents, repeatedly citing the prerogative of states to keep such material confidential. Thus, in spite of recent improvements, lack of access to information has remained a substantial constraint on civil society monitoring and assessment of IMF activities.

A fourth resource constraint on dialogue between civil society and the IMF concerns poor capacities for coordination. For example, the Fund has rarely compensated for some of the shortcomings in its own resources by drawing on the greater expertise and information regarding civic contacts of the World Bank and various UN specialised agencies.

In civil society, meanwhile, the various associations doing advocacy work on the Fund have on the whole not communicated terribly well with one another. Indeed, especially in the South and East, many agencies have been unaware even of each other's existence. Not surprisingly, associations with conformist aims have rarely collaborated in lobbying the IMF with groups that pursue a reformist or radical programme. In addition, however, disagreements regarding aims, strategy, and tactics have sometimes bitterly divided reformists and radicals. Most unconstructive of all, competition for scarce monies has sometimes discouraged NGOs from collaborating together in their IMF work as generously as they ideally would do.

In sum, with better resourcing dialogue between civil society and the IMF could develop much further than it has done to date. Of course, more staff, more funds, more information, and more coordination would not by themselves allow these exchanges to realise their full potential as constructive policy inputs and forces for democratisation of global economic governance. However, it is hard to see how such advances could be achieved in the absence of increased resources of these kinds.

Structural Constraints

The principal reason why greater resources would not by themselves suffice to deepen IMF-civil society contacts is that various embedded structural conditions have also limited the development of these relationships. Some of these constraints have related to institutional organisation. Others have lain in wider social relations.

In respect of its institutional organisation, the Fund has been substantially monolithic, with little division on the inside or porosity towards the outside. IMF officials have pursued many frank policy discussions with one another, but the arguments have remained always within the walls of the building and always within pretty narrow boundaries of 'acceptable' debate. In management style, the Fund has maintained tight central direction and rigorous internal discipline. In these various ways, then, the fairly monolithic character of the institution has discouraged IMF officials from developing a more open dialogue with outside parties, including civic groups.

Difficulties of access to the IMF for civil society organisations have also resulted from the culture of secrecy that has traditionally enveloped monetary and financial regulation. Central banks, state treasuries, and global financial agencies like the Fund have not in the past been attitudinally geared for 'public' relations. To be sure, there are good arguments for some discretion in IMF activities. For instance, advance notice of proposed currency devaluations, interest rate changes, tax alterations, and the like could compromise the success of such measures. However, institutions of monetary and financial regulation like the Fund have tended to drape the cloak of secrecy over much more than sensitive matters. In the process they have also shielded themselves from the degree of public accountability that is usually demanded of other governance agencies in a democracy. True, the IMF has in the 1990s shifted its views on the balance between the need to know and the need for confidentiality in favour of the former. However, an embedded culture of secrecy does not dissolve quickly. Moves toward greater openness have yet to reach all corners of the Fund and fully to change the style of its contacts with civic associations.

A third structural circumstance of the late-twentieth century, namely, the power of neoliberalism, has complicated efforts to reverse the IMF's tendencies towards insularity and secrecy. Neoliberalism refers here, somewhat loosely, to the predominant contemporary worldview according to which globalised market relations will in time create maximal liberty, democracy, prosperity, and peace for humankind as a whole. Broadly speaking, neoliberalism has prescribed:

(a) the abolition of most state-imposed restrictions on cross-border movements of resources (money, consumables, durables, financial instruments, information, communications, *etc.*);
(b) the removal of state controls on indicators of economic value (prices, wages, foreign exchange rates, interest rates, *etc.*);
(c) the contraction of state ownership of productive assets (that is, thoroughgoing privatisation);

(d) the reduction of state provision of welfare needs and greater reliance on voluntary agencies, corporate charity, and market arrangements for social insurances, pensions, *etc.*; and

(e) the universal practice of liberal democracy, in particular the conduct of periodic multiparty elections to representative law-making bodies.

The Fund has ranked among the world's chief proponents of neoliberal globalisation, sometimes even employing religious metaphor in its evangelism. Thus, for example, the Managing Director has exhorted members to heed 'eleven commandments' in a broadly neoliberal framework.[34] Needless to say, conviction politics of this kind are not particularly conducive to two-way dialogue with reformers and radicals who call neoliberal 'truth' into question.

Nor has the IMF had much pressure or incentive to engage in more deeply critical policy explorations with civil society groups. Neoliberalism has been the favoured knowledge of most centres of power in the 1980s and 1990s, including in particular the global financial markets and the major states with whom the IMF has its closest ties. With their endorsement of neoliberal ideas, most business associations and many economic research institutes have had relatively easier entry into the Fund. However, prevailing knowledge/power structures of the day have encouraged the IMF of the 1990s largely to close its ears to unorthodox talk. Indeed, some campaigners for IMF reform have – deliberately or unconsciously – shifted their language in the direction of neoliberalism in order to get at least some hearing from the Fund.

Next to forces of institutional culture and discourse, a further structural circumstance that has limited contacts between the Fund and civic associations has related to social hierarchies: of North over South and East; of propertied and professional classes over poorer and less literate circles; and of men over women. These inequalities were mentioned earlier in the discussion of biases in the IMF-civil society dialogue. The point to stress at the present juncture is that this unequal access has not been accidental. Rather, relations between the Fund and civic groups have reflected broader structural power hierarchies of countries, classes, and genders.

Thus voices of the South and East have tended to play second fiddle in the IMF-civil society dialogue largely because they hold a weaker position generally in the contemporary world political economy. Although the deepest impacts of Fund recommendations have been felt in the South and East, a large majority of the votes, money, staff, and ideas in the institution have come from the North. Likewise, civic associations who maintain contacts with the Fund have mostly had their base in the North. Even in South-North meetings of civil society groups, activists from the North have tended to dominate the proceedings unless delegates from the South have explicitly insisted on having equal say. Although colonial times have passed, Northern solidarity with Southern civil society partners can sometimes still be delivered with patronising tone and paternalistic gesture.

The relative exclusion of other social groups in contacts between the IMF and civil society has similarly had largely structural causes. For example, English fluency, tertiary education, and other socialisation have stood as major class-related prerequisites for participation in the dialogue. Meanwhile patriarchal gender relations have – one presumes – figured significantly in sustaining the overwhelming predominance of men among IMF officials, as in global finance more generally.

A fifth structural inhibition to greater development of relations between the IMF and civil society has been the persistent hold on political thought of the sovereignty norm. Although states have, through contemporary globalisation, lost their effective capacity to exercise supreme, absolute, comprehensive, and unilateral control over their territorial jurisdiction, governments have continued to cling jealously to the *claim* that they always have the final say in governance. Most civic activists and Fund officials, too, have continued to work under the spell of the sovereignty myth. Hence both the IMF and civil society organisations have usually limited their direct contacts to a level that governments would tolerate.

Officials of the Fund have been acutely conscious that their organisation is run at its highest levels (the Board of Governors and the Executive Board) by the collective decisions of its shareholders, the member states. Both by the letter of international law and in the predominant mindset of Fund staff, the IMF is only responsible to governments and not – at least directly – to citizens organised in civic associations. Fund management and staff have been supremely concerned to preserve their relationships with governments and have rarely pursued contacts with civic groups that might disturb those relationships.

Indeed, Fund officials have frequently argued that civic representatives should take issues regarding IMF activities to governments rather than to the Fund itself. In a similar vein, many IMF staff have asserted that 'contact with civil society is really government's job' and that 'it is the responsibility of governments to establish a [participatory] process.'[35]

Thus the extent of IMF outreach to civic associations has often been conditioned by the attitude of the member state whose jurisdiction is involved. When a government has encouraged the Fund to participate in a major public relations effort – as occurred in Venezuela in 1996 – the IMF has been more inclined to undertake it. In contrast, if a government has wished Fund missions and the Resident Representative to keep a low profile, then these officials have generally felt constrained to do so.

Clearly, IMF relations with civil society have involved delicate issues concerning the location of initiative, power, and legitimacy in contemporary governance. That said, Fund officials have perhaps sometimes cited these worries as a way to evade challenges from civic groups. After all, staff have tended to invoke arguments about the state's primacy only in relation to NGOs, and not with respect to business lobbies or academic institutes. Moreover, in practice governments have rarely complained to the IMF about its contacts with civil society. To this extent the Fund has possibly exaggerated the constraints that states pose for dialogue with civil society and invoked the sovereignty principle to its convenience.

If the IMF has sometimes hidden behind the sovereignty card, civic groups have often advanced unsustainable claims regarding their legitimacy. On the whole, civil society associations have attended insufficiently to questions concerning their representativeness, consultation processes, transparency, and accountability. Ironically, some of the organisations that have pressed hardest for a democratisation of the Fund have done little to secure democracy in their own operations. These shortcomings have dented the credibility of many advocacy groups – especially NGOs – and have allowed the IMF and states to take civic associations less seriously than they might otherwise have done.[36]

On questions of representativeness and consultation, for example, the disproportionate weight in civil society of Northerners and middle-class professionals has been stressed earlier. Many activists have had experience neither in the South and East nor at the grassroots. Consultation of notional constituents has often occurred haphazardly at best. NGO campaigners have therefore often appeared in the eyes of the Fund to represent only themselves.

Most civil society groups have also attended insufficiently to issues of transparency in their operations. Many of these organisations have not published annual reports of their activities regarding the IMF. Some have not even prepared a general written statement of objectives for public distribution. Often these associations – again, especially NGOs – have not made clear who they are, where their funds originate, and how they reach their policy positions.

The picture has generally been little better with regard to issues of accountability in civil society organisations. Many countries have lacked adequate mechanisms to ensure the public-interest credentials of NGOs in particular. Too often these associations have been accountable only to a largely self-selected board of trustees, to private funders, and/or to foreign official donors.

These frequent shortfalls in the legitimacy of civil society groups have hampered their access to the IMF. Many Fund officials – especially those who have been reluctant in any case to engage in dialogue with reformers and radicals – have seized on poor democratic credentials as a reason to limit contacts, in terms of both frequency and depth. NGOs in particular are likely to find their influence on the IMF limited so long as they cannot better demonstrate features of consultation, representativeness, transparency, and accountability in their relations with their constituents.

In sum, then, a host of resource limitations and structural constraints have together created substantial inhibitions against the development of wider and deeper dialogue between the IMF and civic organisations. Given the alignment of social forces described above, it is not surprising that the contacts have had the partial, generally shallow, and frequently troubled character described earlier.

Conclusion

This chapter has described a host of relationships that have grown, with only indirect if any involvement by states, between the IMF and organisations of civil society. This development conforms to a wider trend in contemporary governance whereby accelerated globalisation has broken the state's effective monopoly on regulation. In a world in which increasing areas of social life are largely supraterritorial, sovereign governance by territorial states is no longer tenable. Effective and democratic public policy must therefore be constructed at least partly through channels outside the state.

The IMF has tried to fill a number of gaps in governance where state sovereignty has become impracticable in monetary and financial affairs. By the letter of international law, governments have the right to accept or reject Fund stabilisation and adjustment policies, bailouts in financial crises, technical assistance, *etc.* In practice, however, the forces of a globalising world political economy have thoroughly compromised a state's supposed 'free will' in these matters.

Hence it is understandable – and, in terms of effective and democratic policy, right – that various civic associations have pursued direct contacts with the IMF. Yet how well have the relationships that have developed thus far between civil society and the Fund increased efficacy and democracy in global economic governance?

On the positive side, civic groups have offered the Fund many policy inputs, and the IMF has taken steps – inconceivable before the 1980s – to accommodate relations with civil society. New channels of participation have become available. There is potential – some of it already realised – in the Fund's claim that it 'encourages governments to work at consensus-building and two-way communication, including with national NGOs'.[37] Even with its fragility to date, the IMF-civil society dialogue has had some significant impacts, for example, in increasing transparency of Fund operations and in heightening public awareness of macroeconomic issues in a number of countries. Hence the exchanges have arguably contributed to some democratisation of both the Fund itself and of economic policy-making in certain member countries.

That said, on the whole interchanges between civil society and the IMF have so far fallen well short of a fully effective and democratic dialogue.

Many parties have been marginalised or excluded, many contacts have lacked substance, and many exchanges have been insufficiently open and reciprocal. Major resource constraints and large structural barriers have greatly hampered a maturation of the relationships. It is good that these efforts at increased efficacy and democracy in global governance have started, but the process still has a very long way to go.

NOTES

Research for this chapter has been supported through the Global Economic Institutions Programme of the Economic and Social Research Council in the United Kingdom. Interviews were conducted with more than a hundred persons in civil society, the IMF and other official circles in Brussels, Bucharest, Geneva, The Hague, Kampala, London, New York and Washington. I am most grateful for all of this interest in and support for this project. Responsibility for the present assessment of course lies with the author alone.

The chapter is based on research undertaken between September 1996 and May 1998. Interviews were conducted on the condition of non-attribution; thus references below to these conversations do not detail names or venues.

1. See further Manuel Guitián, *The Unique Nature of the Responsibilities of the International Monetary Fund* (Washington, DC: IMF, 1992).

2. These points are broadly developed from Jan Aart Scholte, 'The Geography of Collective Identities in a Globalizing World', *Review of International Political Economy* (Vol. 3, No. 4, 1996), pp. 597–600. For more extensive theorisation of democratic dialogue in post-sovereign world politics, see for example, Chris Brown, *International Relations Theory: New Normative Approaches* (New York, NY: Harvester Wheatsheaf, 1992), and Andrew Linklater, *The Transformation of Political Community: Ethical Foundations of the Post-Westphalian Era* (Oxford: Polity, 1998).

3. For more on this particular conception of globality, see Jan Aart Scholte, 'Beyond the Buzzword: Towards a Critical Theory of Globalization', in Eleonore Kofman and Gillian Youngs (eds.), *Globalization: Theory and Practice* (London: Cassell, 1996), pp. 43–57.

4. See further Jan Aart Scholte, 'The Globalization of World Politics', in John Baylis and Steve Smith (eds.), *The Globalization of World Politics: An Introduction to International Relations* (Oxford: Oxford University Press, 1997), pp. 13–30; Scholte, 'Global Capitalism and the State', *International Affairs* (Vol. 73, No. 3, 1997), pp. 427–52; and Scholte, 'Globalisation and Governance', in Patrick Hanafin (ed.), *Identity, Rights and Constitutional Transformation* (Aldershot: Dartmouth, 1998).

5. For a more detailed account of these developments, see Margaret de Vries, *The IMF in a Changing World, 1945-85* (Washington, DC: IMF, 1986), and Harold James, *International Monetary Cooperation since Bretton Woods* (New York, NY: Oxford University Press, 1996).

6. 'IMF Institute Program 1997', p. 2, and Gérard M. Teyssier, *The IMF Institute in Retrospect and Prospect* (Washington, DC: IMF, 1990).

7. *The Technical Assistance and Training Services of the International Monetary Fund* (Washington, DC: IMF Pamphlet Series No. 43, 1989); *IMF: 50 Facts (30. IMF Technical Assistance to Member Countries)* (Washington, IMF External Relations Department, 1994); and http://www.imf.org/external/np/exr/facts/tech.htm.

8. http://dsbb.imf.org/.

9. IMF, *Annual Report 1966* (Washington, DC: IMF, 1966), p. 133, and http://www.imf.org/external/np/ext/ facts/glance.htm.

10. IMF, *Functions and Organization of the Staff Financial Year 1991* (Washington, DC: IMF Budget and Planning Division, 1990), p. 3; *Annual Report 1997* (Washington, DC: IMF, 1997), p. 226.

11. Treasurer's Department, *Financial Organization and Operations of the IMF*, Fourth Edition (Washington, DC: IMF Pamphlet Series No. 45, 1995), p. 28.

12. *Ibid.*, pp. 45–6.

13. http://www.imf.org/external/np/ext/facts/nab.htm.

14. Lester M. Salamon, 'The Rise of the Nonprofit Sector', *Foreign Affairs* (Volume 73, No. 4, 1994), p. 109.

15. Union of International Associates, *Yearbook of International Organizations 1997/98 Volume I* (Munich: Saur, 1997), pp. 1762–3.

16. UNDP, *Human Development Report 1997* (New York, NY and Oxford: Oxford University Press, 1997), pp. 96–7.

17. See further Peter Willetts (ed.), *'Conscience of the World': The Influence of Non-Governmental Organisations in the UN System* (London: Hurst, 1996), and Thomas G. Weiss and Leon Gordenker (eds.), *NGOs, the UN, and Global Governance* (Boulder, CO: Rienner, 1996).

18. Such details are given in Jan Aart Scholte, *The International Monetary Fund and Civil Society: An Underdeveloped Dialogue* (The Hague: Institute of Social Studies Working Papers No. 272, February 1998).

19. Interview with the author, April 1997.

20. http://www.ipc.apc.org/dgap/

21. Interview with the author, November 1996.

22. Interview with the author, November 1996.

23. See, for example, IIF Working Group on Crisis Resolution, *Resolving Sovereign Financial Crises* (Washington, DC: Institute of International Finance, 1996), and Eurodad/Solagral Seminar on Financial Markets, Paris, 3-4 October 1997 (Unpublished minutes).

24. Interviews with the author, October-November 1996.

25. Correspondence with the author, February 1998.

26. Interview with the author, November 1996.

27. Interviews with the author, October-November 1996.

28. Gertrude Windsperger, 'NGOs and IMF: Shared Goals – Different Approaches', *IMF Staff News* (March 1997), p. 9.

29. Interviews with the author, November 1996 and April 1997.

30. Interviews with the author, October-November 1996, April and July 1997, and May and February 1998.

31. *Annual Report 1997, op. cit.*, in note 10, p. 225.

32. Correspondence with the author, December 1997.
33. *Annual Report 1996* (Washington, DC: IMF, 1996), p. 220; http://www. imf.org/external/ np/obp/orgcht.htm.
34. 'Building a New Global Partnership', *IMF Survey* (Vol. 25, No. 19, 14 October 1996), p. 317. See also 'Partnership for Sustainable Global Growth', Interim Committee Declaration (Washington, DC: 29 September 1996).
35. Interviews with the author, October 1996, March 1997, and May 1998, and Anne Bichsel, 'The World Bank and the International Monetary Fund from the Perspective of the Executive Directors from Developing Countries', *Journal of World Trade* (Vol. 28, No. 6, 1994), p. 151.
36. On these issues see further Anne Bichsel, 'NGOs as Agents of Public Accountability and Democratization in Intergovernmental Forums', in William M. Lafferty and James Meadowcroft (eds.), *Democracy and the Environment: Problems and Prospects* (Cheltenham: Elgar, 1996), pp. 234–55.
37. Windsperger, *op. cit.*, in note 28, p. 8.

Part III

Globalisation and Poverty

5. Reconceptualising 'Gender and Development' in an Era of 'Globalisation'

Marianne H. Marchand

The 'globalisation' and global restructuring *problématique* has become a major concern among students of International Political Economy/International Relations (IPE/IR).[1] Furthermore, although much disagreement exists about the causes, scope, and impact of 'globalisation', as well as its novelty, it is increasingly acknowledged that current processes (and practices) of 'globalisation' encompass socio-cultural and politico-economic dimensions.[2] However, less often explicitly acknowledged in the mainstream and critical literature on global restructuring is its gendered, as well as racialised, nature. Notwithstanding this lack of interest, there is a rapidly growing body of literature which specifically addresses the gender dimensions of global restructuring.[3]

An important contribution to developing gender-analyses of global restructuring has been made by academics specialising in gender and development. Their concern with the 'global' is mirrored by a similar concern among certain development-oriented international groups and networks such as Development Alternatives with Women for a New Era (DAWN), the Network for Gender Oriented Alternative Strategies on Economics (GOALS), the Ost-West Europäisches Frauen Netzwerk (OWEN), and the Network Women in Development Europe (WIDE). However, as M. Patricia Connelly *et al.* argue, this focus on the 'global' is but one of three debates raised within the gender and development field:

> the 1990s pose new challenges. Global restructuring, the rise of new, previously marginalized and often critical voices (especially among women), a growing consciousness of world-wide environmental degradation and the erosion of Northern hegemony have cast doubt on old certainties. Established thinking about development and modernity have run their course. This is true for women and development as well. Neither GAD nor WID problematized western development models, with their tendency to assume a North/South dichotomy. Nor did they adequately address issues of culture and difference.... Addressing the issues of gender and development seems to us to require a return to

major debates about the nature of political and economic power, the role of gender and the character of development.[4]

According to Connelly *et al.*, these three debates (about the gender dimensions of global restructuring, the modernist and growth-oriented underpinnings of the development enterprise, and the complex realities and differences among women in terms of gender, class, race, ethnicity, age, sexual orientation) have not yet come together in a coherent synthesis.[5] Although one may well question the merits of constructing one coherent synthesis, it is nevertheless important to break through the walls of relative (mutual) isolation in which these three debates have developed so far. This article attempts to do just this, by engaging in a critical analysis of the recent emphasis on the 'global' within the gender and development field. This critical analysis will be informed by insights from the three debates, as identified by Connelly *et al.*, and will explore three questions in particular. First, why has there been a partial shift within the gender and development community from more 'micro-oriented concerns' to more 'macro-level' analyses?[6] Second, to what extent is this shift accompanied by changes in discursive practices about gender and poverty in general and, more specifically, in conceptualising empowerment? Third, what does the new focus on global restructuring and the (possible) reconceptualisations of poverty mean for social movements in organising around gender and development/global restructuring issues?

In order to answer these questions, I will highlight, in the next two sections, the recent focal shift towards the 'global' within the GAD field. I will thereby limit myself to the literature which specifically addresses global restructuring.[7] This will be followed by a brief discussion of WIDE, which is specifically addressing the question of organising around gender and global restructuring. Finally, I will provide a critical analysis of the 'global' shift within the GAD field, especially in terms of its conceptual implications, and make some suggestions about fruitfully furthering this endeavour. Indirectly, this critique substantiates the claim of Connelly *et al.* that there are three concurrent, juxtaposed debates within the GAD field, which do not really inform each other. As the critique will reveal, the framing of the 'globalisation issue' by the GAD community has severe drawbacks. For one, identifying women as a 'vulnerable group' and as victims of global restructuring may help to draw the attention of policy-makers to the issue at hand, but it also reifies discursive representations of Third World women as passive, ignorant, and voiceless – thereby ignoring the criticisms formulated by post-colonial feminists about the representation and 'Othering' of Third World women.[8] The second set of criticisms addresses the economistic turn in the GAD field. It is argued that the narrow economic focus on global restructuring is ahistorical and ignores contingent socio-political dimensions of global restructuring. As a consequence, the concept of empowerment is (implicitly) redefined as economic empowerment. Moreover, resistance strategies to global restructuring, such as (feminist) alternative development models, are sought within the confines of economics and economic models. In the concluding section, I will suggest some alternative conceptualisations for addressing the gender and global restructuring *problématique*.

From Gender and Development to Gender and Global Restructuring

It would be erroneous to assume that the GAD community has only recently become interested in questions of global restructuring. The internationalisation of production, as well as the accompanying emergence of a new international division of labour (NIDL) have been among the first issues to receive attention.[9] As early as 1983, June Nash has observed that

> the role of gender in the configuration of this new international arrangement [the new international division of labor] should not be underestimated. The vanguard of industrial investment in the world capitalist system is in the lowest paid segment of those countries paying the lowest wages. Young women in developing countries are the labor force on this frontier just as women and children were in the industrialization of England and Europe in the nineteenth century.[10]

The emergence of Export Processing Zones (EPZs), or free trade zones, which were created from the mid-1960s and early 1970s onwards in parts of South East Asia, Latin America, and the Caribbean, has allowed transnational corporations (TNCs) to shift labour-intensive production processes to low wage countries. As early analyses by feminist scholars have revealed, the interaction of existing (local and corporate) gender ideologies with a demand for a docile, cheap, non-unionised workforce led to the employment of very young women often under appalling working conditions.[11] Although generally reaffirming these early analyses, subsequent research has emphasised differences in terms of employment practices and labour conditions. From the standpoint of many women workers, the TNC subsidiaries have tended to provide slightly better employment conditions (including better pay) than local sub-contracting firms. As Susan Tiano explains, this is also why the electronics sector has been able to attract young(er) and better educated workers:

> multinational companies do not appear to recruit from the most vulnerable sector of the female labor force, as the exploitation thesis maintains. Rather they are able to hire workers whose domestic status and educational attainment give them an advantage in the labor market.

Locally owned establishments, particularly in the apparel industry, typically hire workers whose labor market status is somewhat weaker.[12]

Moreover, working in the EPZs is often the best option locally available to (young) women, and the income they earn sometimes gives them more standing within the family or household.[13] The focus on the NIDL in general, and on the EPZs in particular, is not something that has subsided. On the contrary, various changes, ranging from new employment practices, the introduction of new(er) technologies, new types of industries entering EPZs, new investment and sourcing strategies by TNCs to the rapidly spreading of EPZs, have stirred a renewed interest by the GAD community in the issue.[14]

A second reason why the GAD community has shown an interest in 'global issues' since the early 1980s is related to the growing body of critical scholarship in the field. Early expressions of this critical scholarship, much of which is often seen as a counterpart to dependency theory and world-systems theory, have addressed global gender(ed) inequalities from the start. One example is Maria Mies' *Patriarchy and Accumulation on a World Scale*, which advanced the thesis that women are being exploited on a global scale:

[i]f we look at the new international division of labour from the point of view of women, of women's liberation, we can now say that it is always necessary to look at both sides of the coin, to understand how women at both ends of the globe are divided yet factually linked to each other by the world market, and by international and national capital. In this division, the manipulation of women as invisible producers in the Third World and as atomized, visible yet dependent consumers (housewives) plays a crucial role. The whole strategy is based on a patriarchal, sexist and racist ideology of women which defines women basically as housewives and sex objects. Without this ideological manipulation combined with the structural division of women by class and colonialism, this strategy would not be profitable for capital.[15]

Various schools and perspectives have always coexisted within the GAD field. Since the mid-1980s, however, feminist scholars from South and North working within various critical intellectual traditions increasingly found each other in a perspective which emphasised 'the centrality of economic and political factors, the importance of class, gender relations and the sexual division of labour, particularly women's productive and reproductive labour'.[16] The exchanges in views which engendered the emergence of this so-called GAD perspective[17] were facilitated by the UN Decade for Women which provided meeting grounds at the mid-decade conference in

Copenhagen, as well as the Third UN Women's Conference in Nairobi in 1985. Although, by the mid-1980s, feminists from South and North had found each other in the emerging GAD perspective which challenged the social construction of gender (relations) and called for the empowerment of women in the South, differences in emphasis have remained.[18] In particular, Southern feminists involved in the DAWN network have tended to focus more on issues of colonialism/colonial legacy, race, ethnicity, and culture.[19] Despite these differences, a solid, critical theoretical foundation has been forged from which to engage in a gender-analysis of global restructuring. This foundation consists of the notion that the global economy is embedded in and shaped by various power structures encompassing gender, race, ethnicity, and class relations.

Critical Interventions in the Debates about Global Restructuring

Turning to the first query – that is, the reasons why a shift from 'micro-oriented concerns' to 'macro-level analyses' has occurred – we find that the structural adjustment policies of the 1980s have provided a critical turning point for the way in which gender and development questions are being addressed. On the one hand, because of its all-encompassing nature, the structural adjustment *problématique* has required multi-level gender analyses. On the other hand, structural adjustment has been mirrored by profound political, economic, and social transformations in Central and Eastern Europe, as well as a significant restructuring of the welfare state among the members of the Organisation for Economic Cooperation and Development (OECD). A recognition of these contingent processes is voiced by Isabella Bakker, when she argues that the current restructuring of global economics has had profound effects on social, economic, and political life in both developed and developing countries:

> [r]estructuring can be analysed as a series of cumulative and conjunctural crises in the international division of labour and the global distribution of economic and political power; in global finance; in the functioning of national states that are losing economic and political control of national economies; in the decline of the Keynesian welfare state and the established social contracts between labour, government and business; and in the increasing exploitation of marginal forms of labour performed by women, youth and minorities. The emergence of the global assembly line and, in particular, the growth in the number of informal-sector workers and women's paid work is one of the centrepieces of global restructuring.[20]

Whereas in the mainstream literature there is increasing agreement on the elements of restructuring, this is not accompanied by a recognition of the gendered nature of current structural and institutional transformation(s).[21] The response by the GAD community has been to address this lack of attention and to make the gendered dimensions of global restructuring one of its focal points for analysis and activism.[22] Moreover, this recent turn has led to a dialogue with other feminist scholars who have formulated gender(ed) analyses of the international political economy and have addressed specific issues, such as the flexibilisation of labour, the feminisation of management styles, the gendered dimensions of new technologies, and the erosion of the welfare state.[23]

Taking a closer look at the way in which GAD specialists have addressed the question of global restructuring, we can distinguish at least five types of interventions into the debate.[24] To start, there is considerable emphasis on the need to 'make women visible'. This need is often raised within international policy-making circles, including the United Nations and other international organisations such as the World Bank and the OECD. As Susan Joekes indicates, much of the efforts to make 'women visible' originated with a frustration about the lack of statistical information about women's work and activities:

> [b]ut many activities, particularly in the 'informal' sector, were neglected because of the practical difficulties of collecting information. Women tend to be concentrated in activities of this kind, so they were omitted from the statistical record more often than men. The invisibility of women's work thus became a common complaint among some economists and policy makers.[25]

As a result, and aided by the attention directed at the position and roles of women during the UN Decade for Women (1975–85), various international organisations started to collect statistical data on women's work and activities.[26] With the increasingly widespread adoption of structural adjustment programmes (SAPs) during the 1980s, these efforts were extended towards the gathering of information on, and the development of analyses of, the differential effects of SAPs on men and women. SAPs often include a shift from non-tradeable commodities, such as food production for the domestic market, to tradeable commodities, especially the cultivation of cash-crops for export; a reduction of government funding in areas like health and education, social services, and subsidies for transportation and basic staple goods; as well as a retrenchment of the public sector alongside a significant increase of the informal sector. As the literature reveals, these programmes tend to affect women disproportionately.[27] In these analyses, women are seen as one of the 'vulnerable groups' bearing the brunt of structural adjustment;[28]

that is, they are portrayed as the victims of a process of restructuring which is outside of their reach and by which they are increasingly marginalised and excluded.

In contrast, another approach to 'making women visible' stresses that women are not left outside the processes of global restructuring, but are participating in it while remaining invisible. Kimberly Chang and Lily Ling argue that globalisation consists of a Self and its Other; that is, the 'Western, industrialized, "cosmopolita[n]"' globalisation 1 (G1) and the 'non-Western, non-industrialized "parochia[l]"' globalisation 2 (G2).[29] Analysing the interactions between the public and private spheres of G1 and G2 from a gendered perspective, Chang and Ling claim that

> [t]wo distinctive though interactive globalisation processes operate in the world political economy today. While Globalization 1 (G1) refers to a 'masculinized' high-tech world of global finance, production, and technology, Globalization 2 (G2) represents a 'feminized' menial economy of sexualized, racialized service. It usually involves intimate activities located within the private home: e.g., preparing food, washing soiled clothing and undergarments, tending children, tidying bedrooms, cleaning bathrooms, taking out the garbage. This service economy invites other types of intimacy as well: leaving home, working among strangers, dealing with alienation/harassment/abuse, confronting moral dilemmas. In this sense G2 is G1's 'intimate Other'.[30]

In both mainstream and critical analyses of 'globalisation', the feminised sphere of G2 is being ignored or neglected and should, in the view of Chang and Ling, be made visible.

The second contribution by GAD specialists has been to show the complexity and contradictory nature of global restructruring processes. As their analyses reveal, these processes are embedded in, and refracted through, power structures grounded in ethnicity, race, gender, class, and age, and, therefore, may benefit some while adversely affecting others. Whereas global restructuring leads to increasing inequalities, generally affecting women more than men, it also leads to various forms and degrees of inclusion and exclusion.[31] For example, women may be included economically by taking 'advantage' of new job opportunities provided in the EPZs, but often undergo social and political marginalisation or exclusion.[32] Similarly, the introduction of new management styles or new technologies may well provide new opportunities to selected groups of women. As Cecilia Ng Choon Sim and Carol Yong suggest in their discussion of the gendered impact of information technology (IT) in Malaysia,

[o]n the one hand, it is true that the clerical workforce is slowly becoming feminized, and that lower level data entry operators are largely women, who work under highly stressed conditions. Women's position in the labour force is still secondary and ideologically constructed, and skill polarization by gender will continue to be common. On the other hand, in the Malaysian IT and telecommunications industry, more than in other technological fields, women are slowly making headway into middle level professional and management positions. Malaysian women seem to be taking advantage of the educational system, which is heavily promoting computer studies, although they still predominate in the software programming side while men are in the more lucrative fields such as electronics engineering and management.[33]

As this analysis shows, it is important to acknowledge the complexities and contradictions of global restructruring processes. This is exemplified in those cases where the introduction of new technologies in the service sector has led to growing polarisations, not just by gender, but also by ethnicity, class, and skills.[34]

Third, in the view of various scholars, the scope and reach of 'globalisation' require multi-level gender analyses. According to Diane Elson, it is imperative to go beyond gender differentiation at the household or micro-level, to analyse how gender biases are constituted at the meso- and macro-levels. She argues that these biases occur at the meso- and macro-levels, because institutions, actors, and policies become gender-bearers.[35] In other words, institutions such as markets, firms, and public sector agencies are gendered through their embeddedness in social (gendered) norms and networks.[36] Elson suggests that the GAD community needs to understand and research the interconnectedness of economic restructuring in order to develop 'feminist strategies for enabling economic analysis at these three levels to contribute toward the empowerment of women, rather than the perpetuation of their subordination'.[37] This entails more than opening up the black-box of the household to reveal how the impact of structural adjustment policies is differentiated at this level, resulting in increased demands on, for example, the time and resources of women. It also involves feminist analyses of the extent to which new economic institutions, emerging in the wake of the retrenchment of the public sector, reflect male-biases. Similarly, macro-economic policies need to be challenged for taking the 'reproductive economy' for granted.[38]

One area in which linked, multi-level analyses are being pursued is that of trade. This focus on trade corresponds with the emergence of the new trade agenda in the wake of the Uruguay Round, which includes issues like the establishment of the World Trade Organisation, trade-related intellectual property rights and investment measures, environmental concerns, and the emergence of 'New Regionalism' (the instutionalisation of regional politico-economic activities). The importance of developing a gender analysis of trade and the new trade agenda is indicated by Janice Goodson Førde:

> [m]acro-economics is central to development policy and practice as the use of the present market liberalization and economic growth model witnesses. Trade policies are central to the rationale and implementation of economic stabilization and structural adjustment policies. Therefore, trade policies and the new trade agenda after the Uruguay Round of the GATT in 1994 are tools of development which have gender specific effects on men and women. International and regional trade policies must be monitored, analyzed, and influenced in order to enhance and not worsen women's economic prospects.[39]

Joekes concurs, arguing that 'women may be especially vulnerable to the disruptive effects of trade', and urging 'gender activists' to 'press for policies to ensure that women are – at the very least – not disadvantaged in the distribution of benefits from trade'.[40] According to Joekes, however, trade expansion will also engender some positive effects in the areas of income and employment generation. For instance, in parts of Latin America, Asia, and, to a lesser extent, Sub-Saharan Africa, job creation has occurred in the areas of light manufacturing, services, and quasi-industrial horticultural production. It is in these sectors, particularly when job creation is stimulated by labour-intensive operations in EPZs, that women have been able to find employment.[41] Likewise, trade expansion has provided new opportunities for local traders in foodstuffs. Where, as in Sub-Saharan Africa, trade liberalisation and structural adjustment policies have led to an increase in domestic food prices, women traders are in a position to benefit.[42] In sum, Joekes suggests that international trade is not an inherently gendered process and that women may very well benefit from trade expansion. For her, the only rationale for gender-sensitive intervention in the area of international trade is to counteract its possible negative distributive effects for women.[43]

For the fourth type of intervention, GAD specialists have joined other feminist scholars in various efforts to identify gender biases in conceptualisations of global restructuring. Two strands of theoretical challenges have been pursued thus far. The first focuses on gender biases in neoclassical economic thought and is thereby informed by the epistemological and ontological critiques of mainstream (neoclassical) economics by feminist economists.[44] These feminist critiques have addressed some of the basic assumptions upon which neoclassical economics in general, and the 'new home economics' in particular, have been constructed.[45] For instance, feminist economists question the central assumption of rational economic man, which would predict the behaviour of individuals in the marketplace, for reflecting

a very narrow understanding of human behaviour. This concern is voiced by
Paula England in the following passage:

> [t]here are androcentric biases in the deep theoretical structure of
> neoclassical economics. Three of the most basic assumptions
> underlying economic theory are that interpersonal utility comparisons
> are impossible, that tastes are exogenous to economic models and
> unchanging, and that actors are selfish (have independent utilities) in
> markets. I argue that each of these assumptions flows from a
> separative model of human nature that has become a focus of criticism
> by feminists across a number of disciplines. I call the model
> 'separative' because it presumes that humans are autonomous,
> impervious to social influences, and lack sufficient emotional
> connection to each other to make empathy possible. This is how they
> are presumed to behave in 'the economy' or the 'market'.[46]

Gary Becker, Nobel laureate and a major representative of 'new home
economics', argues, however, that there is some room for empathy or altruism
in the daily lives of rational individuals. In his view, altruism among family
members stimulates not only a high degree of specialisation and division of
labour between men and women, but also leads to 'an efficient allocation of
resources in families'. Such altruism would not work in the market place
however, because it is less 'efficient'.[47] The assertion that rational economic
man can be competitive and individualistic in the marketplace, but will be
altruistic within the confines of the household, has also been met with the
challenge by feminist economists that it does not provide a very realistic
picture of human behaviour and intra-household dynamics. Nancy Folbre
formulates the major feminist objections to the views of Becker on intra-
family altruism in the rather humourous introduction to her book, *Who Pays*
for the Kids?

> Traditional neoclassical theory stars Rational Economic Man. Call him
> Mr. REM, for short. His tastes and preferences are fully formed; his
> personal and financial assets are given. He is a rational decision-maker
> who weighs costs and benefits. He processes perfect information
> perfectly. All his decisions are motivated by the desire to maximize his
> own utility – to make himself happy. In the competitive marketplace,
> where he constantly buys and sells, he is entirely selfish, doesn't care
> at all about other people's utility. In the home, however, he is entirely
> altruistic, loves his wife and children as much as his very self. The
> same goes for Mrs. REM, who is like him in every respect, except for
> a different set of biological assets. Both Mr. and Mrs. love to
> calculate, to choose, to buy and sell. Can there be any exploitation, any

oppression in their world? Only if some Big Brother, like the state, restricts their choices. What is their home life like? Pretty nice, because both of them want the same things – they (and all the little baby REMs) have a joint utility function. No fights over the dinner table, no buying and selling in the living room, either. Funny, it sounds sort of like utopian socialism in one family.[48]

Finally, mainstream economics has been under considerable attack for focusing narrowly on the productive or 'commodity' economy and paid work, thus neglecting the reproductive or 'care' economy and unpaid work.[49] GAD specialists have in part relied on these critiques to develop their own critical analyses of development policies.[50] Wendy Harcourt suggests that the claims of feminist economics regarding the need to analyse the interrelatedness of productive and reproductive labour has contributed to the acknowledgement in development policy circles that women's work (and time) is not infinitely elastic.[51] In addition, as the discussion of WIDE will reveal, these feminist critiques of neoclassical economics have also provided the foundation for developing gender-oriented conceptualisations and strategies towards a framework of alternative economics.

The second challenge to gender biases in conceptualisations of global restructuring has been informed by feminist and post-modernist critiques of dichotomous thinking in Western social sciences. Various feminist IR scholars have suggested that, within the context of current global restructuring, the economy is increasingly associated with masculine values and identified as a masculine(ised) space. Alternatively, the economy has been represented as a dualistic space consisting of a dominant masculine sphere (the export-oriented internationally competitive side) and a subordinate feminine sphere (the domestic economy which includes older industries, the small business sector, and the health and care sector).[52] In the words of Anne Sisson Runyan,

[t]he neoliberal ideology upon which it [the process of global restructuring] rests is based on a masculine model of the market which privileges the actions of so-called economic men, who, if unfettered by state regulation and 'feminine' concerns about social welfare and ecological sustainability, can provide the engines of growth – growth primarily for corporate and other economic elites.[53]

Compared to challenges posed by feminist economists to neoclassical economics, feminist IR critiques of global restructuring have received less attention within the GAD community. As I will show in my critical analysis of the GAD interventions under discussion, this is partly due to the (narrow) framing of global restructuring as a primarily *economic* problem. Moreover, this observation also substantiates the claim by Connolly *et al.* that there are various prevalent discourses within the GAD community which do not really overlap.[54]

A fifth type of GAD intervention has been constituted by the rather distinct voices of Maria Mies, Veronika Bennholdt-Thomsen and Claudia von Werlhof, as well as Vandana Shiva.[55] Of all the interventions by the GAD community, these authors have formulated the most radical critique of global restructuring. They set out to challenge the 'global capitalist-patriarchal model of accumulation' for being premised upon the exploitation of women, colonial peoples, and nature.[56] Whereas Mies *et al.* focus on the 'housewifezation' of women in the industrialised world as a counterpart to the exploitation of Third World women, Shiva links the exclusion and exploitation of women to a shift in economic thinking:

> [b]efore the emergence of [the] modern patriarchal paradigm of economi[c]s, it was assumed that national economic affairs could be conceived of as merely extensions of the housekeeper's budget. Similarly, 'oecologie' suggested that the living organisms of the earth constitute a single economic unit resembling a household or a family dwelling intimately together. With 'home' as the metaphor for both ecology and economics, there was no hierarchical divide between domestic production and commodity production for exchange and trade, or between nature's economy, the sustenance economy and the market economy.[57]

However, as Shiva argues, the emergence of capitalism led to the displacement of the home metaphor as an interpretive frame for economics. Instead, the trade metaphor was introduced, and with it, economic value was redefined in terms of exchange: only those goods and activities which can be traded are assigned economic value, while non-tradeable goods and activities are rendered 'unproductive'.[58] According to Shiva, 'both the marginalisation of women's work and nature's work are linked to how the metaphor of "home" was reconstituted as the domain where no economic value is produced'.[59] In other words, Shiva and Mies *et al.* argue that the marginalisation and exploitation of the labour of women is tied to its invisibility in economic models and social theory.[60]

Not surprisingly, the interventions of the GAD community in the debates about global restructuring are grounded in earlier theoretical traditions within the field. For example, the WID perspective informs most, although not all, efforts to 'make women visible'.[61] This is also true for some of the work done in the area of trade, especially when it is connected to the objective of providing women with better access to the market without aiming to transform the gendered nature of the latter. In contrast, the concerns voiced by Shiva and Mies *et al.* are more reflective of some of the earlier radical and socialist feminist concerns. These interventions, which directly address the complex and contradictory nature of global restructuring and challenge its theoretical underpinnings, tend to have an affinity with the GAD perspective. Obviously, these differences should not be exaggerated, as the interventions tend to be complementary rather than oppositional.

A review of the five interventions reveals some additional interesting features. Despite the variety of issues raised by GAD specialists, most authors are concerned with the feminisation of poverty, often addressed in terms of (increased) marginalisation or exclusion of women. This issue is most explicitly raised by Mies *et al.* and Shiva. However, the question of empowerment tends to receive less immediate attention. Where authors address the question of empowerment in the context of a broader analysis of global restructuring, they seem to be at odds as to its meaning. For Joekes, empowerment entails the securing of better access to the market for women in general. More specifically, she argues that 'gender activists and NGOs' should focus on such issues as reducing the 'gender wage gap' and on gaining access for women in those (trade-related) sectors of the economy which yield a 'high return'.[62] Others, including Elson, Harcourt, and Gita Sen, emphasise the transformative aspects of empowerment. On various occasions, these authors have argued for the need to link the grass-roots empowerment of women to multi-level feminist analyses of global economic restructuring.[63] On the one hand, as Sen indicates, this entails the need to translate the successful strategies for empowerment of women at the micro-level, such as the Self Women's Association in India (SEWA), to the macro-level:

> [there] is the continuing need for women's empowerment. An important lesson of the experiences with development policies and projects is that much that is worthwhile does not get done unless there is a concerted demand for it. This is especially true for gender equity and female poverty where the social and cultural barriers against even a recognition of the problems are strong. But can the positive experiences with empowering strategies in micro projects be translated into empowerment that will generate major restructuring at the macro level? This is the challenge ahead.[64]

On the other hand, it involves the linking of feminist strategies based on critical analyses of meso- and macro-level economic policies to the empowerment of women at the grass-roots. In the words of Elson, it is important to examine

> how concepts of the micro, the macro, and the meso are used by orthodox and critical economists in discussions of economic policy

reform; and the extent to which these concepts recognize gender. We also consider some feminist strategies for enabling economic analysis at these three levels to contribute towards the empowerment of women, rather than the perpetuation of their subordination.[65]

Yet, as my next discussion of WIDE will reveal, it is not an easy task to pursue transformative empowerment (strategies) within the context of global restructuring. Moreover, as the WIDE example will illustrate, the dominant discourse of the GAD community on, and framing of, the question of global restructuring is dangerous in that it may actually lead to the *disempowerment* of women and men at the grass-roots.

'GAD' Activism and Global Restructuring: The Example of WIDE

As indicated above, the analytical interventions discussed in the previous section have informed various attempts by GAD activists to develop gender-oriented analyses and strategies towards a framework for alternative economics. Many of these efforts have been pursued within the context of the Women's Global Alliance for Development Alternatives, consisting of Southern and Northern women's networks, and as part of the preparations for the Fourth World Conference on Women in Beijing (1995). The work of the Global Alliance has been described as 'an ongoing process through which women's networks have begun to share analyses and develop joint strategies in order to shift the development paradigm towards gender-equitable, sustainable and caring development'.[66] WIDE, as one of the founding members of the Global Alliance, has been involved in formulating economic alternatives to counteract the current hegemony of neoclassical economics. In this section, I will give a brief overview of these efforts.

At its 1994 annual meeting in Amsterdam, WIDE[67] established a Working Group on Alternative Economics which set out to analyse processes of global restructuring from a European perspective, that is, within Western and Eastern Europe. Its second objective was to develop economic alternatives on the basis of this analysis.[68] This rather unusual shift in focus for a network which, up to that moment, had been preoccupied with North-South relations found its roots in discussions with Southern networks. In particular, representatives of DAWN argued that, for a comprehensive understanding of global restructuring, it was important to analyse the changes taking place within the OECD region.[69] In response to this request, WIDE and three other networks based in Canada and the United States jointly wrote a framework paper entitled 'Wealth of Nations – Poverty of Women', in preparation for Beijing.[70] As the introduction to the framework paper reveals, the exercise of writing it was an eye-opener for those involved. First, the authors became more acutely aware of the similarities and differences across the OECD region and their own relative ignorance of many of these issues. Second, the authors concurred with the observation of DAWN representatives for the need to develop a critical global analysis of economic restructuring or adjustment.

This framework paper has been followed by the position paper by WIDE entitled 'Toward Alternative Economics from a European Perspective', which was published only a few weeks before the Beijing Conference.[71] Informed by feminist critical economics, this paper embarks upon a critique of macro-economic theory, and uses this critique, as well as a brief overview of the experiences of European women, to develop its 'alternative economics from a European perspective'. The alternative economics of WIDE encompasses four elements:

(1) prioritising people: 'all activities would have to be regarded not for their profit maximizing capacity, but rather for their ability to improve the quality of peoples' lives, to care for people and the planet';[72]
(2) reconceptualising and reorganising paid and unpaid work, to ensure 'an alternative vision of society and of a human centred development that incorporates women's experiences....' This would also entail new indicators to 'gauge true workloads';[73]
(3) promoting human sustainable development, which requires a 'shift in development thinking, economic analysis and policy making', to address the 'link between the worldwide ecological crisis and current economic and social policies';[74]
(4) demanding accountability: 'international financial and trade institutions as well as governments need to be made accountable and brought under UN monitoring and control mechanisms, including the establishment of codes of conduct for transnational corporations'.[75]

The final part of the WIDE position paper discusses the strategies needed to bring about this visionary human-centred alternative development framework. Unfortunately, this part of the paper is not very well developed and suggests only two strategies for change: forming alliances with other networks and lobbying for policy changes in the four above-mentioned issue areas.

In the aftermath of Beijing, WIDE has started to focus on trade issues and gender.[76] This focus coincides with the emerging interest among researchers in developing a gender analysis of the new trade agenda. Unfortunately, WIDE has not yet been able to develop a coherent analysis or set of strategies in this area. This issue was also raised at the 1996 annual meeting, when WIDE officers and its Secretariat were challenged for allowing others to set its agenda on gender and trade. In particular, some participants took issue with a gender analysis of trade which takes existing (economic) trade theories as a starting point.[77] Instead, it was argued that the starting point for a gender analysis should be women's different experiences with, and roles in, trade, that is, as (local) traders, market women, entrepreneurs, and as employees in export industries.[78] These criticisms indicate some serious contradictions in the attempts of WIDE to formulate a critical analysis of global restructuring as well as transformative empowerment (strategies). These contradictions are most clearly reflected in the WIDE position paper:

> despite the authors' attempt to put people first and to include European women's lives in their analysis, they still fall in the trap of a top-down approach. This is possible because the analysis is guided by the attempt to refute and reject neoclassical economic theory whereby the accounts of women's lives take on an instrumental role (rather than being the *focus* of the analysis). In so doing, the WIDE position paper takes neoclassical economics as a *starting point* and tries to formulate an alternative economics in oppositional dualistic terms.... For instance, profit maximizing and care are seen as incompatible.[79]

Ironically, the instrumental role which the lives of women and men play in rejecting neoclassical economic theory is not reversed in the alternative economic framework of WIDE. In contrast to the stated objectives, the lived (diverse) realities of women and men continue to play an instrumental role in the alternative human-centred economics of WIDE; that is, they do not occupy centre stage. In other words, the everyday experiences of women, men, and children are being relegated to a subordinate and dependent position within WIDE's own analytical framework, which renders it impossible to serve as the foundation for developing transformative empowerment strategies at the grass-roots.

This brief overview of current discussions in WIDE illustrates that its recent shift towards the 'global' has been controversial. In particular, representatives of women's groups at the grass-roots are increasingly expressing a sense of exclusion and alienation from the new agenda of WIDE. Some of the additional (epistemological and ontological) reasons will be addressed in the next section.

A Critical Assessment

Having explored the 'global' turn of the GAD community, and some of its implications for conceptualising transformative empowerment and women's organising, this article now turns to a critical analysis of this shift. The shift towards the 'global' within the GAD field appears to provide interesting and significant insights into processes of global restructuring, and could therefore inform critical IR/IPE scholarship in this area. Likewise, feminist IR/IPE insights into processes and practices of global restructuring, as well as into gendered constructions of 'global' economic and political spaces, could also inform GAD scholarship. Before embarking upon such a constructive engagement, however, the new directions within the GAD field need to be subjected to a critical assessment. This critical assessment focuses on the question of knowledge production, and in particular, the framing of the gender and global restructuring *problématique* and the accompanying suggested alternatives and/or alternative economic framework(s). The critique is informed, first, by a conceptualisation of global restructuring as involving contingent processes and practices of transformation which need to be historicised as well as contextualised. Second, the critique is informed by a concern about the power of representation and 'Othering'.

Following the direction of the UNICEF report, *Adjustment with a Human Face*, many authors discussing the effects of global restructuring on women refer to them as a 'vulnerable group'. Arguing that global restructuring affects women generally more adversely than men is problematic for several reasons. Such a statement tends to obscure more than it reveals, because it does not allow for any differentiation among women and men in terms of class, race, ethnicity, age, nationality, and education. In other words, the term 'vulnerable group', in itself, does not provide a very sound basis for feminist activism or gender-sensitive policy-making. Moreover, the term evokes a very powerful image reinforcing earlier representations of Third World women as traditional, voiceless, dependent and passive beings.[80] According to Jane Parpart,

> [t]his construction/representation of Third World women has been reinforced by the current economic crisis, which has highlighted the characterization of women in the South as the *vulnerable* 'other', victimized by retrogressive traditions and economic ineptitude of Third World economies. The Commonwealth Expert Group on Women and Structural Adjustment publicized the phrase 'vulnerable groups' to describe the dire consequences of SAP policies for women and other disadvantaged groups in the South.... This evocative phrase became a rallying cry for development experts wishing to challenge World Bank policies, particularly from UNESCO.... While an effective weapon against the Bank, this language has further entrenched the image of the helpless, premodern, vulnerable Third World woman.[81]

The categorisation of women as being mainly the (passive) victims of global restructuring backfires in that it leads to their discursive disempowerment, and ignores or neglects the strategies of survival and resistance in which women at the grass-roots are involved on a daily basis.

Another major limitation of various GAD contributions to the debates about global restructuring is that they reflect an economistic turn in the (GAD) literature. Yet, the economistic framing of global restructuring has gained considerable influence in current policy debates, as can be gleaned from the following passage in the formal statement (prepared by networks of women from the South and North), entitled 'Quality Benchmark for Beijing: An Economic Framework':

> [t]he inherent gender bias in economic thinking and policy assumes that the reproductive work women do is without cost or economic value. At the same time most women are excluded from the potential or hypothetical benefits that economic growth could bring, and their contribution, on which these benefits are based, remains invisible. Being most vulnerable to the world economic crisis, women are at the forefront of the challenge to the present model of development. Standing at the crossroads of production and reproduction, their perspectives are crucial to achieving equality, equity, peace, environmental protection and human-centred development.[82]

Because the new economistic direction of GAD has received considerable attention, it is important to subject it to a critical assessment. Obviously, this is not to suggest that there is no need for critical feminist analyses of the economic dimensions of global restructuring. However, when these analyses inform, for instance, the formulation of alternative strategies, they should be embedded in a much more comprehensive analysis of contingent economic, social, political, and cultural processes and practices of global restructuring.

The economistic framing of global restructuring by GAD has several dimensions. First, global restructuring is understood in economic terms, and solutions or alternatives are sought within the confines of economics and economic models. An example of this is Elson's suggestion to link micro-, meso-, and macro-levels of analysis.[83] She argues that, in order to develop 'feminist strategies for enabling economic analysis',[84] it is important to acknowledge

> that the key issue we need to address in attempts to engender macro-economic policy reform is not pre-existing customs and traditions which discriminate against women, but one-sided emphasis by reformers on paid work in the 'productive economy', and a neglect of unpaid work in the 'reproductive economy'.[85]

Similarly, as the example of WIDE illustrates, GAD activists are formulating strategies to counter the gendered effects of global restructuring by developing an alternative *economic* framework based on feminist critiques of the gender biases in neoclassical economic thought.

As the discussion reveals, these GAD interventions focus primarily on the economics of global restructuring, and do not address the contingent socio-political and cultural dimensions in a comprehensive analysis. Contrasting the narrow focus of these contributions are the comprehensive analyses of scholars like Chang and Ling, Saskia Sassen-Koob, or Swasti Mitter and Sheila Rowbotham.[86]

A second dimension of a (feminist) economistic approach is its failure to historicise and contextualise processes of global restructuring, leading to analyses which employ universal categories and cannot adequately incorporate differences. This ahistorical approach is exemplified by Elson's analysis. She claims that

> feminist critical economics argues that the operation of economic reform at micro-, meso- and macro-levels is male-biased, serving to perpetuate women's relative disadvantage, even though the forms of that disadvantage vary between different groups of women and are disrupted and change in the course of policy reform. Most economic theory, whether orthodox or critical, is also male-biased, even though it appears to be gender-neutral. The male bias arises because theory fails to take adequate account of the inequality between women as a gender and men as a gender.[87]

What is interesting about this passage is that, although Elson recognises differences among women, these are differences in *relative disadvantage*. Moreover, these differences and possible changes are brought about by policy reforms, and are not linked to the positionalities of men and women in terms of ethnicity, race, class, sexuality, and religion. Elson's difficulty in raising the issue of difference in her critique stems from the major subject of her criticism: neoclassical economic theory. One of the basic assumptions of neoclassical economic theory is that economies are fundamentally driven by universal laws about supply and demand: it does not really matter where (and when) these economies are situated, because they all exist and function through the activities of selfish rational actors, who enact these universal laws by buying and selling goods in the marketplace. Although Elson strongly refutes neoclassical economic theory (as well as critical institutional economics), she does not really challenge some of its universal claims. Instead, addressing the need for economic policy reform, she argues her points in ahistorical and universal categories herself:

> [a] feminist critique of economic policy reform at the macro-level can be developed in terms of an analysis of how economic policy reform

treats the interdependence between the 'productive economy' and the 'reproductive economy', between making a profit and meeting needs, between covering costs and sustaining human beings.[88]

Although Elson recognises the need to differentiate among groups of women in the earlier passage, being caught in the universalistic logic of economic theorising, she fails to do so in this one. This becomes especially problematic, as feminist critical economics is intended to lay the groundwork for 'feminist strategies for enabling economic analysis'.[89]

A third dimension of the economistic approach is its widespread use of dualistic categorisations or dichotomies like productive/reproductive work, paid/unpaid labour, and commodity/care economy. Various feminist and post-modernist scholars have argued that binary opposites or dichotomies are embedded in Western Enlightenment thinking.[90] These scholars have criticised their use, because they tend to obscure shades of difference, in particular experiences which do not fit into a dualistic grid. For instance, the categorisation of paid/unpaid work presupposes only two types of labour: productive or remunerated work in the cash economy and reproductive work in the household. Yet, this categorisation leads to the invisibility of what is now often referred to as the triple role of women, which includes their work in the household, the cash economy, and the community.[91] As GAD specialists have argued, the activities of, in particular, women at the community level are not only distinct from their work in the household and in the cash economy (and should thus be recognised as such), but they often constitute vital survival strategies for the entire community.[92] Dichotomies have also been challenged because the first term is generally valued over the second, leading to the creation of hierarchies. In its critique of neoclassical economic thought, feminist critical economics has needed to address the invisibility of the second term, as well as the often implicit hierarchisation between the two terms. Yet, in its efforts to make the care economy, reproductive labour, and unpaid work visible in mainstream economic analysis, feminist critical economics may well have fallen into the trap of 'dichotomy reversal' when formulating its alternative economics framework. Behind the attempt to promote an alternative economics, which prioritises a 'caring economy', lurks the danger of a female sphere or maternalist approach. Emphasising the primary attachment of women to the caring or reproductive economy tends to essentialise women and their roles as those of mother, wife, and nurturer. In other words, promoting a 'caring economy' creates certain tensions in that it denies differences among women as well as men, and that it may lead to a valuation of the feminine, but not necessarily to changes in the gendered division of labour.

The narrow focus of the economistic approach has repercussions for the empowerment of women and for the development of strategies to counter ongoing processes of global restructuring. For one, this approach tends to emphasise the economic empowerment of women at the expense of socio-political dimensions of empowerment, such as self-reliance and participatory decision-making. Moreover, as the previous section on WIDE illustrates, feminist critical economics may partially fail its objective of formulating 'enabling economic analysis'. Its conceptual challenges to neoclassical economics lead to fairly abstract discursive accounts and position papers. Although this may serve the lobbying efforts of WIDE with institutions of the European Union, it also excludes and disempowers people who are not very familiar with the vocabulary of economists. WIDE is trying to address this problem by starting an economic literacy campaign among its members. This does not, however, resolve the fundamental problem of WIDE, expressed by representatives of women's groups at the grass-roots: how to develop strategies to counter and transform current processes of global restructuring. As long as its strategies are informed by narrow economistic analyses of global restructuring, this dilemma will not be resolved. In order to develop alternative strategies and identify points of intervention, WIDE needs to engage in a comprehensive analysis of global restructuring which would include conceptualisations of the complexities of power and changing power relations.

Towards a New 'GAD' Analysis of Global Restructuring?

The shift towards the 'global' by the GAD community has resulted in interesting and refreshing insights into processes of global restructuring. Yet, as the previous discussion has shown, this shift has not been unproblematic. It is therefore imperative that we build upon the work that has already been done, and embark upon analyses which take into account the complexities and contingent nature of global restructuring. This would involve the need to contextualise and historicise processes of global restructuring, and would include the exploration of how debates about global restructuring interface with, for instance, concerns about difference(s), gendered and racialised representations of the 'global', and the 'Othering' of Third World women. The importance of such analyses is not just to develop a better understanding, but also to create a broader basis for formulating alternative strategies which are sensitive to differences. A shared conceptual starting point for such analyses may be the notion that processes and practices of global restructuring are represented as involving the breaking down of an 'old order' and the construction of a 'new one' (or 'new ones'). The social construction of the new 'global' order is mediated through structures of, and practices around, class, gender, ethnicity, race, sexual orientation, and religion, which makes contextual and historical analyses imperative.[93] As Janine Brodie suggests, past experience indicates that this restructuring involves the (re)negotiation of several boundaries, namely the state/market, the international/national, and the public/private.[94] Given the complexities of current processes of global restructuring, I would argue that the negotiation of boundaries is even more extensive than Brodie suggests, and involves boundary shifting and construction among several contingent and sometimes overlapping spaces and spheres. These include the state/market/civil society spheres, the international/national spheres, the global/local spheres, as well as the public/semi-public/private/semi-private realms. The acknowledgement of boundary negotiation and shifting would allow us to ask the following questions: what shifts in power are occurring and where is power located? What kind of power is exercised and how? Who are the bearers of power and of what kind of power? How are various boundaries gendered, racialised, and classist? How are various domains or spaces gendered/racialised/classist? These and other questions would enable us to identify certain critical points of intervention (in terms of boundary construction), and to link various strategies to the (explicit) negotiating of these socially constructed boundaries and spaces. For example, a critical analysis of the internationalisation of the state allows us to track shifts in power among and within bureaucratic agencies and from national to regional institutions, or alternatively, to analyse the (gendered) implications of a devolution of power to the local level. At the same time, it allows us to identify (new) loci and sources of power in the market as well as in civil society, such as informal business networks. On the basis of such analysis, we can also address how the exercise of power is gendered and the extent to which various institutions are gender bearers.

In sum, a more holistic analysis of global restructuring, which emphasises its complexities, contingencies, and contradictions is needed. Only then can we identify critical points of intervention to renegotiate various boundaries and address the multiple dimensions of empowerment.

NOTES

I wish to thank the two anonymous *Millennium* reviewers and Mridula Udayagiri for their very helpful comments on earlier versions of this article. I have also benefitted from questions and reactions to earlier presentations on this topic at the Institute of Social Studies in The Hague, at the *Millennium* 25th Anniversary Conference, and at Dalhousie University, Canada.

1. I have placed inverted commas around 'globalisation' because it is a very imprecise term and is used too much as a blanket statement. Moreover, it has received a certain ideological connotation through the way in which proponents have (discursively) employed it. I prefer the term global restructuring, as it explicitly refers to a process of (partially) breaking down an old order and attempting to construct a new one, regardless of who or what is involved and whether this 'new order' actually materialises. Note that this 'new order' is not

necessarily superior to the old one and that it does not necessarily involve a concerted effort to design and give meaning to this 'new social construct(s)'. In sum, global restructuring entails the contingent social, political, economic, and cultural transformation(s) of the old world order into a new one; this involves the increased functional integration of economic activities (including the integration of financial markets and the emergence of a neo-fordist mode of production) which has been enabled by new communication technologies, the internationalisation of the state, and the emergence of a global civil society, increased individualisation as well as mass-mediated images and representations of the emergence of a global culture and a global village. See, for example, Robert W. Cox, *Production, Power, and World Order* (New York, NY: Columbia University Press, 1987); Peter Dicken, *Global Shift: The Internationalization of Economic Activity*, Second Edition (London: Paul Chapman Publishing, 1992); and Malcolm Waters, *Globalization* (London: Routledge, 1995).

2. See, in particular, Eleonore Kofman and Gillian Youngs (eds.), *Globalization: Theory and Practice* (London: Pinter, 1996), and Waters, *op. cit.*, in note 1.

3. See, for instance, the volume prepared by Jeanne Vickers, *Women and the World Economic Crisis* (London: Zed Books, 1991); Lourdes Benería and Shelley Feldman (eds.), *Unequal Burden: Economic Crises, Persistent Poverty, and Women's Work* (Boulder, CO: Westview Press, 1992); Nanette Funk and Magda Mueller (eds.), *Gender Politics and Post Communism* (London: Routledge, 1993); Nahid Aslanbeigui, Steven Pressman, and Gale Summerfield (eds.), *Women in the Age of Economic Transformation* (London: Routledge, 1994); Isabella Bakker (ed.), *The Strategic Silence: Gender and Economic Policy* (London: Zed Books/North-South Institute, 1994); Susan Joekes and Anne Weston, *Women and the New Trade Agenda* (New York, NY: UNIFEM, 1994); Rae Lesser Blumberg, Cathy A. Rakowski, Irene Tinker, and Michael Montéon (eds.), *EnGENDERing Wealth and Well-Being: Empowerment for Global Change* (Boulder, CO: Westview Press, 1995); Eva Haxton and Claes Olsson (eds.), *Women in Development: Trade Aspects on Women in the Development Process* (Stockholm: United Nations Youth and Student Association of Sweden, 1995); and Kimberly Chang and Lily H.M. Ling, 'Globalization and its Intimate Other: Filipina Domestic Workers in Hong Kong', paper presented at the annual meeting of the International Studies Association, San Diego, CA, 16–21 April 1996. See also the papers that were presented at the international conference on 'Gender and Global Restructuring: Shifting Sites and Sightings', Research Center for International Political Economy and the Belle van Zuylen Institute, University of Amsterdam, 12–13 May 1995.

4. M. Patricia Connelly, Tania Murray Li, Martha MacDonald, and Jane L. Parpart, 'Restructured Worlds/Restructured Debates: Globalization, Development and Gender', *Canadian Journal of Development Studies* (Special Issue, 1995), p. 18. The acronyms GAD (Gender and Development) and WID (Women in Development) refer to two distinct approaches within the 'gender and development' field. The GAD approach emphasises the need to challenge and transform how the social construction of gender and gender relations informs the perpetuation of inequalities between men/women and masculine/feminine. The WID approach aims at integrating women more fully into the mainstream of the development process, and thereby does not question the direction or character of

this development (process), as such. For a more detailed overview, see Caroline O.N. Moser, *Gender Planning and Development: Theory, Practice and Training* (London: Routledge, 1993), pp. 55–77, and Jane L. Parpart and Marianne H. Marchand 'Exploding the Canon: An Introduction/Conclusion', in Marianne H. Marchand and Jane L. Parpart (eds.), *Feminism/Postmodernism/ Development* (London: Routledge, 1995), pp. 1–22.

5. Connolly, Li, MacDonald, and Parpart, *op. cit.*, in note 4, p. 32.
6. For clear statements about this shift in concerns, see, for example, Diane Elson, 'Micro, Meso, Macro: Gender and Economic Analysis in the Context of Policy Reform', in Bakker (ed.), *op. cit.*, in note 3, pp. 33–45, and Jeanne Vickers, *op. cit.*, in note 3, p. 11. For the purposes of this article, the gender and development community includes practitioners, activists, and academics. In the rest of the article, I will use the terms GAD community and GAD specialists to indicate those working within the field of gender and development. See also footnote 4 on terminology.
7. For now, this excludes analyses of feminist internationalism because very few authors have directly addressed the role and contributions of feminist internationalism/ international feminism to debates concerning an emerging global civil society.
8. See, for instance, Marnia Lazreg, 'Feminism and Difference: The Perils of Writing as a Woman on Women in Algeria', *Feminist Studies* (Vol. 14, No. 1, 1988), pp. 81–107; Chandra Mohanty, 'Under Western Eyes: Feminist Scholarship and Colonial Discourses', *Feminist Review* (Vol. 30, Autumn 1988), pp. 61–88; and Marchand and Parpart (eds.), *op. cit.*, in note 4.
9. The term new international division of labour (NIDL) is used to describe the internationalisation of production, which involves the relocation of industries from the core of the global economy to the periphery and semiperiphery. The term was first introduced by Stephen Hymer, but received widespread attention after the publication of Folker Fröbel, Jürgen Heinrichs, and Otto Kreye, *The New International Division of Labour* (Cambridge: Cambridge University Press, 1980). For a concise overview of the development of the concept of NIDL, see Dicken, *op. cit.*, in note 1, pp. 124–5.
10. June Nash, 'Introduction', in June Nash and María Patricia Fernández-Kelly (eds.), *Women, Men and the International Division of Labor* (Albany, NY: State University of New York Press, 1983), p. x.
11. *Ibid.*, passim.
12. Susan Tiano, 'Maquiladoras in Mexicali: Integration or Exploitation?', in Vicky Ruiz and Susan Tiano (eds.), *Women on the United States-Mexican Border: Responses to Change* (Boston, MA: Allen and Unwin, 1987), pp. 87–8. Note that the electronics sector is mostly concentrated in the hands of TNC subsidiaries.
13. See, for example, María Patricia Fernández Kelly, *For We Are Sold, I and My People: Women and Industry in Mexico's Frontier* (Albany, NY: State University of New York Press, 1983); Lourdes Benería and Martha Roldán, *The Crossroads of Class and Gender: Industrial Homework, Subcontracting and Household Dynamics in Mexico City* (Chicago, IL: The University of Chicago Press, 1987); Ruiz and Tiano (eds.), *op. cit.*, in note 12; Fiona Wilson, *Sweaters: Gender, Class and Workshop-based Industry in Mexico* (London: Macmillan, 1991); and Leslie Sklair, *Assembling for Development: The Maquila Industry in Mexico and the*

United States, Updated and Expanded Edition (San Diego, CA: Center for US-Mexican Studies, University of California at San Diego, 1993).

14. See, for example, Patricia A. Wilson, 'The New Maquiladoras: Flexible Production in Low-Wage Regions', in Fatemi Khosrow (ed.), *The Maquila Industry: Economic Solution or Problem* (New York, NY: Praeger, 1990), pp. 135–58; María Patricia Fernández Kelly, *Political Economy and Gender in Latin America: The Emerging Dilemmas* (Washington, DC: The Woodrow Wilson Center Latin American Program Working Papers, Number 207, 1994); Kathryn Kopinak, 'Gender as a Vehicle for the Subordination of Women Maquiladora Workers in Mexico', *Latin American Perspectives* (Vol. 22, No. 1, 1995), pp. 30–48; Swasti Mitter and Sheila Rowbotham (eds.), *Women Encounter Technology: Changing Patterns of Employment in the Third World* (London: Routledge, 1995); and Cecilia Ng Choon Sim and Anne Munro Kua (eds.), *New Technologies and the Future of Women's Work in Asia*, Workshop Report, 13–16 September 1994, Malaysia (Maastricht: UNU/INTECH Publication, 1995).

15. Maria Mies, *Patriarchy and Accumulation on a World Scale: Women in the International Division of Labor* (London: Zed Press, 1986), p. 142.

16. Connelly, Li, MacDonald, and Parpart, *op. cit.*, in note 4, p. 29.

17. For an outline of the GAD perspective, see note 4.

18. Connelly, Li, MacDonald, and Parpart, *op. cit.*, in note 4, p. 29.

19. Gita Sen and Caren Grown, *Development, Crises and Alternative Visions: Third World Women's Perspectives* (London: Earthscan Publications, 1988).

20. Isabella Bakker, 'Introduction: Engendering Macro-economic Policy Reform in the Era of Global Restructuring and Adjustment', in Bakker, (ed.), *op.cit*, in note 3, p. 2.

21. *Ibid.*, p. 1.

22. For examples of titles, see note 3.

23. See, for example, Cynthia Enloe, *Bananas, Beaches and Bases: Making Feminist Sense of International Politics* (Berkeley, CA: University of California Press, 1990); J. Ann Tickner, *Gender in International Relations: Feminist Perspectives on Achieving Global Security* (New York, NY: Columbia University Press, 1992); V. Spike Peterson and Anne Sisson Runyan, *Global Gender Issues* (Boulder, CO: Westview Press, 1993); Marianne H. Marchand, 'Gender and New Regionalism in Latin America: Inclusion/Exclusion', *Third World Quarterly* (Vol. 15, No. 1, 1994), pp. 63–76; Sandra Whitworth, *Feminism and International Relations* (London: Macmillan, 1994); Kofman and Youngs (eds.), *op. cit.*, in note 2; Jan Jindy Pettman, *Worlding Women: A Feminist International Politics* (London: Routledge, 1996); Saskia Sassen-Koob, 'Issues of Core and Periphery: Labour Migration and Global Restructuring', in Jeffrey Henderson and Manuel Castells (eds.), *Global Restructuring and Territorial Development* (London: Sage, 1987), pp. 60–87; Bakker (ed.), *op. cit.*, in note 3; Doreen Massey, *Space, Place, and Gender* (Minneapolis, MN: University of Minnesota Press, 1994); and Mitter and Rowbotham (eds.), *op. cit.*, in note 14.

24. It is important to note that various authors have formulated several (types of) interventions in a single article or book. In other words, the work of some authors is being used as example for more than one type of intervention.

25. Susan P. Joekes/INSTRAW, *Women in the World Economy: An INSTRAW Study* (New York, NY and Oxford: Oxford University Press, 1987), p. 4.

26. See, for instance, United Nations, *The World's Women 1985: Trends and Statistics*, First Edition (New York, NY: United Nations Publications, 1985); Organisation for Economic Cooperation and Development, *Shaping Structural Change: The Role of Women* (Paris: OECD Publications, 1991); United Nations, *Women in a Changing Global Economy: World Survey on the Role of Women in Development* (New York, NY: United Nations Publications, 1994); United Nations, *The World's Women 1995: Trends and Statistics*, Second Edition (New York, NY: United Nations Publications, 1995); and United Nations Development Programme, *The Human Development Report 1995* (New York, NY: United Nations Publications, 1995). See also the five reports of the ECA, ECE, ECLAC, ESCAP, and ESCWA regions by the United Nations Industrial Development Organisation, entitled *Participation of Women in Manufacturing: Patterns, Determinants and Future Trends. Regional Analysis. [...] Final Report* (Vienna: UNIDO, 1995).

27. Commonwealth Expert Group on Women and Structural Adjustment, *Engendering Adjustment for the 1990s* (London: Commonwealth Secretariat, 1989); Vickers, *op. cit.*, in note 3; Benería and Feldman, (eds.), *op. cit.*, in note 3; and Lois Woestman, *World Bank Structural Adjustment and Gender Policies: Strangers Passing in the Night – Fleeting Acquaintances or Best Friends?* (Brussels: EURODAD and WIDE, 1994).

28. Vickers, *op. cit.*, in note 3. The term 'vulnerable groups' was first introduced in the UNICEF study by Giovanni A. Cornia, Richard Jolly, and Francis Stewart (eds.), *Adjustment with a Human Face, Volume I: Protecting the Vulnerable and Promoting Growth* (Oxford: Oxford University Press, 1987).

29. Chang and Ling, *op. cit.*, in note 3, pp. 7–8.

30. Chang and Ling, *op. cit.*, in note 3, p. 1.

31. See, for example, Marchand, *op. cit.*, in note 23; WIDE, NAC, Alt-WID, and CRIAW, 'Wealth of Nations – Poverty of Women', paper presented at the 'Globalization of the Economy and Economic Justice for Women' Workshop at the Economic Commission for Europe (ECE) Regional Preparatory Meeting of the Fourth World Conference on Women, Vienna, 13–15 October, 1994.

32. Marchand, *op. cit.*, in note 23, pp. 70–3.

33. Cecilia Ng Soon Sim and Carol Yong, 'Information Technology, Gender and Employment: A Case Study of the Telecommunications Industry in Malaysia', in Mitter and Rowbotham (eds.), *op. cit.*, in note 14, p. 201.

34. Swasti Mitter, 'Beyond the Politics of Difference: An Introduction', in Mitter and Rowbotham (eds.), *op. cit.*, in note 14, p. 11.

35. Elson, *op. cit.*, in note 6, pp. 39–42.

36. *Ibid.*

37. *Ibid.*, p. 33.

38. *Ibid.*, pp. 38–42.

39. Janice Goodson Førde, 'Trade Aspects of Women's Role in the Development Process, Cairo – Copenhagen – Beijing', in Haxton and Olsson, (eds.), *op. cit.*, in note 3, p. 12.

40. Susan Joekes, 'A Gender Perspective on Development and International Trade', *ICDA Journal* (Vol. 3, No. 2, 1995), p. 83.

41. *Ibid.*, p. 84.

42. *Ibid.*, p. 90.

43. *Ibid.*, pp. 81–93.
44. See, for example, Susan F. Feiner and B. Roberts, 'Hidden by the Invisible Hand: Neoclassical Economic Theory and the Textbook Treatment of Race and Gender', *Gender and Society* (Vol 4, No. 2, 1990), pp. 159–81; Marianne A. Ferber and Julie Nelson (eds.), *Beyond Economic Man: Feminist Theory and Economics* (Chicago, IL: University of Chicago Press, 1993); Nancy Folbre, *Who Pays for the Kids?* (London: Routledge, 1994); Edith Kuiper and Jolande Sap (eds.), with Susan Feiner, Notburga Ott, and Zafiris Tzannatos, *Out of the Margin* (London: Routledge, 1995); and Julie Nelson, *Feminism, Objectivity and Economics* (London: Routledge, 1996).
45. For the debates between advocates of (neoclassical) new home economics and feminist economists, see Nancy Folbre (ed.), *The Economics of the Family, The International Library of Critical Writings in Economics, Volume 64* (Cheltenham: Edward Elgar Publishing, 1996).
46. Paula England, 'The Separative Self: Androcentric Bias in Neoclassical Assumptions', in Ferber and Nelson (eds.), *op. cit.*, in note 44, p. 37.
47. Gary S. Becker, 'Altruism in the Family and Selfishness in the Market Place', *Economica* (Vol. 48, February 1981), p. 10.
48. Folbre, *op. cit.*, in note 44, p. 18.
49. See Feiner and Roberts, *op. cit.*, in note 44; Folbre, *op. cit.*, in note 44; Kuiper and Sap, (eds.), *op. cit.*, in note 44; and Nelson, *op. cit.*, in note 44. The terms 'commodity economy' and 'care economy' are used by Diane Elson in 'Women and Global Economic Restructuring: Towards Solutions', in *Final Report of the Expert Group Meeting on Women and Global Economic Restructuring*, prepared by Joanna Kerr (Ottawa: The North-South Institute, 1994), pp. 7–11.
50. See Wendy Harcourt, 'The Globalisation of the Economy: An International Gender Perspective', *Development: Focus on Gender* (Vol. 2, No. 3, 1994), pp. 6–14, and Diane Elson, 'Visions of Alternative Economics from a Feminist Perspective', *WIDE Bulletin: Defying Marginalisation, On the Road from Beijing* (March 1996), pp. 4–10.
51. Harcourt, *op. cit.*, in note 50, p. 7.
52. Charlotte Hooper, 'Masculinist Practices, Multiple Masculinities and Change in the Global Gender Order', paper presented at the international conference on 'Gender and Global Restructuring: Shifting Sites and Sightings', Research Center for International Political Economy and the Belle van Zuylen Institute, University of Amsterdam, 12–13 May 1995; Chang and Ling, *op. cit.*, in note 3; Anne Sisson Runyan, 'Women and the Neoliberal Agenda of the North', in Haxton and Olsson, (eds.), *op. cit.*, in note 3, pp. 104–17; Marianne H. Marchand, 'Selling NAFTA: Gendered Metaphors and Silenced Gender Implications', in Eleonore Kofman and Gillian Youngs (eds.), *op. cit.*, in note 2, pp. 253–70.
53. Runyan, *op. cit.*, in note 52, p. 105.
54. Connolly, Li, MacDonald, and Parpart, *op. cit.*, in note 4.
55. Maria Mies, Veronika Bennholdt-Thomsen, and Claudia von Werlhof, *Women: The Last Colony* (London: Zed Press, 1988), and Vandana Shiva, 'WTO, Women and the Environment: An Ecological and Gender Analysis of "Free Trade"', in Haxton and Olsson, (eds.), *op. cit.*, in note 3, pp. 16–44. See also Maria Mies and Vandana Shiva, *Ecofeminism* (London: Zed Press, 1993).

56. Mies, Bennholdt-Thomsen, and von Werlhof, *op. cit.*, in note 55, pp. 1–5, and Shiva, *op. cit.*, in note 55, pp. 21–4.

57. Shiva, *op. cit.*, in note 55, p. 21.

58. *Ibid.*, p. 26.

59. *Ibid.*, p. 26.

60. Mies, Bennholdt-Thomsen, and von Werlhof, *op. cit.*, in note 55, p. 1, and *ibid.*, pp. 21–4.

61. An important exception to this is the paper by Chang and Ling which has not only more in common with the GAD approach, but also brings some post-colonial feminist concerns about 'othering' into the discussion about global restructuring. See Chang and Ling, *op. cit.*, in note 3.

62. Joekes, *op. cit.*, in note 40, p. 92.

63. Elson, *op. cit.*, in note 6; Harcourt, *op. cit.*, in note 50; and Gita Sen, 'Poverty, Economic Growth and Gender Equity: The Asian and Pacific Perspectives', in Noeleen Heyzer and Gita Sen (eds.), *Gender, Economic Growth and Poverty* (New Delhi: Kali for Women, 1994).

64. Sen, *op. cit.*, in note 63, p. 25.

65. Elson, *op. cit.*, in note 6, p. 33. See also Harcourt, *op. cit.*, in note 50, pp. 12–13.

66. Wendy Harcourt, Lois Woestman, and Louise Grogan, *Towards Alternative Economics from a European Perspective* (Brussels: WIDE, 1995), p. 3.

67. WIDE was founded in 1985, in the aftermath of the UN Third World Conference in Nairobi, and 'is a European Network of gender and development activists and researchers working in non-governmental development organisations and research institutes in Europe'. See *ibid.*, p. 3.

68. Personal minutes of the meeting.

69. Personal minutes of the meeting.

70. WIDE, NAC, Alt-WID, and CRIAW, *op. cit.*, in note 31.

71. Harcourt, Woestman, and Grogan, *op. cit.*, in note 65. For a more detailed analysis of the WIDE position paper, see Marianne H. Marchand, 'The New Challenge: The Gender and Development Community Goes "Global"', *Connections* (No. 3, September 1996), pp. 16–19.

72. Harcourt, Woestman, and Grogan, *op. cit.*, in note 66, p. 10.

73. *Ibid.*, p. 11.

74. *Ibid.*, p. 15.

75. *Ibid.*, p. 17.

76. *WIDE Bulletin*, *op. cit.*, in note 50, pp. 21–3 and 29. The concern with gender and trade issues was first voiced at the 1995 annual meeting of WIDE in Brussels. The 1996 annual meeting in Bonn was entirely dedicated to 'Women and Trade'.

77. It should be noted that Joekes delivered one of the keynote addresses at the 1996 annual meeting of WIDE.

78. Personal minutes of the meeting.

79. Marchand, *op. cit.*, in note 71, p. 18.

80. Much has been written on colonial discursive practices and representation(s) of Third World women. See, for instance, Lazreg, *op. cit.*, in note 8; Mohanty, *op. cit.*, in note 8; Special Issue on 'Feminism and the Critique of Colonial Discourse', *Inscriptions* (Nos. 3/4, 1988); and Marchand and Parpart (eds.), *op. cit.*, in note 4.

81. Jane L. Parpart, 'Deconstructing the Development "Expert": Gender, Development and the "Vulnerable Groups"', in Marchand and Parpart (eds.), *op. cit.*, in note 4, pp. 221–43.

82. 'Quality Benchmark for Beijing: An Economic Framework', reprinted in *Remaking the Economy: Some Readings on Women's Economic Perspectives*, ISIS International-Manila Information Pack (Quezon City: ISIS International-Manila, 1995), pp. 69–70.

83. Elson, *op. cit.*, in note 6; see also my previous discussion of Elson's work, in the second part of this article. It should be noted that Elson's work is taken as an example because it has had a significant influence on WIDE's activism.

84. *Ibid.*, p. 33.

85. *Ibid.*, p. 43.

86. See Chang and Ling, *op. cit.*, in note 3; Sassen-Koob, *op. cit.*, in note 23; and Mitter and Rowbotham (eds.), *op. cit.*, in note 14.

87. Elson, *op. cit.*, in note 6, pp. 38–9.

88. *Ibid.*, p. 41.

89. *Ibid.*, p. 33.

90. Parpart and Marchand, *op. cit.*, in note 4.

91. Moser, *op cit.*, in note 4, pp. 27–36.

92. *Ibid.* Women's community work is often directed at improving the living conditions in the neighbourhood, by starting soupkitchens, for instance, or by pressuring local town councils to provide basic services to the neighbourhood, such as paved roads, garbage collection, water, and electricity.

93. See discussion on global restructuring in note 1. See also Janine Brodie, 'Shifting Boundaries: Gender and the Politics of Restructuring', in Bakker (ed.), *op. cit.*, in note 3, pp. 46–60.

94. *Ibid.*, pp. 52–8.

6. Internationalising Economic and Environmental Policy: Transnational NGO Networks and the World Bank's Expanding Influence

Paul J. Nelson

Networks of nongovernmental organisations (NGOs) which focus on development, the environment, economic policy, and human rights have become important actors in policy and funding debates for the multilateral development banks, particularly the World Bank. They raise issues of environmental impact, economic and social justice, political participation, and the rights of minorities (sometimes majorities), generally excluded from national and global decision-making, in a domain of cooperation and governance once managed solely by governments.

Recently, much attention has been given to both the World Bank and NGOs. In the years surrounding the World Bank's fiftieth anniversary, its resource-mobilisation and project-financing roles, environmental record, development 'paradigm', internal 'culture', and expanding role in global governance have all drawn comment from scholars and practitioners.[1] Like the World Bank, NGO networks have attracted scholarly attention to the expanding range of actors participating in international policy processes. Recently, this has included critical study of accountability and performance in NGO networks.[2]

This article probes the relation between the political strategy of three NGO networks – environment, poverty, and structural adjustment – and policy results in the Bank. The memberships of the networks overlap somewhat, but they are distinct in strategy and agenda, particularly at the level of their coordinating NGOs in Washington. The theme that unites them most strongly is the call for greater popular participation as the key to just and sustainable political and economic systems. Much NGO advocacy has sought to open World Bank and government policy processes to direct popular influence, making participation both the medium and message.

The two principal arguments of this article revolve around this participation. The first is that the distinct political approaches of NGO networks have advanced three different images of participation in international decision-making. The three vary most importantly in the extent

148

to which they involve international participants in the global decision- and policy-making process.

The second argument is that the World Bank has interpreted and managed the various demands and 'versions' of participation of the networks, accepting and embracing greater international roles that are proposed for it in environmental regulation, while essentially rejecting calls for reduced participation in making national economic policy. The Bank has sought to move from being a target of NGO criticism to position itself as a lever, an ally, or even a leader in urging change among its borrowing governments. In the process, the Bank has adopted and adapted the language of popular participation, rendering it amenable to its own structure and mandate. In a period of growing influence and authority, even pressure from NGO critics has helped to expand the range of influence of the Bank. The authority of the Bank to prescribe policy and institutional changes in several fields has been increasingly accepted. This is a change which adds to the diversity of the fields of influence of the Bank, even while strengthening its capacity to regulate the economic policies that are central to its mandate.

The World Bank can largely be understood as an agent of what Stephen Gill has called 'disciplinary neoliberalism'.[3] The Bank has, since 1980, assumed the role of designer, financier, and enforcer of a neoliberal vision of integration among national economies. Bank conditionality (and other incentives) have encouraged and financed an economic liberalisation which, as Gill argues, does not as yet have deep roots in the political economies of most of the Bank's borrowers.[4] The Bank has developed an expanded and deepened capacity for monitoring and is equipped to advise and regulate its borrowers' policy behaviour.

To construct a more complete image of the World Bank, an understanding of its 'disciplinary' role should be complemented with an emphasis on the Bank as an organisation, subject to external pressure, and neither internally monolithic nor static. Holding the two perspectives together permits a critical understanding of reform currents within the organisation; these currents should be seen in the context of its larger role. At the same time, it permits a critical view that does not dismiss or ignore policy change in environmental or social practice. While acting as a monitor and enforcer of neoliberal reform, the World Bank has also become the principal international agency to which NGOs appeal for influence over borrowing countries' environmental and social policies. The more activist posture of the Bank in these issues adds a dimension to its role in development policy and finance, without diminishing its leadership in promoting neoliberal reform.

The first part of the article addresses the networks. A brief description is followed by an outline of the operational meaning of participation in the platforms and strategies of the networks. Part II analyses the response of the World Bank to these challenges. Part III raises issues for influence and accountability among international organisations, states, and internationally organised citizenry.

Transnational Civic Actors Meet Internationalised Government

While thousands of NGOs have been involved in UN global summits, such as the 1992 Earth Summit in Rio de Janeiro, a much smaller number has become involved in international advocacy with the World Bank in a sustained way.[5] Their number, while large and growing, is not vast, and observation and generalisation is possible. This analysis describes three loose networks around the themes of environment, poverty, and structural adjustment, and examines their distinct forms of organisation and advocacy. The focus is on international NGOs (INGO) based in the industrialised capitals, particularly in Washington, the level at which the networks are most separable and identifiable. Although distinctions among the networks are being eroded somewhat, each is still clearly identified with an agenda, strategy, and core membership.

Describing the Networks: Participants, Origins, Agendas, and Records

The groups of NGOs reviewed here are loosely coordinated networks of diverse origins with activities that together amount to a common, collective agenda. They have varied claims to legitimacy, employ varied modes of action, and respond to a variety of constituencies. They are held together by shared values, shared political experience, funding and other project agreements, and joint participation in international gatherings.

These transnational networks can fruitfully be analysed in terms of the issues on which they focus: each organisation has a social, environmental, political, or other mission, and treats change at the World Bank as a means of accomplishing that mission.[6] I emphasise their common focus on the World Bank as an institution in order to isolate and analyse the roles of international organisations and of NGOs in international regimes, and the relationships between the two sets of actors. Changes in policy and practice at the World Bank also influence other aid donors, a fact that its NGO critics have recognised.[7]

NGOs have organised and mobilised themselves differently to seek influence on environment and infrastructure, poverty, and structural adjustment.[8] Despite evolving relationships among community-based organisations (CBOs), NGOs, governments, the World Bank, and other transnational actors, Washington-based NGOs have remained the 'apex' organisations, articulating and negotiating on most issues. A sketch of the three networks follows.

Environment and Infrastructure

In 1983, several US-based environmental NGOs, including Friends of the Earth, the Environmental Defense Fund, National Wildlife Federation, and Sierra Club, began a campaign to force reforms in World Bank lending.[9] The campaign began with a series of critiques of major infrastructure projects, usually involving forced resettlement of communities for large-scale dam construction.[10] Working with overseas affiliates and with environmentalists in the regions, they lobbied the US Congress, and met with the staff of the Bank to raise awareness about 'problem' projects and to accelerate environmental reforms.[11] European organisations such as the German NGO *Urgewald, Ecologist* (United Kingdom), and national offices of Friends of the Earth have also been active.[12]

The agenda of the campaign was initially concerned with protecting river basins, preserving tropical forests and biodiversity, and promoting demand reduction and efficiency in energy lending. However, three related issues have come to equal, and sometimes eclipse, these conservationist themes: involuntary resettlement of communities for dam projects, protection of indigenous peoples' lands, and accountability and transparency at the World Bank.

The US-based advocates quickly encountered independent local efforts by NGOs, unions, and CBOs to protect livelihoods and lands from the effects of major dams, slum clearance, and power plant projects.[13] The alliances they have formed are usually temporary and purposive, intended to accomplish a specific political objective. In the process, however, enduring contacts have been built which I characterise as a network. Although the alliances may not have regular, systematic exchanges, or institutional hubs (some do), they endure and evolve, and are periodically reactivated for a new round of advocacy.[14]

Southern participation began in each instance with a campaign around a project or loan.[15] In general, the participants are either federations of community organisations, national-level organisations, or both. Among the early project conflicts that launched the network and established its methods were Polonoroeste in Brazil, Singrauli energy projects and the Sardar Sarovar dam in India, and the Kedung Ombo Dam in Indonesia.[16]

These efforts, along with international human rights campaigns, are among the best illustrations of what Margaret Keck and Kathryn Sikkink call the 'boomerang' effect: a NGO network appeals to international governmental organisations in order to bring pressure to bear on a national government.[17] Working with international NGO partners, national NGOs appeal to an international organisation, in this case the World Bank, to bring pressure to bear on their own government. The strategy can compensate for weak political influence in the national arena, and take advantage of international norms on subjects such as indigenous peoples' rights or rainforest protection that may make the Bank more sensitive to critique than are most borrowing governments.

Poverty

Like most development financiers and aid donors, the World Bank affirms that all of its lending is intended to assist in the reduction of poverty.[18] However, many NGOs argue that the Bank, and other donors, should focus more of their resources on directly improving the welfare of poor people and expanding their access to productive assets.

NGO advocacy around poverty reduction grew in the 1970s, along with the rising fashion of 'New Directions' in development aid. The NGO effort, almost exclusively Northern-based, argued through the 1980s for a stronger focus on poverty, for more social sector lending, and increasingly, for public participation in project planning and implementation.[19] Among the INGO participants have been Oxfam (UK and US), Bread for the World (US), Church World Service (US), Community Aid Abroad (Australia), Christian Aid (UK), Save the Children Federation, World Vision International, CARE (US and Canada), RESULTS (US), and NOVIB (Netherlands).[20]

Advocacy around poverty has gradually developed greater North-South coordination, around a shifting set of institutional loci. In the early 1980s, efforts were generally loosely coordinated at best: Bread for the World advocated US legislation forcing greater poverty 'targeting' in World Bank lending; the Development Bank Assessment Network, a Washington-based cooperative effort, pressed for greater dialogue between US-based NGOs and the Bank; and a number of European and US-based NGOs pressed for new approaches in urban sector projects.[21]

Poverty advocacy became more international when, in 1984, the World Bank agreed to meet regularly with a standing consultative committee of NGOs. The NGO-World Bank Committee became an official international venue for discussing poverty and participation issues in the Bank. The Committee helped to build relationships among NGOs around poverty-related policy issues, but was largely ineffective, in the 1980s, in winning changes in practice at the Bank. The relative ineffectiveness of the committee reflects some of the problems of international cooperation on broad policy issues. Members found it difficult to sustain communication and campaigning between semi-annual meetings; the committee had relatively weak links to the broader NGO communities in each of the regions; further, a relatively loose agenda, until 1988, allowed many meetings to be so diffuse that there was little planned campaigning for particular policy changes.[22]

The first visible result came with the initiation by the Bank of a three-year 'participation learning process', which energetically documented and promoted participatory methods to Bank staff.[23] Following the approval of a modest set of proposals by the board of the Bank in 1994,[24] two NGO centres adopted the task of monitoring their implementation. One, the NGO Working Group on the World Bank, initiated annual regional meetings in Asia, Africa, and Latin America and the Caribbean, with the aim of exploring the practice and implications of expanded participation in Bank-financed operations.[25]

A second effort, initiated by the Washington-based advocacy group Bread for the World, has sought to mobilise NGO pressure on the Bank to implement its commitments to expanded participation. The project produces an occasional newsletter, *News and Notices for World Bank Watchers*, monitors budgetary and organisational changes within Bank headquarters, and seeks to focus attention on making the country planning process of the Bank (Country Assistance Strategies) more participatory.[26]

North-South NGO partnerships in anti-poverty advocacy tend to arise not in struggles over particular projects, but from relationships formed in funding and implementing projects or through collaborating in international meetings. Since 1993 alone, these partnerships have given rise to several developments: a NGO network from among NGO participants in the Bank's participation learning process; mailing list networks of NGOs constructed from participants in discussions of operational collaboration with the World Bank, sponsored by InterAction and by the Forum of African Voluntary Development Organizations (FAVDO); follow-up efforts among NGOs participating in the World Summit on Social Development; and a NGO group advising and monitoring the Bank's new initiative of lending to micro-enterprises, the Consultative Group to Assist the Poorest (which in turn emerged from a Bank-sponsored international meeting on World Hunger in 1993).[27] Often, the NGOs which have the staff and capacity to engage in policy discussions are national or regional consortia.[28]

Structural Adjustment

NGOs have criticised the effects of orthodox adjustment plans on income distribution, public services to the poor, resource depletion, and food self-reliance.[29] Many also object to the lack of broad national participation in framing economic policy, and some advocate specific alternative programmes.[30] Participants based in the industrialised countries have included the Development Group for Alternative Policies (US), several of the Oxfam organisations, the Inter-Church Coalition on Africa (Canada), World Wildlife Fund (US), Christian Aid (UK), and NOVIB (Netherlands).[31]

NGOs responded slowly in the early 1980s to the initial structural adjustment loans given by the Bank. Some of the early criticism from Northern NGOs focused mainly on the new balance-of-payment loans, with policy conditions, as a distraction and dilution of the commitment of the Bank to basic human needs lending.[32] Others did recognise and highlight the essentially new level of influence that adjustment lending offered to the Bank, but coordinated discussions on a global scale emerged only in the mid-1980s, in conjunction with the increasing concern of UNICEF with the impact of World Bank-supported national economic policies.[33] NGOs met in September 1987 for a UN-NGO Workshop on Debt and Adjustment, assessed the impact of the economic crisis, and 'discussed alternative approaches and strategies'.[34] Beginning in 1988, the NGO Working Group on the World Bank made adjustment one of its two agenda items.[35] Further, one of the largest NGO gatherings devoted to the subject took place in Washington in 1992, when 100 NGOs from 46 countries met in hopes of developing more coordinated and effective strategies.[36]

NGOs have employed strategies devised to influence public opinion, such as publishing critiques and videos, and have also relied upon direct lobbying, in the form of letter-writing campaigns to parliaments and the Bank and dialogue with Bank staff. NGO networks have produced case studies of country experiences with adjustment, including a widely distributed study of Mexico, commissioned by the NGO Working Group on the World Bank.[37]

NGOs meeting in preparation for the 1994 World Summit on Social Development argued for an international review of the adjustment experience.[38] Here, as in other episodes of the adjustment campaign, NGOs found themselves allied with UN agencies whose proclamations met with relatively little response from the World Bank.[39] US-based NGOs, in their first opportunity, in 1995, to meet with World Bank President James Wolfensohn, proposed a new approach, which is now in process. The NGO proposal for a joint Bank-NGO review of structural adjustment experience, based on country studies involving local NGOs and the Bank, has been accepted and is under development. The NGOs formed an international steering committee that reflects a widespread hope in the possibility that empirical, cooperative review may be more effective with the Bank under its new leadership than it has been in the past.[40]

Most countries undergoing adjustment programmes have experienced vigorous national debate, sometimes tied to national opposition politics, and usually including NGOs.[41] However, the most active participants in international networks addressing the World Bank directly are from a handful of countries including Mexico, Nicaragua, Ecuador, Philippines, India, Ghana, and South Africa.

The Networks Evolve

NGO networks are not static. Engagement with the Bank and other agencies has helped to produce a convergence, conceptually, among environmental, 'sustainable development', anti-poverty, and human rights work. Such a convergence is apparent in the struggles over development in the Narmada river valley, which has been represented as a human rights and development policy issue, while advocacy has remained essentially within the environmental network.[42] Advocacy around the 1996 political crisis in Nigeria also brought together the concerns of human rights and environmental organisations about land rights, oil exploration, political prisoners, detention, and summary execution.[43]

Despite the increasing conceptual integration of the agendas of the networks, there continues to be little coordination among them in agenda planning, information sharing, or advocacy. Development advocates, for instance, gave formal support but little effort to the information and inspection panel reforms initiated by environmental campaigns. Environmentalist critics agree with much of the critique of export-oriented economic strategy, but have not entered extensively into the adjustment debate.[44] Advocates in Washington continue to organise their campaigning, information exchange, and constituency-building along the lines of environment, development, and structural adjustment.

The networks have no overall coordinating body or forum. Several recent meetings have proposed to bring together participants and expand the dialogue among the networks. However, each has been temporary and partial.[45] It is no surprise that NGOs lack a single global congress or secretariat: the participants are not given to establishing central or hierarchical authority. What is notable is the relative lack of sustained cooperation among the campaigns. Common initiatives are rare; joint meetings and communication not routine; the networks continue to have access to largely distinct contacts at the World Bank; and the networks remain distinct at Washington level.[46] The '50 Years is Enough!' campaign in the United States includes many of the environment and structural adjustment network participants, and is the most sustained example of cooperation. Much of the advocacy of the campaign, however, continues under the separate themes of its platform.[47]

Some Southern NGOs experience tensions between their participation in NGO networks and the views they share with their own governments. Differences erupted in 1992 among NGOs over funding of the concessional lending arm of the World Bank, the International Development Association (IDA), when some Southern NGOs resisted efforts led by US environmentalists to make funding of IDA conditional on various reforms. While US NGOs cite their responsibility to US constituents and their frustration with the pace of reform, many NGOs based in the borrowing countries want their INGO supporters to give full support to IDA, and press for reforms on a separate track.[48]

Some Southern NGOs, and others based outside the United Sates, have taken initiatives that reduce somewhat the role of Washington-based NGOs as the principal representatives of the networks to the World Bank. The Bank has expanded its contact with NGOs in borrowing countries, but other NGOs are also increasing their direct representation in Washington. The Oxfam affiliates, the Forum of African Voluntary Development Agencies (FAVDO), a forum of Swiss development NGOs, and CARE-Canada have established Washington offices for direct liaison with the Bank. Caribbean NGO activist Atherton Martin proposed a Southern NGO Secretariat in Washington for the same purpose.[49]

All of these dynamics suggest that the NGO networks are evolving alliances with specific purposes, indeterminate structures, and sporadic and *ad hoc* coordination. The role of US-based organisations as spokespersons at the apex of the networks is challenged and modified by recent developments, but remains intact.

Three Meanings of 'Participation' for International Governance and Organisation

The one central area of convergence, vital to the agendas of all three networks, is promoting 'participation'. What is of interest here is not the stated definitions, but the operational meaning of participation in the agenda and strategy of each campaign. The participants of the three networks could agree, in general, on a definition of popular participation as it should be practiced. All three networks seek, through advocacy with the Bank or governments, to increase the opportunities for people affected by World Bank activities to make their needs and priorities heard, and to increase the propensity of the Bank to listen and respond.

The important difference arises not at the level of the definition of, or commitment to, local participation and empowerment, but in the three strategies' distinctly different implications for participation and influence in decision-making on economic and environmental policy. The environmental campaign expands the field of participation by bringing national development policy issues into international venues. The anti-poverty campaign calls for changes in World Bank priorities and practice, in order to expand the effective participation of the poor in projects. Adjustment campaigns aim to reduce Bank influence on policy, and to reassert the authority of domestic actors.

The environment and infrastructure campaign supports communities in resisting or shaping World Bank-financed projects that affect their lands or livelihoods. International support for campaigns against the Narmada River projects in India, the Arun III Hydroelectric Project in Nepal, and a series of projects encouraging colonisation in Rondônia, Brazil, brought the concerns of relatively small populations (relative to the intended 'beneficiaries') to international arenas.[50] Campaigns have included local resistance, direct lobbying in Washington by INGOs, and INGO facilitation of visits to the Bank and US Congress by local activists.

The campaign asserts the rights of local communities and organisations to be informed of plans that affect their livelihood and to participate in project conception and design. Leaders of the environmental campaign proposed and won a modest liberalisation of the information disclosure policy of the Bank in 1993, as well as the creation of an independent inspection panel to hear citizen complaints against the Bank.[51] Internationalising domestic policy issues has appealed effectively to international norms where natural resource management has implications for global issues (such as biodiversity, rainforest cover, greenhouse gasses), and where human rights and cultural rights norms favour protection of indigenous peoples' lands and practices.[52] National development policy decisions are opened to international participation.

Anti-poverty campaigning also calls for new policies and practices by an international actor (the World Bank) to allow and encourage greater local participation in Bank-financed activities. Local-level participation in project planning and implementation is a major focus of the dialogue between development NGOs and the Bank. Here, participation is framed as a process of active involvement of stakeholders in a particular project, encouraged and facilitated by methods and practices that have gained some currency among development assistance professionals.[53]

NGOs have pressed for participatory approaches at the Bank both directly and indirectly. Every public controversy over a 'problem' project sends the message that investments can be implemented more smoothly if affected communities are consulted.[54] Not surprisingly, the clearest and earliest directives of the Bank regarding participation were in the controversial project areas of involuntary resettlement and indigenous peoples.[55]

Some development NGOs have collaborated with the World Bank on projects, usually as implementing agents in projects financed by World Bank loans to governments.[56] In so doing, they have promoted participatory methods among Bank staff. In 1994, the Bank initiated a series of meetings between international, and then Southern NGO staff, and Bank staff, to discuss procedural and logistical issues in their working relations.[57] NGOs have also argued for a broad understanding and vigorous implementation of participation Bank-wide. Some World Bank staff have credited discussions in the NGO-World Bank Committee with inspiring the internal participation learning process of the Bank.[58]

The implicit meaning of participation in the adjustment network is nearly the opposite of strategy of the environmental networks. NGO critics of adjustment treat neoliberal economic policy primarily as an artifact of the World Bank and International Monetary Fund (IMF), and call for greater national control over economic policy.[59] Whatever the limitations of national political systems, they implicitly argue that citizen participation is more likely to be effective without overpowering leverage from the World Bank.[60]

The NGO critique, whether it is of public sector job loss, reduced social benefits, export-oriented exchange rate policies, or the privatisation of public and parastatal enterprises, has a common refrain: effective citizen participation in making economic policy is being thwarted by the Bank.[61] The extent of the effect of the Bank on the national politics of these decisions, of course, varies widely.[62] However, the influence of the Bank over the basic shape of economic policy often creates at least the perception of effective disenfranchisement for those who oppose it.

NGO critiques of adjustment have addressed the erosion of democratic traditions and the reinforcement of repressive and unrepresentative regimes, and have called for a 'new, more democratically determined approach' to development strategy.[63] In addition to calling for a more open, participatory approach, US-based, international, and some African NGOs have often called for reduced adjustment lending or an end to conditionality.[64]

As with other issues, NGOs do not address adjustment with a single voice. Another line of NGO critique demands not a smaller World Bank role, but a more benign one. Some call for 'positive conditionality' to promote, among other things, food self-reliance and reduced military spending.[65] However, the nationalist and populist argument described above is the more significant theme, particularly among NGOs with ties to the transnational network.

In some countries, the critique of adjustment is closely linked to opposition politics. Whether nationally-based protest is closely tied to opposition to a sitting government (as in Mexico), or is focused principally on the Bank and IMF as international perpetrators (as in the Philippines and many sub-Sahara African countries), the critique calls for new and broader popular participation.

The three NGO campaigns have sought to expand the participation and influence of local actors in Bank-financed projects and policy initiatives. The participation sought is in each case local, but the three have distinctly different approaches to the role of international actors. International intervention (by a reformed and closely-monitored World Bank) is the route to expanded participation in environmental and anti-poverty campaigns. While critical of the Bank, they assign it new roles and duties. In calling for the opposite – less adjustment lending and less conditionality – the campaign on adjustment makes a different sort of political demand. The diverse responses of the Bank are the subject of the next section.

The World Bank: Selecting, Adapting, Adopting
the NGO 'Participation' Agenda

The roles of the World Banks as regulator, financier, and coordinator of official aid donors, give it an important place in the institutional framework that governs the increasingly globalised international economy. However, far from being static or monolithic, the World Bank is a dynamic, complex institution that weighs, balances, interprets, and reshapes mandates and pressure from diverse constituents. States, financial institutions, private contractors, civil society groups, internal actors, and its own leadership are all elements of the operating environment of the Bank, shaping its approach to the varied calls for 'participation'.

The World Bank interprets, adapts, and positions itself in response to NGO pressure. Confronted with potent new criticisms, the Bank has often managed to adapt sufficiently to shift from being the target of the critics, to claim a new status as an ally or even a leader in the effort. The Bank often responds actively, and in different ways, to its NGO critics on the themes of environment and infrastructure, poverty, and structural adjustment. The World Bank has tended to embrace 'participation' that strengthens the international role in policy and project decisions, and that promotes local involvement in project management. It has largely resisted a call for sharply expanded domestic initiative and participation in national economic policy.

This section sketches the pattern of interpretation, adaptation, and adoption, and discusses its significance for international development and governance. The diverse NGO network strategies are one significant factor in the pattern of change and resistance to change at the Bank.[66] The interpretation of the policy and practice of the Bank that follows rests on the premise that it is an entity with imperatives, priorities, and strategies of its own, not merely a creation and servant of states. It protects its productive processes, shapes and conforms to social 'myths' that are the standards for evaluating its work, and selects and manages information to create and maintain the analytic world in which it works.[67] Even as the role of the Bank in enforcing the disciplines of debt service, adjustment, and austerity grew, proponents within the Bank pressed for more participatory methods for project and analytical work.

Reviewing the pattern of adaptation, adoption, or resistance to change allows a more complete interpretation of the World Bank as an agent of disciplinary neoliberalism. It modifies the interpretation of the Bank as an agent of the neoliberal project by emphasising currents of internal initiative and influence that shape the policy and practice of the Bank. At the same time, it reinforces the interpretation by showing the steadfastness with which the economic policy reform agenda is maintained and strengthened in the face of popular challenge. External criticism, including the diverse demands for more open and participatory operation, can force policy change at the Bank, but the organisation has retained substantial control over the nature and institutional impact of policy changes. Most significantly, the Bank has resisted the critique of adjustment lending that would both diminish its influence and undercut its role in the implementation of neoliberal policy.

The pattern of change takes on added significance when one considers the influence of the World Bank among donors and other development practitioners. The Bank exerts intellectual leadership through publications, training, and collaboration with other donors. In addition, it plays a more political and direct coordinating role; it manages, chairs, and often reports from the coordinating meetings of government aid donors that consider the economic plans of borrowers and that craft a common policy. The growth of this coordinating role in the 1980s created what Peter Gibbon calls a 'new aid regime' in which bilateral programmes follow the World Bank on a coordinated, orthodox path.[68]

Environment and Infrastructure: Accepting International Authority, Establishing and Defining Accountability

The environmental strategy has been effective in forcing policy change at the Bank. While NGO critics remain dissatisfied with institutional arrangements and implementation, this section will argue that resettlement, energy lending, and information disclosure policies have been changed significantly in the past decade. The NGO appeal to international norms and authorities, with strong support from the US government, has led to significant policy changes and to some changes in practice and organisational structure. The World Bank has clearly accepted the call to a significant role as an environmental regulatory authority.[69] The resettlement procedures of the Bank include requirements for consultation of affected groups and restoration of incomes and livelihoods when populations are resettled.[70] New sectoral lending policies have been adopted in key sectors (such as forestry and energy), and a new independent inspection panel has been created.[71]

However, this accomplishment in Bank policy is not an assurance that consultation leads to influential participation and greater accountability, or that borrowers are constrained by the policies and procedures of the Bank. The 1994 review by the Bank found that consultation was almost always carried out, but in no case had resettlement met the requirement of restored incomes, and that borrower governments routinely failed to implement steps agreed in the project.[72]

Consultation can lead to influence and accountability when other conditions are present. Heavy surveillance and pressure by the World Bank can help to ensure that agreed-upon standards are implemented. An internal paper outlining 'Regional Remedial Action' on resettlement cautiously observes that 'difficulties' arise 'when borrowers [lack] commitment to the resettlement activities', and notes that the Bank must maintain an 'intensity of supervision' to improve such implementation.[73] Vigorous, sustained protest by affected communities, with international support, has encouraged such supervision. A NGO commentary on the 1994 resettlement review argues that 'nearly all the cases' cited as positive examples of Bank influence in a resettlement operation required 'extraordinary' local resistance, and that neither borrowers nor the Bank 'revise[d] any project willingly'.[74]

NGO advocates intended that the new information disclosure policy and inspection panel would facilitate such pressure, and the 1994 review of portfolio performance by the Bank states ominously that, now, 'individual resettlement plans, which have improved substantially...can be challenged on every detail of the relation between policy and planning'.[75] What impact have the institutional changes had on normal practice in the Bank? Most infrastructure projects now eliciting protest have been under development for several years, and one can only speculate as to how they would have been different if they had been designed under the present circumstances. This pipeline effect[76] makes it almost impossible to assess impact 'on the ground' in the short term.

One can, however, report the responses of member governments. Their apparent willingness and ability to thwart Bank guidelines for resettlement suggests that many states recognise that, even as governments need the finance and seal of approval of the Bank for controversial projects, the Bank also needs to continue to disburse funds, particularly to major borrowers.[77] Do the new disclosure policy and inspection panel change this bargaining situation? The inspection panel cannot rule on the performance of governments in implementation, so it has no immediate, direct effect on the incentives for governments. However, the threat of an appeal could make the Bank more reluctant to finance problematic projects, and encourage staff to be more insistent on government implementation of agreed steps in resettlement. While the board of the Bank effectively blocked a proposed investigation of the Brazilian Planofloro project, an investigation and report by the panel was significant in Wolfensohn's cancellation of the Arun III project in August 1995.[78]

Participation as Project Methodology: Embracing the Policy, Testing the Practice

Participation as project methodology is, for the World Bank, the most tractable of the NGO approaches to participation. As with the environmental campaign, the NGO effort has called for greater staff sensitivity to non-economic (in this case social) considerations, and has sought to shift the practice of the Bank towards more participatory methods. Like the environmental strategy, the participation effort implies restrictions on the practice of the Bank, as well as potential new influence for the Bank over the policy and institutions of borrowers. The call for improved practice can be rendered consistent with internal concerns regarding government capacity and local 'ownership' of Bank-financed projects and initiatives. When couched in the language of economic effectiveness, rather than in that of political values, the participation agenda permits the Bank to align itself with proponents of participation, and to involve NGOs in implementing projects that many governments increasingly cannot manage.[79]

Official policy on participation is a patchwork of statements in various documents. Consultation of affected groups and communities is explicitly mandated in operations involving involuntary resettlement or affecting the lands of indigenous peoples, in social investment funds, and in environmental impact assessments for projects rated as 'Category A' (environmentally sensitive).[80] Consultation is encouraged in many other sectors and settings, including poverty reduction projects, emergency recovery loans, agricultural pest management, the forestry sector, and in dealing with 'gender issues in development'.[81] Participation is supported in many senior management statements, and is now sometimes discussed in non-project activities such as poverty assessments, environmental action plans, and the development of country assessment strategies. Wolfensohn's presidency has created an unforeseen new demand for the services of the (few) participation and NGO specialists of the Bank.[82]

During the late 1980s, a core of supporters on staff promoted participatory methods as general practice or in particular sectors.[83] This pro-participation core grew during a three-year 'participation learning process', an internal series of reviews and workshops that involved practitioners from NGOs, universities, and governments in a process of collecting experience to make the case to Bank staff for participatory methods.[84] The board approved most elements of the modest recommendations of the learning group; these included intensive monitoring of 19 'flagship projects', efforts to 'mainstream' participation in policy dialogue with governments, training and incentives to encourage a 'culture of participation', and the creation of a high-level oversight group.[85] Regional action plans have been developed, and limited special funding was made available for staff to cover the extra costs of participatory measures in project preparation.[86] An extensive Participation Sourcebook is available to staff, featuring principles and case studies of 'best practice'.[87]

The Social Development Task Group of the Bank represents the most extensive foray into the social and political dimensions of promoting participation in development projects.[88] Responding in part to NGO calls for World Bank help in securing an 'enabling environment' for NGOs and community organisations in borrowing countries, the Bank has engaged the services of the Center for Not-for-Profit Law to develop a model set of statutes and regulations for NGO and voluntary associations.[89] The objective is to reduce red tape and regulatory restrictions on operation, in parallel to the efforts of the Bank in the for-profit private sector. The recommendations, which aim to influence local law at a level of great detail, represent one of the paradoxes of the NGO efforts: by seeking to change World Bank practice, advocacy has dramatically expanded the range and the depth of its influence.[90]

The implementation record of the Bank demonstrates both achievements and limits. NGO involvement, often taken as a proxy for community participation, has grown rapidly since 1988, approaching half of all projects in two recent years.[91] The terms of NGO involvement and their influence over the shape of projects are subject to debate. During the 1980s and early 1990s, more than three-quarters of NGO involvement in Bank-financed projects consisted solely of implementing a component of a project designed by Bank and government officials.[92] World Bank reports emphasise increasing NGO involvement in project design, claiming that up to half of NGO involvement now includes influence over project design.[93] However, a review of the project documents shows this claim to be inflated: half of the NGO 'design' in 1991–93 refers, in reality, either to NGO design of a 'subproject' which is to be submitted to a project-financed fund for support, or to the contribution by NGOs to the design of the 'social fund' intended to cushion the impact of adjustment reforms on 'vulnerable groups'.[94] Most NGO and community involvement is arguably a form of directed participation in which consultation and promotion of community activity helps to mobilise the social energy needed to make a project succeed.

Much of the responsibility for the character of NGO involvement in projects rests with the NGOs themselves, most of which have been willing to accept involvement in a project, and the funding it offers, on the terms of the Bank, without articulating a strategy for influence over government or Bank practice.[95] The new initiative of InterAction to encourage US-based NGOs to enter into project collaboration with the Bank recognises the weakness, to date, of the operational influence of NGOs on participation at the Bank, and proposes to stimulate more strategic participation by its NGO members.[96]

Further, there are extensive organisational, managerial, political, and professional barriers to further implementing participatory methods at the Bank. Among the barriers, some of which are now discussed within the Bank, are the following: a process for project development and approval ('Project cycle') that makes amendment and pilot efforts difficult; organisational incentives that favour rapid disbursement of funds; staff career incentives and monitoring and evaluation systems that do not emphasise and reward efforts at expanding participation; the demands of borrowers for fewer delays in loan preparation; and a pervasive tendency to control the course of project implementation.[97] These limits aside, the efforts of the Bank have drawn favourable notice from critical observers.[98] While some of the positive impression may stem from the vigorous promotion and dissemination by the Bank of its participation studies, the real change that has transpired represents the pragmatic approach of the Bank to implementing its projects in an era of shrinking governments.

Adjustment and National Economic Policy: Tightening Accountability, Building 'Ownership'

For 15 years, the World Bank has used training, publications, national policy dialogue, and financial leverage to help create substantial consensus in official circles around a package of liberal economic reforms known as structural adjustment.[99] Despite this so-called 'Washington Consensus', and despite more than a decade of implementation of liberalisation in most of the Bank's borrowing countries, the hold of neoliberalism on economic policy in many countries remains tenuous, and the Bank and other donors continue to promote their implementation through loan conditions.[100]

The central position of the Bank in debt management and adjustment has made it a lightning rod for criticism, and has compelled it to devise a response to its critics in order to reconcile its adjustment lending with its expressed priority for poverty reduction and sustainable development. It has done so both by defending adjustment as a poverty-reduction strategy and by refining its adjustment lending practice. Its defence has gone beyond the counterfactual argument that conditions for the poor could only have been worse without adjustment, to argue that some adjustment loans are now essentially 'poverty-focused'.[101] A review of the 'poverty-focused' conditions cited by the Bank, however, suggests that what is occurring is not a refocusing of the loan conditions of the Bank towards reducing poverty, but an assertion that the liberal reforms of the Bank (such as labour market deregulation in Côte d'Ivoire and Zimbabwe, or the privatisation of land rights in Mozambique) are, in themselves, poverty-reduction tools.[102]

The practice of supporting adjustment has evolved significantly in response to the evaluations of the Bank itself, as well as to criticism regarding social impact and implementation. This evolution has not changed the general economic model, nor has it shifted the practice of the Bank towards a less intrusive international role. Indeed, it has tended to tighten borrower accountability to the Bank. The response of the Bank has also featured five steps to improve the implementation and impact of the reform packages: the attachment of fewer conditions to any one loan, and the prescription of their implementation in greater detail; the making of social safety nets as the norm in adjustment packages; the promotion of the institutional capacity to implement reforms and attract investment, under the rubric of 'good governance'; the creation of room for consultation in some of the research ('economic and sector work') that precedes adoption of sectoral and country aid strategies; and the encouragement of public dissemination of the adjustment strategy and its anticipated benefits. Without entering into the debate about the merits of these changes, how do they respond to the appeal for greater domestic participation?

Social safety nets are probably neutral with respect to participation in making economic policy. Acute needs and reduced state capacities in many countries have led to the creation of funds to finance employment and social welfare benefits, and civic mobilisation and NGO management of projects have been features of many of these funds.[103] The political significance of these funds has been the recognition by the Bank of the need to support liberalising governments by financing compensatory measures to cushion short-term losses of employment and social services by 'vulnerable' and politically volatile groups.[104] Adopting more narrowly-focused and specifically-defined conditions is an explicit effort to increase borrower accountability to the World Bank for the implementation of reforms. The 1988 review by the Bank of its adjustment lending signalled this shift, noting the relatively low proportion of loan conditions that were 'fully implemented during the loan period', and arguing for more focused and detailed conditions.[105] It is thus arguably a further shift of authority and initiative towards the Bank.

The attention of the Bank to 'good governance' issues since the early 1990s is a third response to criticism of adjustment lending. The Bank's influential treatment of 'governance' highlights transparency, accountability, legitimacy, and participation.[106] The origins of the Bank's interest in good governance include its frustration in winning implementation of agreed-upon conditions for adjustment plans throughout the 1980s. According to David Williams and Tom Young, the Bank recognised that its limited success had partly to do with 'political considerations.... [T]he experience of adjustment lending led the Bank to take account of political factors such as interest group pressure and government legitimacy'.[107] The Bank's interest in increasing governments' capacities to implement politically difficult policy changes means that 'good governance' is in large part about the capacity to implement 'good economic policy'.

Finally, the Bank has taken a few steps to encourage participation in its 'economic and sector work': research that forms the basis for Bank and government policy agreements, and documents Bank-related policy formation. Bank-sponsored planning activities that form the framework for projects – poverty assessments, social assessments in sectors as well as projects, and National Environmental Action Plans (NEAP) – have all been cited as processes that can benefit from expanded participation.[108] A limited number of poverty assessments and social assessments have been carried out in a deliberately participatory fashion, at the initiative of determined Bank staff.[109] However, the model – national policy planning in a complex field with strong international interest – has not been applied in general to economic policy-making. Expanded participation in setting economic policy is not likely to promote consensus and 'ownership', but is likely to raise thorny issues of the distribution of assets and income, social services, and entitlements. The Bank, and most of its borrowers, prefer that economic policy remain a matter of apolitical technical expertise, rather than of participatory politics.[110]

Recognising the need for a 'broader commitment to reform' in societies undergoing adjustment, the Bank has begun to encourage governments to disseminate information about the planned reforms.[111] The strategic interest of the Bank is freely stated: to 'minimize [the] vulnerability [of adjustment programmes] to derailment by those who stand to lose from the reforms', and to encourage an 'increase in power of the interest groups that will benefit from reforms in the course of adjustment'.[112] Efforts have been varied, including a television broadcast, in Togo, of a meeting in which World Bank staff presented the outline of the Country Assistance Strategy of the Bank to civil servants.[113]

Despite the initiatives in social assessment, NEAPs, and poverty assessment, the evolving practice of adjustment lending of the Bank has tended to strengthen accountability to the lender. Its formative and coordinating role in adjustment policy lends credence to the arguments of Robert Cox, Jonathan Cahn, and Stephen Gill that the governance responsibilities of the state are being assumed or severely impinged upon by international actors such as the World Bank.[114]

Conclusions: Influence and Accountability

The advocacy strategies of transnational NGO networks have contributed to a pattern of changes in policy and practice at the World Bank. Appeals to international norms and authority on environmental and resettlement policy have led the Bank to accept an expanded role and influence over environmental policy among its borrowers. Calls for new practice and priorities in poverty and social policy, focusing on popular participation in Bank-financed activities, have helped to encourage the Bank to embrace participation as a policy, while implementing its practice in a highly selective manner. Calls for a diminished World Bank role in structural adjustment have contributed to changes in the practice of adjustment lending, but these changes have tended to tighten the accountability of borrowers to the Bank for implementing adjustment policy, rather than expanding the national role in setting policy directions.

This pattern of change has contributed to three trends in international interactions on environmental and economic policy. First, INGOs and some industrialised country governments have asserted active roles, largely through the influence of the World Bank, in environmental and resource management issues in borrowing countries. Some of the leverage exercised through the US government may be diminished by the growing reluctance of the United States to meet its financial obligations to the Bank.[115] However, the pattern of INGO and Northern government influence over the environmental policy of the Bank and its borrowers is firmly in place.

Second, NGOs have pursued an agenda that designates the World Bank to monitor and regulate borrower government practice. The environmental critics of the Bank have, in effect, won it a larger role in defining adequate environmental safeguards and promoting the adherence of borrowers to them. What began as a NGO effort to check the lending by the Bank for environmentally destructive projects has become a source of influence for the Bank over borrowers. Adding the 'green' lustre to its reputation has helped the Bank to give balance to its higher profile as promoter and regulator of the neoliberal reform project. Initiatives in popular participation, while less prominent, have also helped to win the cooperation of some development NGOs that remain critical of many aspects of the Bank's practice.

In theory and practice these developments require greater subtlety in interpreting and strategising about the World Bank. Recognising the currents of change in environmental and social policy, and the internal constituencies that support them, reveals the organisation as being more dynamic and less monolithic than its critics sometimes imply. Viewing these trends against the central importance for the Bank of neoliberal reform allows analysts and advocates to place the reforms in context and to maintain a clear focus on the limitations and likely points of resistance to reform. One is hardly tempted to refer to the practice of 'disciplinary' environmentalism at the Bank, or a 'disciplinary' role in promoting participation. The Bank does now exercise influence over the policy and practice of borrowers in these fields. However, it does not involve the intensity of either promotion or monitoring which the Bank has given the neoliberal project. That promotion, monitoring, and oversight has been supplied largely by the NGOs.

The strengthening effect on the Bank also raises an issue for the 'boomerang' strategy, whereby NGOs appeal to international organisations in order to influence their own governments. When repeated appeals succeeded at the Bank, one result has been a stronger Bank and, arguably, diminished national control over certain areas of policy. Whether this effect is short- or long-term, and what its implications are for the national development and influence of NGOs and civil societies, remain to be seen. One likely effect is to aggravate the problem of the dominance of donors over the policy-making and implementation process of many of the poorer and more aid-dependent countries, especially in Africa. The problem, described as lack of government 'ownership' in development circles, is outlined most vividly in a recent study of the relations between Tanzania and its aid donors.[116]

Third, official discourse continues to define poverty alleviation as consistent with the neoliberal reform agenda of the Bank. Social sector lending is highlighted as the partner of international economic integration in a new generation of market-driven, World Bank-regulated growth with equity. As state functions are redefined, national governments are compelled to accept a greater local governmental and civic role in managing social services and development projects. This trend offers the possibility of more decentralised and responsive public services, but it comes, at least in the smaller and poorer countries, at the cost of expanded accountability to aid donors, including the Bank.

The World Bank, then, has grown from its role in project finance to adjudicator and financier of domestic compliance with international environmental norms; coordinator of an international aid regime and the economic policy conditions attached to adjustment; and, to a limited extent, arbiter of standards of 'good governance' that promote the transparency of states to the Bank, and their ability to host international investment.

International NGO networks have won significant battles over individual projects, World Bank practice, and information disclosure and the independent inspection panel. They have won a role for themselves in certain spheres of international policy-making, and in mobilising public participation and maintenance of externally funded projects. Their support for local and national NGO protest efforts has also helped excluded minorities gain access to international fora. As their influence expands, they increasingly confront the need to make their voice and agenda demonstrably representative of Southern priorities and needs. How they respond will significantly affect the legitimacy they are assigned by international organisations such as the Bank and Southern NGOs.

However this challenge is met, it seems likely that NGO advocacy will continue to promote the internationalisation of some policy areas. In the process, previously excluded constituencies win international support and leverage over government policies. As they enter into dialogue with the World Bank and other international agencies, however, they confront the tension between gaining influence through international leverage, and surrendering national prerogatives in major policy arenas. The recent trend points to the curious wedding of expanded participation in international arenas and shrinking discretion in national governance.

NOTES

Thanks to the John D. and Catherine T. MacArthur Foundation for research support, to the project on International Organisations and 'Good Governance', directed by the Facultad Latinoamericana de Ciencias Sociales (FLASCO) in Argentina and supported by the Ford Foundation, and to two anonymous referees who provided helpful comments on an earlier version of this article.

1. On the environmental record of the World Bank, see Bruce Rich, *Mortgaging the Earth: The World Bank, Environmental Impoverishment, and the Crisis of Development* (Boston, MA: Beacon, 1994). On internal culture, see Paul J. Nelson, *The World Bank and Non-Governmental Organizations: The Limits of Apolitical Development* (London: Macmillan, 1995). On governance, see David Williams and Tom Young, 'Governance, the World Bank and Liberal Theory', *Political Studies* (Vol. 42, No. 1, 1994), pp. 84–100. On the development paradigm, see Jo Marie Griesgraber and Bernard Gunter (eds.), *Development: New Paradigms and Principles for the Twenty-first Century* (London: Pluto, 1996).

2. On NGOs in general, see John Clark, *Democratising Development: The Role of Voluntary Organisations* (West Hartford, CT: Kumarian, 1991), and Julie Fisher, *The Road from Rio: Sustainable Development and the Non-Governmental Movement in the Third World* (Westport, CT: Praeger, 1993). On the politics of transnational networks, see Kathryn Sikkink, 'Human Rights, Principled Issue-Networks, and Sovereignty in Latin America', *International Organization* (Vol. 47, No. 3, 1993), pp. 411–41, and Thomas E. Princen and Matthias Finger, *Environmental NGOs in World Politics: Linking the Local and the Global* (London: Routledge, 1994). Critical studies include Jonathan Fox and David Brown (eds.), *The Struggle for Accountability: The World Bank, NGOs, and Grassroots Movements* (Cambridge: MIT Press, forthcoming 1997), and Michael Edwards and David Hulme (eds.), *Beyond the Magic Bullet: NGO Performance and Accountability in the Post-Cold War World* (West Hartford, CT: Kumarian, 1995).

3. Stephen Gill, 'Globalisation, Market Civilisation, and Disciplinary Neoliberalism', *Millennium: Journal of International Studies* (Vol. 24, No. 3, 1995), pp. 399–423.

4. *Ibid.*, pp. 401–2.

5. A global strategy meeting held in October 1995, for instance, involved 80 NGOs from 29 countries. Twenty-six were based in the United States. See 'NGO MDB Strategy Meeting – List of Invitees', Bank Information Center, 13–15 October 1995, Harpers Ferry, WV. The NGO Working Group on the World Bank (NGOWG), a principal forum for discussion of participation and social policy, involves 26 NGOs. With five NGOs replacing members at the end of their five year terms annually, the NGOWG has involved a total of perhaps 70 NGOs since its establishment in 1984. See Jane G. Covey, 'Critical Cooperation? Influencing the World Bank Through Policy Dialogue and Operational Cooperation', in Fox and Brown (eds.), *op. cit.*, in note 2, Chapter 3.

6. The case for the 'issue network' framework is made in Sikkink, *op. cit.*, in note 2.

7. The World Bank is nearly the sole focus of adjustment advocacy; anti-poverty advocates devote at least as much attention to the major bilateral donors as to the Bank. The environmental network discussed here has broadened its focus somewhat to deal with the regional development banks, USAID, and the UN Development Program, but still devotes most of its effort to the World Bank. On the regional banks, see Antonio Quizon and Violeta Q. Perez-Corral, *The NGO Campaign on the Asian Development Bank* (Manila: ANGOC, 1995). On the Inter-American Development Bank in particular, see Paul J. Nelson, 'Transparency, Accountability, Participation: Implementing New Mandates at the World Bank and Inter-American Development Bank', paper prepared for the FLASCO-Argentina Project on International Organisations and Good Governance, February 1996.

8. Networks have also been active in global climate change, including the Global Environment Facility, and in the role of the Bank in agreements related to greenhouse gases, human rights, and debt relief. This article discusses the three networks that offer the longest continuous records of advocacy involving diverse (North and South) NGO actors. Human rights advocates, principally the Lawyers' Committee for Human Rights and Human Rights Watch, have led an effort to compel the Bank to consider human rights performance in its lending decisions, to use its influence with governments in specific cases of rights abuses, and to broaden internal procedural reforms. Some argue for a change in the Charter of the Bank to mandate consideration of human rights performance. See, for example, Jerome Levinson, 'Multilateral Financial Institutions: What Form of Accountability?', *The American University Journal of International Law and Policy* (Vol. 89, No. 1, 1992), pp. 39–64. However, many human right advocates focus instead on reforms such as human rights impact assessments, and on the call for judicial reform under the 'governance' rubric. The major interest of the Bank in judicial reform is the creation of a reliable, consistent system to adjudicate contracts. Nonetheless, rights advocates have seized the opening to press for attention to judicial corruption, arbitrariness, criminal procedure, and arrest and detention practices. See Lawyers Committee on Human Rights, *The World Bank: Governance and Human Rights* (New York, NY: Lawyers Committee, 1993).

9. For histories of this campaign, see David Wirth, 'Partnership Advocacy in World Bank Environmental Reform', in Fox and Brown (eds.), *op. cit.*, in note 2, Chapter 2; Rich, *op. cit.*, in note 1; and Barbara Bramble and Gareth Porter, 'Non-Governmental Organizational Organizations and the Making of US International Environmental Policy', in Andrew Hurrell and Benedict Kingsbury (eds.), *The International Politics of the Environment* (Oxford: Clarendon, 1992), pp. 313–53. All three articles are by participants, past or present, in Washington-based environmental NGO offices. The analysis of this article focuses on one aspect of the environmental effort to influence the Bank. Another network, dealing with biodiversity, global climate change, and the administration of the Global Environment Facility, is not treated here.

10. Some early NGO criticism of these projects is collected in Stephen Schwartzman, *Bankrolling Disasters* (Washington, DC: Sierra Club, 1986).

11. Other participants include the World Wildlife Fund, the International Union for the Conservation of Nature, the Center for International Environmental Law, and Greenpeace.

12. Participants are identified based on participation in one of several meetings and communications in the network webs. Agendas are recorded in a set of work plans submitted to an October 1995 coordinating meeting hosted by the Bank Information Center, a Washington-based NGO. For more information on the meeting, see note 5.

13. See, for example, the account in Rich, *op. cit.*, in note 1, pp. 120 and 149–52.

14. In 1993, Washington-based environmental NGOs, for example, sought support for structural and procedural reforms at the Bank from national NGOs who had been involved in past campaigns to block projects. Kay Treakle, Program Director for Early Warning Systems, Bank Information Center, interview by Paul Nelson, 5 December 1995, Washington, DC.

15. Schwartzman, *op. cit.*, in note 10; Patrick McCully, *Silenced Rivers: The Ecology and Politics of Large Dams* (London: Zed Books, 1996), pp. 299–308.

16. Schwartzman, *op. cit.*, in note 10.

17. Margaret Keck and Kathryn Sikkink, *Activists Without Borders: Transnational Advocacy Networks in International Politics*, draft book manuscript.

18. World Bank, *World Development Report 1980* and *World Development Report 1990* (New York, NY, and Oxford: Oxford University Press), and James D. Wolfensohn, 'People and Development', Address to the Board of Governors of the World Bank Group, Washington, DC, 1 October 1996, p. 10.

19. See, for example, Independent Group on British Aid, *Real Aid: A Strategy for Britain* (London: Independent Group on British Aid, 1982), and Paul Nelson, 'Development Aid: An Agenda for Change', *Bread for the World Background Paper Number 86* (Washington, DC: Bread for the World, 1986).

20. Participants are identified by their participation in the NGO Working Group on the World Bank, or in the November 1993 Conference on World Hunger hosted by the World Bank.

21. See US Public Law 95–118, *The International Financial Institutions Act*, Title XI: Targeting Assistance to the Needy. The urban sector advocacy is recounted in Development GAP, 'NGO-World Bank Urban Sector Workshop', Memorandum to 'the NGO Committee', 21 December 1981. Other efforts are noted in Douglas Hellinger, 'NGOs and the Large Aid Donors: Changing the Terms of Engagement', supplement to *World Development* (Vol. 15, supplement, Autumn 1987), pp. 135–43.

22. Nelson, *op. cit.*, in note 1; Marcos Arruda, 'NGOs and the World Bank: Possibilities and Limits of Collaboration', paper based on an oral presentation to the seminar, World Bank and NGOs: Operational and Policy Approaches for Collaboration (mimeo), 1993; and Covey, *op. cit.*, in note 5.

23. World Bank, *Report of the Participation Learning Group* (Washington, DC: World Bank, 1994).

24. The participation reforms are discussed below.

25. See Society for Participatory Research in Asia, *Report of the Asian Regional Meeting of the NGO Working Group on the World Bank, March 20–24* (New Delhi: PRIA, 1995); ALOP (Asociación Latinoamericana de Organizaciones de Promoción), 'Spring Meetings of the LAC NGO Working Group on the World

Bank, Proceedings', Santafé de Bogotá, 24–25 April 1995; InterAfrica Group, 'Recommendations of the African NGO Consultation on IDA 11', Addis Ababa, 11 January 1995.

26. On the Country Assistance Strategy effort, see *News and Notices for World Bank Watchers* (No. 12, 1996). A third and relatively new effort has been initiated by InterAction, the Washington-based consortium of US NGOs. InterAction seeks to encourage an expanded operational collaboration by US development NGOs and their Southern partners, with the aim of promoting and monitoring participatory approaches. See InterAction, 'Promoting Popular Participation at the World Bank through InterAction's World Bank Project', (Washington, DC: InterAction, 1996).

27. On the participation learning group, see World Bank, *The World Bank and Participation* (Washington, DC: World Bank, 1994), Annex VI. On InterAction and FAVDO efforts, see InterAction, *op. cit.*, in note 26, and FAVDO, 'World Bank-NGO Africa Round Table Meeting', 30 January 1996. On the CGAP, see Lawrence Yanovitch and Dennis Macray, 'The Multilateral Development Banks and the Microfinance Sector', prepared for the Congressional Task Force on the US and the Multilateral Development Banks, 30 July 1996. On NGO participation in the conference on World Hunger, see World Bank, *Annual Report 1994* (Washington, DC: World Bank, 1994).

28. Among the active regional NGO consortia are ALOP (Asociación Latino-Americana de Organizaciones de Promoción (based in San Jose, Costa Rica), ANGOC (Asian NGO Coalition, based in Manila), and FAVDO (Forum of African Voluntary Development Organizations, based in Dakar).

29. The Development GAP, *The Other Side of the Story* (Washington, DC: Development GAP, 1993); Oxfam UK and Ireland, 'Structural Adjustment and Inequality in Latin America: How IMF and World Bank Policies have Failed the Poor' (mimeo), September 1994; The Development GAP, *Structural Adjustment and the Spreading Crisis in Latin America* (Washington, DC: Development GAP, 1994).

30. For examples from Jamaica and Thailand, see Norman Girvan, 'Empowerment for Development: From Conditionality to Partnership', in Jo Marie Griesgraber and Bernhard G. Gunter (eds.), *Promoting Development: Effective Institutions for the Twenty-First Century* (London: Pluto Press, 1995), pp. 23–37.

31. For purposes of identifying the members of the network, NGOs represented at a 1992 Washington meeting on structural adjustment are considered participants, as are members of the Adjustment working group of the NGO Working Group on the World Bank, and of the African Women's Economic Policy Network.

32. See, for example, Jonathan Sanford, *Status of the Poverty Alleviation Focus of the International Development Association* (Washington, DC: Congressional Research Service, 1984), p. 22.

33. Regionally, African NGOs reached common positions and coordinated action somewhat earlier, largely embracing and advocating the 1980 Lagos Plan of Action and the 1989 Economic Commissions for Africa 'Alternative Framework', and meeting in 1990 in parallel to the United Nations Program of Action for African Economic Recovery and Development. For a summary of these African initiatives see Taoufik Ben Abdallah and Isabelle Mamaty, 'Africa's Debt Crisis: Events and Proposals Since 1980', *African Environment*

(Vol. 7, No. 1, 1994), pp. 25–41.

34. 'UN-NGO Workshop on Debt, Adjustment and the Needs of the Poor', Final Statement, Oxford, 19–22 September 1987. The meeting involved 58 representatives of 36 national NGOs from 22 countries, and 10 INGOs and NGO networks.

35. NGO Working Group on the World Bank, *Position Paper of the NGO Working Group on the World Bank* (Geneva: NGO Working Group on the World Bank, 1989), p. i.

36. See The Development GAP, *The Other Side of the Story, op. cit.*, in note 29.

37. Carlos Heredia and Mary Purcell, *The Polarization of Mexican Society: A Grassroots View of World Bank Economic Adjustment Programs* (Washington, DC: The Development GAP and Equipo Pueblo, 1994).

38. Martin Khor, 'Summit Slams SAPs', *Bank Check Quarterly* (No. 9, September 1994), p. 5.

39. On the World Summit on Social Development, see Martin Khor, 'Development: Social Summit Draft Calls for SAPs Review', Third World Network release, 31 August 1994. On a recent World Bank response to United Nations initiatives, see Martin Khor, '"Don't Tell Me What To Do" Says World Bank Chief to UN', *Third World Economics* (No. 16, 31 July 1995), pp. 2–4.

40. For an outline of the study see the memo of the World Bank, 'World Bank-NGO Review of Bank-Supported Policy Reform Programs and Exploration of Options for the Future', (Washington, DC: World Bank, April 1996). The NGO steering committee members represent African Women's Economic Policy Network, FOCUS on the Global South (Thailand), the Bank's External Gender Consultative Group, FUNDE (El Salvador), ALOP (Latin America), Rede Brasil (Brazil), IBASE (Brazil), Public Services International, Oxfam International, Inter-Church Coalition on Africa (Canada), Friends of the Earth (United States), and The Development GAP (United States).

41. See, for example Joan M. Nelson, 'The Politics of Long-Haul Economic Reform', in Joan M. Nelson (ed.), *Fragile Coalitions: The Politics of Economic Adjustment* (Washington, DC: Overseas Development Council, 1989); Paul Mosley, Jane Harrigan, and John Toye, *Aid and Power: The World Bank and Policy-based Lending, Volume I* (London: Routledge, 1991); and Robin Broad, *Unequal Alliance: The World Bank, The IMF and the Philippines* (Berkeley, CA: University of California, 1988).

42. On the Narmada experience, see William Fisher, *Toward Sustainable Development? Struggling over India's Narmada River* (Armonk, NY: M.E. Sharpe, 1995). Indonesia's NGO campaign and its international support group are exceptional in their thorough integration of development, environment, adjustment, and human rights issues.

43. See James Riker, 'State-NGO Relations and the Politics of Sustainable Development in Indonesia: An Examination of Political Space', paper presented at the Annual Meeting of the American Political Science Association, Washington, DC, 2–5 September 1993. On Nigeria, see Aaron Sachs, 'Dying for Oil', *Worldwatch* (Vol. 9, No. 3, 1996), pp. 11–21.

44. The efforts of the World Wildlife Fund to document resource impacts of adjustment are the notable exception. See David Reed, *Structural Adjustment and the Environment* (Boulder, CO: Westview Press, 1992).

45. Recent meetings have included consultations at the time of a UN preparatory conference for the World Summit on Social Development (January 1995), and a coordinating meeting sponsored by the Bank Information Center (October 1995).

46. In the absence of an authoritative institutional voice, NGO efforts rely heavily on a variety of bases of legitimacy at the World Bank, mostly informal. These forms of legitimacy, including representation of Southern views, expertise, designation (as member of an official consulting body), and a domestic (US) political constituency, appear almost always in combination. Balancing their diverse constituencies and sources of legitimacy produces tensions and ambiguities in the messages of the networks about participation. 'Participation' in the environmental campaign focuses on minority voices, but actual voices in the dialogue with the Bank are usually those of Northern environmentalists. In the poverty debate, some Northern NGOs seek opportunities for project collaboration – and funds – as well as broader changes in World Bank policy and practice. Adjustment advocates confront the tension between radically shrinking the policy-making role of the Bank and forcing it to promote a different set of policy conditions.

47. The campaign operates through working groups on adjustment, debt, gender, and environment. Its efforts at public mobilisation, through, for example, telephone or postcard campaigns to the US Treasury or the World Bank, cross over the working group lines and call for action by all participating organisations. Congressional lobbying, however, has been done almost exclusively by working groups.

48. For an account, see Nelson, *op. cit.*, in note 1. IDA is only one example. On trade and environmental issues more generally, see Andrea C. Durbin, 'Trade and Environment: The North-South Divide', *Environment* (Vol. 37, No. 7, 1995), pp. 37–41, and Iqbal Asaria, 'North Must Lead to Change Lifestyle', *Third World Resurgence* (No. 28, 1994), pp. 7–8.

49. Atherton Martin, 'Address to the Conference on Global Hunger', Washington, DC, 30 November 1993.

50. Daniel Bradlow, 'The Panel's Investigation of the Arum Dam in Nepal', Memorandum to World Bank Inspection Panel Interest Group, 8 March 1995 (Washington, DC: Washington College of Law, 1995), and Margaret Keck, 'Brazil: Planafloro in Rondônia: The Limits of Leverage', in Fox and Brown (eds.), *op. cit.*, in note 2.

51. On information disclosure, see World Bank, 'Disclosure of Operational Information' (Washington, DC: World Bank, 1993); Lori Udall, 'The World Bank's Revised Information Policy and New Inspection Panel: Public Accountability or Public Relations?', in John Cavanagh, Daphne Wysham, and Marcos Arruda (eds.), *Beyond Bretton Woods: Alternatives to the Global Economic Order* (Boulder, CO: Pluto, 1994), pp. 145–54; and Christopher H. Chamberlain and Martha L. Hall, *The World Bank's Revised Information Disclosure Policy: A Report on Content and Accessibility* (Washington, DC: Bank Information Center, 1995). On the inspection panel, see Ibrahim F.I. Shihata, *The World Bank Inspection Panel* (New York, NY: Oxford, 1995); Bradlow, *op. cit.*, in note 50; and Nelson, *op. cit.*, in note 7.

52. Human rights advocates argue that no form of participation in national development is fully possible without the assurance of basic social and political freedoms, and they have urged the World Bank to join in the effort to enforce these rights. In so doing, they seek to stretch the self-definition of the Bank as apolitical by forcing it to recognise the political implications of lending to governments with poor human rights records. On this theme, see David Gillies, 'Human Rights, Democracy and "Good Governance": Stretching the World Bank's Policy Frontiers', paper prepared for the President, International Centre for Human Rights and Democratic Development, Montreal, 1992.

53. See, for example, Bhuvan Bhatnagar and Aubrey C. Williams (eds.), *Participatory Development and the World Bank: Potential Directions for Change* (Washington, DC: World Bank, 1992).

54. The importance of participation in projects with 'adverse potential social consequences' is highlighted in World Bank, *The World Bank and Participation* (Washington, DC: World Bank, September 1994), p. 28.

55. See Operational Directive 4.20 on indigenous peoples and Operational Directive 4.30 on involuntary resettlement, available from the World Bank Public Information Center.

56. Nelson, *op. cit.*, in note 1, Chapter 4.

57. Interaction with NGOs on the Bank's Project Cycle, 7–8 July, 1994 hosted by the World Bank; author's observations. Records are on file at the office of the Forum of African Voluntary Development Organizations, Washington, DC.

58. See, for example, Aubrey Williams, coordinator of the Participation Learning Group activities of the Bank, in a presentation at InterAction, 9 September 1996. See also World Bank, *Cooperation Between the World Bank and NGOs: 1991 Progress Report* (Washington, DC: World Bank, 1 April 1992), p. 16.

59. See notes 63 and 64.

60. This critique has a parallel in the scholarly literature. Jonathan Cahn, arguing that the World Bank has become a 'governance institution', traces increasingly intrusive interventions by Bank conditionality into institutional, legal, and even constitutional issues in borrowing countries. Robert W. Cox argues that the expanded role of the Bretton Woods institutions in economic policies is part of a general 'internationalization of the state' in the 1980s and 1990s. See Robert W. Cox, 'Multilateralism and World Order', *Review of International Studies* (Vol. 18, 1992), pp. 161–80, and Jonathan Cahn, 'Challenging the New Imperial Authority: The World Bank and the Democratization of Development', *Harvard Human Rights Journal* (Vol. 6, 1993), pp. 159–93.

61. See note 63.

62. Mosley, Harrigan, and Toye, *op. cit.*, in note 41.

63. Carlos Heredia and Mary Purcell, 'Structural Adjustment in Mexico: The Root of the Crisis', in *Structural Adjustment and the Spreading Crisis in Latin America* (Washington, DC: The Development GAP, October 1995), p. 10. See also Karen Hansen-Kuhn, 'Structural Adjustment in Costa Rica: Eroding an Egalitarian Tradition', in The Development GAP, *op. cit.*; and 'Summary of Testimony on the Effects of Structural Adjustment Programs Presented at the International Peoples' Tribunal to Judge the G-7', organised by the Pacific Asia Resource Center, Tokyo, 3–4 July 1993.

64. For US NGOs, see 'IDA 10 Position Paper', 26 March 1992, p. 7. See also Church World Service and Lutheran World Relief, 'The International Development Association: Flawed but Essential', statement to the House Banking Committee, Subcommittee on International Development, Finance, Trade, and Monetary Policy, 5 May 1993, pp. 3–4; Mazide N'diaye, letter to World Bank President Lewis Preston, 30 October 1992, on behalf of the NGO Working Group on the World Bank; and South-South-North Network, 'African NGOs Call for Change in IMF and World Bank Policies', *Third World Resurgence* (No. 49, 1994), pp. 28–31.

65. On this distinction among the critics of the Bank in general, see Lisa Jordan, 'The Bretton Woods Challengers', in Griesgraber and Gunter (eds.), *op. cit.*, in note 1, pp. 75–88.

66. Internal changes shape the direction of change as well. Notably, an internal 1992 critique of the loan portfolio of the Bank established the urgency of reforms that enhance borrowers' 'ownership' of, or commitment to, Bank-financed projects. The report found that 37 per cent of the portfolio of the Bank was performing poorly, and highlighted the lack of ownership as a major weakness. However, the report does not specify whose 'ownership' and participation – that of government ministries, commercial interests, or civil organisations – is most urgently to be encouraged and heeded: a central and contested question among NGOs, governments, and the Bank. See World Bank, 'Effective Implementation: Key to Development Impact', report of the Portfolio Management Task Force of the World Bank (Washington, DC: World Bank, 1992).

67. The 'new institutionalist' school of organisational sociology analyses social myths and their role in establishing standards by which institutions are judged and accredited. For a key theoretical statement, see Paul J. Dimaggio and Walter W. Powell, 'The Iron Cage Revisited: Institutional Isomorphism and Collective Rationality in Organizational Fields', *American Sociological Review* (Vol. 48, No. 2, 1983), pp. 147–60. For an application of this approach to the World Bank, see Nelson, *op. cit.*, in note 1.

68. Peter Gibbon, 'The World Bank and the New Politics of Aid', mimeo of a report, Scandinavian Institute of African Studies, 1993.

69. See World Bank, *Striking a Balance: The Environmental Challenge of Development* (Washington, DC: World Bank, 1989), and World Bank, *Mainstreaming the Environment: The World Bank Group and the Environment Since the Rio Earth Summit, Fiscal 1995* (Washington, DC: World Bank, 1995).

70. Carlos R. Escudero, *Involuntary Resettlement in Bank-Assisted Projects: An Introduction to Legal Issues* (Washington, DC: World Bank, 1988), and World Bank, 'Resettlement Review' (Washington, DC: World Bank, 1994).

71. On the inspection panel, see Udall, *op. cit.*, in note 51, and Shihata, *op. cit.*, in note 51.

72. World Bank, 'Annual Report on Portfolio Performance' (Washington, DC: World Bank, 1994), and World Bank, *op. cit.*, in note 58.

73. World Bank, 'Final Report: Regional Remedial Action Planning for Involuntary Resettlement' (Washington, DC: World Bank, 18 May 1995), pp. 39 and 46.

74. 'General Comments on "Resettlement and Development"', unsigned document appended to a letter from 16 US-based NGOs to then-Secretary of the US Treasury Lloyd Bentsen, 22 April 1994.

75. World Bank, *op. cit.*, in note 58, p. 36.

76. Jonathan Fox and L. David Brown, 'Taking Stock of Change: Pressure and Response *vs.* Interests and Inertia at the World Bank', in Fox and Brown (eds.), *op. cit.*, in note 2, Chapter 13.

77. The so-called 'disbursement imperative' is not only a chorus of the critics of the Bank. As the environmental responsibilities of the Bank grew, *The Economist* notes that the role of the Bank as 'a compulsive lender sits uneasily with its new job as custodian of the environment'. *The Economist* (Vol. 330, No. 1, 1989), p. 44.

78. On Planofloro, see Keck, *op. cit.*, in note 50. On Arun, see Lori Udall and Lori Pottinger, 'World Bank Cancels Arun III', *Bankcheck Quarterly* (No. 12, 1995), p. 1.

79. On participation and the language of economic effectiveness, see Nelson, *op. cit.*, in note 1, pp. 166–72. On participation and state capacities, see, for example, Carmen Malena, *Working With NGOs* (Washington, DC: World Bank, Operations Policy Department, 1995), pp. 21–2.

80. World Bank, *The World Bank and Participation* (Washington, DC: World Bank, 1994), Annex 4, pp. 1–2.

81. *Ibid.*

82. Comments by John Clark, World Bank NGO liaison staff to NGO Working Group on the World Bank, Washington, DC, October 1995. For examples of senior management support, see Lewis Preston, 'Foreword', *The World Bank and Participation*, (Washington, DC: World Bank, 1994), and 'A New Environmental Sensitivity at the World Bank – Highlights from World Bank President James Wolfensohn's Speech at the World Resources Institute Dinner in Washington, DC, March 1996' (Washington, DC: World Resources Institute, 1996). The call for participatory methods in drafting Country Assistance Strategies is stated most authoritatively in the draft funding agreement for IDA-11, quoted in Nancy Alexander, 'News and Notices for World Bank Watchers' (No. 12, 1995), p. 28.

83. See, for example, Michael Cernea, 'Farmer Organizations and Institution Building for Sustainable Development', *Regional Development Dialogue* (Vol. 8, No. 2, 1987), pp. 1–19, and Samuel Paul, 'Governments and Grassroots Organizations: From Co-Existence to Collaboration', in John P. Lewis (ed.), *Strengthening the Poor: What Have We Learned?* (New Brunswick, NJ: Transaction Books, 1988), pp. 61–71.

84. On the importance of such internal-external alliances, see Veena Siddharth, 'Gendered Participation: NGOs and the World Bank', *IDS Bulletin* (Vol. 26, No. 3, 1995), pp. 31–8, and Nüket Kardam, 'Development Approaches and the Role of Policy Advocacy: The Case of the World Bank', *World Development* (Vol. 21, No. 11, 1993), pp. 1773–86.

85. On participatory poverty assessments, see World Bank, 'Implementing the World Bank's Strategy to Reduce Poverty' (Washington, DC: World Bank, 1993), and subsequent annual poverty reports. On the flagship projects, see 'Project Flagships', internal World Bank memo, 1995. On participation initiatives in general, see World Bank, *The World Bank and Participation* (Washington, DC: World Bank, 1994).

86. Malena, *op. cit.*, in note 79, p. 51.

87. World Bank, *Participation Sourcebook* (Washington, DC: World Bank, 1995).
88. Social Development Task Group, 'Task Group Report: Social Development and Results on the Ground' (Washington, DC: World Bank, 1996).
89. Williams, *op. cit.*, in note 58.
90. International Center for Not-for-Profit Law, 'The Blueprints Project', Issue Paper (Farmington, CT: ICNL, 1995).
91. World Bank, *Cooperation Between the World Bank and NGOs: FY 1994 Progress Report* (Washington, DC: World Bank, 1995), p. 2.
92. Nelson, *op. cit.*, in note 1, Chapter 4.
93. World Bank, *Cooperation Between the World Bank and NGOs: 1993 Progress Report* (Washington, DC: World Bank, 1994).
94. Nelson, *op. cit.*, in note 1, Chapter 4.
95. Michael Edwards and David Hulme, 'Too Close for Comfort? The Impact of Official Aid on Nongovernmental Organizations', *World Development* (Vol. 24, No. 6, 1996), pp. 961–74.
96. InterAction, *op. cit.*, in note 26.
97. For a review of the project collaboration record and organisational issues, see Nelson, *op. cit.*, in note 1.
98. Matthias Steifel and Marshall Wolfe, *A Voice for the Excluded: Popular Participation in Development* (London: Zed, 1994), pp. 222–3.
99. From the World Bank, see Country Economics Department, The World Bank, *Adjustment Lending: An Evaluation of Ten Years of Experience* (Washington, DC: World Bank, 1988), and Country Economics Department, The World Bank, *Adjustment Lending and Mobilization of Private and Public Resources for Growth* (Washington, DC: World Bank, 1992). An enlightening country study of World Bank influence is Robin Broad, *op. cit.*, in note 41, on the Philippines. Mosley, Toye, and Harrigan, *op. cit.*, in note 41, is the best overview of the power relations involved in the negotiation and (non)implementation of adjustment policies.
100. Gill, *op. cit.*, in note 3. On the 'Washington Consensus', see John Williamson, 'Democracy and the Washington Consensus', *World Development* (Vol. 21, No. 8, 1993), pp. 1329–36.
101. For the counter-factual argument, see World Bank Country Economics Department, *Adjustment Lending and Mobilization of Private and Public Resources for Growth*, Policy and Research Series, No. 22 (Washington, DC: World Bank, 1992). 'Poverty-focused' adjustment loans are reported most extensively in World Bank, *Poverty Reduction and the World Bank: Progress and Challenges in the 1990s* (Washington, DC: World Bank, 1996), Annex B.
102. Nelson, *op. cit.*, in note 1, pp. 22–5.
103. ALOP, *op. cit.* in note 25, and Lynn Khadiagala, 'A Qualitative Review of Social Funds: Strengths, Weaknesses, and Conditions for Success', draft internal World Bank document, 1994.
104. On this recognition at the Bank, see Helena Ribe, Soniya Carvalho, Robert Liebenthal, Peter Nicholas, and Elaine Zuckerman, *How Adjustment Programs Can Help the Poor: The World Bank's Experience* (World Bank Discussion Papers, No. 71, 1990), and Joan Nelson, 'The Politics of Long-Haul Economic Reform', in Joan Nelson (ed.), *Fragile Coalitions: The Politics of Economic Adjustment* (Washington, DC: Overseas Development Council, 1989), pp. 3–26.

105. World Bank, Country Economics Department, *Adjustment Lending: An Evaluation of Ten Years of Experience* (Washington, DC: World Bank, 1988), pp. 15 and 60–4.

106. World Bank, *Governance and Development* (Washington, DC: World Bank, 1992).

107. Williams and Young, *op. cit.*, in note 1, p. 89. The efforts of human rights advocates to expand the Bank's working definition of good governance to include internationally recognised political and human rights has been treated delicately at the Bank; the General Counsel of the Bank has articulated a carefully crafted interpretation of the proscription in the charter of the Bank against interference in the political affairs of members. See the World Bank legal opinion 'Prohibition of Political Activities', 11 July 1995, available from the World Bank Public Information Center.

108. On social assessments, see Gloria Davis, 'Social Assessment', internal World Bank memo, 1994. On poverty assessments, see World Bank, *Annual Report 1995* (Washington, DC: World Bank, 1995), pp. 22–3 and 60. On NEAPS, see World Bank, *Mainstreaming the Environment* (Washington, DC: World Bank, 1994), pp. 82–4.

109. World Bank, *Poverty Reduction and the World Bank: Progress in Fiscal 1994* (Washington, DC: World Bank, 1995), pp. 5–8.

110. For an outline of the preferences of donors for apolitical development, see James Ferguson, *The Anti-Politics Machine: 'Development', Depoliticization, and Bureaucratic Power in Lesotho* (Cambridge: Cambridge University Press, 1990). On the World Bank, see Nelson, *op. cit.* in note 1, Chapter 6.

111. World Bank, *Adjustment in Africa: Reforms, Results and the Road Ahead* (Oxford: Oxford University Press for the World Bank, 1994), pp. 217–18.

112. *Ibid.*

113. Reported in *News and Notices*, *op. cit.*, in note 26, p. 28.

114. Gill, *op. cit.*, in note 3; Cox, *op. cit.*, in note 60; and Cahn, *op. cit.*, in note 60.

115. I have argued elsewhere that the environmental networks' reliance on the US government as the chief proponent of reforms on the World Bank Board creates tensions for US-based NGOs. This close cooperation has identified the network with a government whose participation in World Bank governance is often unfavourably viewed as heavy-handed and unilateral. Ongoing collaboration with the US government may also have steered the agenda of the network towards the issues on which the United States is willing to act, giving the US government curiously strong influence over the agenda of an international NGO network. See Nelson, *op. cit.*, in note 7.

116. Gerald Helleiner, Tony Killick, Nguyuru Lipumba, Benno J. Ndulu, and Knud Erik Svendsen, *Report of the Group of Independent Advisers on Development Cooperation Issues Between Tanzania and Its Aid Donors* (Copenhagen: Danish International Development Agency, 1995).

7. Globalisation and Poverty in South Asia

Mustapha Kamal Pasha

South Asia presents stark antinomies of accelerated integration into a globalising world economy. Despite the growing visibility of a much-heralded middle class,[1] want and destitution remain pronounced markings of social existence in this region.[2] Deprivation serves as a durable feature of rural society,[3] and, in the absence of radical improvements in the condition of the urban poor, migration flows to the cities continue to accentuate the social divide between the haves and the have-nots.[4] Obscured by the rhetoric of neoliberal globalisation, issues of poverty, destitution, or inequality are now subordinated to debates over economic reform.[5] Questions of governance, focusing on analyses of faltering democratisation projects in politically unstable environments, predominate.[6] Despite variance in the political form, a remarkable convergence is growing among the dominant classes in South Asia in the recognition that globalisation is inescapable.[7] Adjustment to its drum-beat is considered the only viable bridge to the future.[8]

Globalisation underscores basic changes in the global political economy, occasioned by the rise of new social forces, a massive restructuring of international economic relations, the internationalisation of the state,[9] and the emergence of novel sources and patterns of both wealth and stratification on a world scale.[10] On a neoliberal view, now popular amongst policy-makers and transnational classes alike,[11] globalisation realises the evolutionary dream of establishing a universal market-based order. Against the backdrop of the collapse of communism and the end of the Cold War, of the democratic revolutions in Eastern Europe and the dismantling of the Soviet Union, and of the delegitimation of the socialist alternative both as norm and development strategy, this order appears inescapable.[12] Rationalised by an ideology of competitiveness, liberalisation, and privatisation, economic globalisation via the market offers to its advocates the assurance of a brave new world of prosperity and material attainment.[13]

The apparently universal appeal of neoliberalism under the unstoppable march of 'globalisation' is matched only by the grand antinomies of its particularisation. In local and regional contexts, therefore, one is likely to uncover contradictory and uneven processes of growth and decline, integration and fragmentation, homogenisation and localisation.[14] The promise of material salvation is intensely refuted by the simultaneous presence of grotesque concentrations of wealth and privilege, on the one hand, and an unprecedented scale of poverty, squalor, inequality, and marginalisation, on the other. Above all, globalisation exposes vast populations in virtually all parts of the world to a relentless market rationality,[15] furthering already existing disparities and deepening social destitution.

Globalisation ultimately fortifies those with privilege. Premised on a market-based order, the new global political economy is closed to those who cannot be valorised.[16] Even those sectors of production, finance, and exchange that are least competitive are now forced to participate in a globalising market.[17] The effects of economic restructuring are pronounced not only in exacerbating income differentials, but in giving poverty a poignant cultural expression. Given culturally-sanctioned notions of affluence, it deepens the social divide and muddles the quest for self-respect, identity, and meaning. Tied to poverty are new forms of identifications of wealth and want, and forms of polarisation based on inclusion and exclusion in a transnational, commodity-based cultural economy.[18]

The major effect of the internationalisation of both economy and state for poverty in South Asia is captured in the new mood regarding poverty alleviation. Once *the* critical, if not primary, goal of economic development,[19] the eradication of poverty now appears a distant aspiration. The explicit incorporation of 'security nets' in liberalisation drives is a tacit acknowledgement of this thinking.[20] At the same time, as the state internationalises, the burden of poverty alleviation is increasingly placed on civil society, the latter being equated with the domain and activity of nongovernmental organisations (NGOs).[21] The emergence of the 'new poor'[22] under *structural adjustment* has given NGOs a more legitimate role in a climate of public retrenchment.

Neoliberal globalisation raises important issues beyond economic restructuring. It signals a reorientation towards the role of the state, namely, new state-society complexes and, more generally, the status of the state in international relations.[23] Curiously, the neoliberal penchant for promoting a market-based order, private capital, and non-state agents in place of social planning, public spending, and the role of a developmental state coincides with the liberal advocacy of civil society and global civil society (GCS) as the new social spaces for overcoming the conceit of statist thinking in politics as well as development. Civil society and GCS are seen as sites for realising individual freedom, establishing governance, and building community.[24] Liberal variants of both International Relations (IR) theory and Development Studies (DS) appear to share this new mood: a shift away from statist discourses of power and planning to an emphasis on new structures, agents, and processes in civil society.[25]

This article explores the implications of neoliberal globalisation for poverty in South Asia. Underlining the tenuous character of economic liberalisation, this paper examines the relation of a market-driven order to poverty alleviation. In a refurbished context, the burden of poverty alleviation may be changing, not necessarily by design, but by default, given the structural imperatives of economic liberalisation and its uneven effects.[26] A new orthodoxy may be elevating NGOs as providers of security nets and poverty alleviation.[27] This article contends that, in the face of disorganised labour movements, the growing fragmentation of post-colonial political coalitions once committed to 'national development', and the deepening of debt peonage, the state is being restructured.[28] Revising the social compact that once minimally guaranteed the alleviation of gross injustices, without necessarily undoing the structures of inequality, no longer seems politically intolerable.[29] Internationalisation and the reconstitution of the *social compact* in South Asia, it is argued, are likely to have a negative impact on inequality and poverty. Without democratised participatory structures and a state fully committed to redressing inequality and poverty, the gains from economic globalisation are likely to centre around those with power and influence, rather than around the dispossessed. The stress on agents in civil society, notably NGOs, fails to tackle the question of structural inequality; the latter lies at the root of poverty.

By way of critique, this article links economic globalisation to the new liberal mood in IR theory. It is argued that the emergence of a seemingly new form of transnational life, or GCS, with an amplified role for non-state agents, notably NGOs, is highly problematic. Against unequal patterns and effects of globalisation, the assurances of GCS and the rise of non-statist modalities of world civic life appear quite extravagant. An understanding of the perils of restructuring in South Asia tends to confirm the frailty of these liberal claims. To contextualise, this article begins with a brief discussion of implicit notions of Third World poverty in recent variants of IR theory and DS. This is followed by an examination of the (neo)liberal agenda in IR theory. Finally, the paper investigates the effects of economic globalisation on poverty alleviation in South Asia.

Third World Poverty

Though separated by academic convention and practice, liberal IR and development theorists both carry similar assumptions concerning the socio-temporal world: the common dream of building a better world and the placing of faith in a universally shared human capacity to attain that dream.[30] Initially, liberal theorists sought to realise this dream in the political organisation of (the) state(s).[31] By comparison, developmentalists solicited its actualisation *via* wealth creation.[32] Against these modular trajectories, the Third World, recognisable through its poverty, has stood as a *naturalised* world, outside civilised society, yet amenable to transformation from the outside.[33] Conceptions of Third World poverty in extant IR theory, as well as in DS, have emanated from a common perspective: the poorer regions of the world are simply closer to the natural world. More to the point, the cultural and *relational* attributes of the 'poor' are seen mainly as biological, not as a social state or condition.[34] With antecedents in post-Enlightenment thinking, both liberal IR and development theories embody the *modern* promise of overcoming natural determination: (international) politics as an escape from a Hobbesian state of nature; development as a triumph over a state of savagery.[35] Against the fiction of nature, IR theorists have generally promoted the idea of an international society.[36] The concept of development has, itself, been premised on an acceptance of a pre-civil phase in societal evolution. In either case, the notion of nature has been central, an hypothetical condition preceding society, but also rationalising the need for society. Historically, the role of 'nature' in post-Enlightenment thought has been performed by the living societies of the Third World.[37] More charitable variants of this view do acknowledge the existence of society in Third World areas, but also signify its deficiency regarding crucial dimensions of established social life, such as political sovereignty or wealth.[38]

Theories of IR have mainly advanced a discourse on space.[39] By contrast, development theories have promoted a discourse on time, generally viewing the Third World as a transitional phase between nature and society.[40] The consequence of this latter demarcation is to reduce time to space; nominal and empty stages replace actual movement.[41] Hence, the notion of the 'Third World' itself conflates spatial and temporal properties, economically poor non-Western regions 'over there' (in space) representing a prior stage (in time) of development of society 'over here'. In recent development thinking, this view may be changing.[42] IR theory, however, continues to resist acknowledging the naturalism of its basic formulation.[43] Reinforced by power, habit, and memory, IR theorists have generally failed to problematise the theoretical status of the Third World in their accounts of *international* politics, except as the silent other.

Though enjoying common antecedents in post-Enlightenment thinking, liberal IR theory and DS have engaged different objects, actors, and processes. IR theorists have generally been concerned with the *political* organisation of space. Development theorists have been preoccupied with the task of theorising the *economic* transition of the Third World to 'society'. Yet, indeed, it is the Third World that provides the bridge between DS and IR theory: the discussion of 'developing areas' usually takes the form of 'low politics', a liberal corrective to the realist agenda.[44] On the other hand, DS has been, until quite recently, generally oblivious to unequal global structures of power and wealth.[45]

The New Agenda

In the context of globalisation, the agenda of liberalism is being smuggled back into IR theory.[46] Globalisation shifts the focus away from the naturalist antecedents of international society to 'civil' society. The liberal recognition of commonality and integration across porous boundaries challenges the realist construction of (world) order as a solution to the problem of anarchy.[47] The project of overcoming natural determination is no longer seen as a 'national' enterprise, but as intrinsic to international relations.[48] Yet, in this putatively new universe, it is unclear whether the Third World will graduate from its naturalised state.

Within the broader context of transnational politics, there is an emphasis on GCS, a loose umbrella term encompassing the domain of 'sovereignty-free' actors with transnational scope.[49] The focus on new global actors and processes in the international system appears to redirect IR into areas directly conditioned by agents *outside* the state, ostensibly demolishing the traditional wall separating the affairs of the state and society. A key implication of invoking the metaphor of anarchy for IR is the denial of human agency in the constitution of international society.[50] Liberalism promises a different vision: human agency is imbricated in the constitution of the world.[51] The idea of GCS foregrounds this alternative logic: the simultaneous acceptance of universality as a preferred world and the recognition of human capacity for its realisation.

Challenging the realist predilection to subsume international relations under inter-state relations,[52] the recent discourse of GCS clearly directs attention towards the emergence of an autonomous domain of non-state activity at the global level. A new global civic consciousness permeates the world system alongside 'world civic politics'.[53] With the appearance of transnational networks among new global actors, sovereignty is under threat. According to Ronnie Lipschutz, for instance, this non-state domain is 'a parallel arrangement of political interaction' built around new global networks outside the state system.[54] Following the liberal promise of internationalism, Lipschutz equates this autonomous realm to the 'leaking away of sovereignty'.[55] By contrast, M.J. Peterson envisages an 'international civil society', an alternative to GCS, to signify 'the various types of societal actors operating across the boundaries of variously structured countries'.[56] However, Peterson's 'international civil society' is composed of 'several interlinked civil societies', not a singular entity.[57] GCS basically denotes the acknowledgement of new forms of transnational political activity.[58] Generally absent here, however, is the pervasiveness of market-based processes at the global level.[59]

Liberal notions of GCS parallel the neoclassical view of the relation of the individual to society. In neoclassical economics, the (sovereign) individual is prior to society.[60] Similarly, to its proponents, GCS is the composite of spatially dispersed Robinson Crusoes. Aspirations of a shared community of interests provide an escape from the strictures of realist (Hobbesian) pessimism. However, the basis of a GCS is interest, not social connectedness. Like preferences in neoclassical economic thought, interests are the point of departure for transnational social life. To put it differently, the image of atomistic individuals provides the starting-point of association for proponents of GCS and social contractarians alike.[61] At best, individuals are bound by interests before they organise themselves as an international society.

GCS proponents assume an international society of states, but add an additional layer of transnational civic relations,[62] without examining the implications of a realist characterisation of the world order. Social relations inspired by the fear of anarchy and those that presuppose mutuality take international relations in quite different directions.[63] GCS supporters find no contradiction in reconciling the opposing images. To the extent that practices *outside* the state system can be aggregated, the idea of GCS is adduced. However, essential to GCS is a tacit acknowledgement of the existence of an inter-state system, not its absence. By implication, sovereignty foregrounds GCS. Yet, proponents of GCS fail to recognise the significance of the idea of sovereignty to their own discourse.[64] Lipschutz's parallel arrangement of political interaction,[65] for instance, only confirms the centrality of an extant inter-state system which lends a foundation to GCS. To be certain, an analytically non-statist notion of GCS would require a radical remapping of the architecture of world politics, and, minimally, a reconsideration of the so-called Hobbesian problematic, not its subsumption in an expanding menu of international relations.

In essence, the idea of GCS is a liberal recasting of world politics in a period of globalisation. Unwilling to accord determinacy to capitalism in organising social life in late modernity, GCS provides an ideal compromise between the state system and world society.[66] Missing in both discourses is the narrative of inequality. *Via* GCS, however, the liberal dream of expanding freedom through voluntary association and the confidence in surmounting natural constraints reappears.[67] The focus on non-state actors as vehicles of change and transformation, therefore, is not coincidental. Liberal proponents of GCS tend to reject the state in favour of non-state actors who create a realm of voluntary association, in both domestic and global affairs. GCS works *via* analogy: the notion of civil society at the domestic level is extended to the global level.[68]

Liberal proponents of GCS fail to transcend the limits imposed by utilitarianism. In selecting the modalities of realising the dream of free association, interests guide the slippery passage to a universal society, not the recognition of a common good. Generally, there is little or no mention of either differentiation within the South or the basic divide between rich and poor regions. Specifically, the notion of either production or property (and the distribution of power based on property) does not enter the GCS discourse.[69] Furthermore, by failing to *historicise* global inequality between and among regions, the GCS formulation ends up swallowing the Third World in its idealisation of international relations.

Advocates of GCS fail to fully appreciate the *asymmetrical* character of globalising structures that may come in the way of actualising universality and affirming human agency.[70] Recent discussions of an emerging GCS, presumably post-, non-, or anti-realist, tend to duplicate the problem of the marginalisation of the so-called Third World in IR. Liberal discussions generally neglect how global structures are implicated in exacerbating inequality and poverty.[71] GCS formulations envisage a liberal universe, ahistorical in content and oblivious to inherent hierarchies of power and wealth.[72] Taking the notion of 'society' as a product of interests, not as a form of capitalist relations on a global scale, liberal proponents of GCS empty out imbalances between social forces.[73] Proponents of GCS also designate NGOs as the principal agents of its design and praxis, without situating their relational context in an uneven global political economy. The GCS discourse effectively precludes the possibility that the central issue of the marginalisation of vast populations in the global political economy could occupy centre-stage in IR theory. A different form of (liberal) hegemony may, instead, be replacing the conceit of a West-centred inter-state system.[74]

In the context of globalisation, talk of an emerging GCS also legitimises the assault on the Third World state. This is the site where the neoliberal agenda of economic globalisation and GCS formulations overlap. Enfeebled by internal tensions and pressured to *globalise*, the state becomes incapable of denying an augmented role to non-state agents. Once the state loses favour in circles of global power and control, civil society can be promoted, especially in its narrowly conceived form of non-state or non-governmental actors.[75] Privileging agents in civil society introduces new forms of initiative, without providing an adequate appreciation of their structural location and function in the global political economy.

Often tied to global capital and its disciplinary institutions (for example, the IMF and World Bank),[76] or its *humanised* expression in philanthropic organisations, non-state actors do not offer an alternative for transformation. Even in the best of circumstances, they work towards reform without upsetting global structures.[77] In the act of reforming society, they can also (unwittingly) undermine the state that gives coherence to society. The process of deepening transnational links is pregnant with the possibility for eroding the autonomy of civil society in the Third World, as the latter increasingly comes under the sway of forces beyond its (national) control.

Following Robert Cox,[78] the realignment of the state under conditions of globalisation is complemented by the role of both transnational actors and their dominant classes in the Third World. Placed within the context of the growing power of global capital,[79] non-state transnational actors are both acquiring the capacity to challenge the sovereignty of Third World states and reconstituting domestic civil society.[80] While most non-state actors enjoy neither power nor privilege in the Third World,[81] those with transnational patronage now may have the occasion to acquire both power and privilege.[82]

The new 'partners-in-development', the non-state transnational network of Northern-based NGOs[83] and their local counterparts, embody the *reformist* side of the globalising ideology of self-help, liberalisation, state retrenchment, private initiative, and participation outside regular political channels.[84] Generally more sympathetic to the new rules of the global game – efficiency and privatisation – these organisations are accountable to their sponsors, not their constituents.[85] In this GCS blueprint of fostering civil society in the Third World, the emphasis lies on establishing an autonomous sphere of development which may even involve organisations critical of the role of international disciplinary institutions.[86] For several Third World intellectuals, NGOs with transnational links promise a more 'progressive' avenue to channel their talent outside the state.[87] Given their relative financial autonomy *vis-à-vis* the state, some NGOs can afford to pursue agendas that do not coincide with 'national' goals.[88] International financial institutions, in turn, now press host states to relax their laws to accommodate the formation of new NGOs.[89] With a background of an over-centralised state, which sees development as 'an administrative project',[90] the lure of popular participation is quite attractive. Yet, a reordering of state-society relations may be the new *conditionality* behind the emphasis on 'governance', 'civil society', and 'grassroots' democracy.[91] Without built-in safeguards against economic restructuring, agents in civil society are now asked to play a more pivotal role to soften the impact of globalisation by establishing poverty alleviation programmes, building infrastructures, and providing social services.[92]

Globalisation and South Asia

Poverty has often provided South Asia with its distinctiveness as a Third World area in Western imagination.[93] Discounting these essentialised representations, the extent of poverty is staggering by any measure. The scale of deprivation, or the absence of capacity to overcome deprivation is palpable. World Bank estimates, for instance, place nearly 50 per cent of the rural poor in Bangladesh below the 'poverty-line', the nutritional referent of basic subsistence in mainstream development thinking.[94] By global comparison, figures for the scope of rural poverty in other countries in the region are also sobering: Nepal (61 per cent)[95], India (51 per cent), and Pakistan and Sri Lanka (both 29 per cent).[96] Allowing for regional, ethnic, and gender-based variations, the picture is more dismal for some areas, as in India's southern 'states' (provinces), such as Bihar, parts of Baluchistan in Pakistan, and for Indian Tamils in Sri Lanka.[97] Over one-half billion people fall in the category of the 'absolute' poor in South Asia, with over 400 million in India alone.[98] Largely an extension of rural poverty, but acquiring a life of its own, urban poverty is hard to calculate. As a floating population buried in slums, the urban poor provide the most palpable evidence of maldevelopment in South Asia. While rural poverty may be opaque to the outside world, globalisation renders urban squalor and poverty visible. With different magnitudes, Dhaka, Calcutta, Bombay, or Colombo embody human tragedy, but also congeal the structures of inequality in the region: the pavement and slum dwellers, alongside sky-scrapers and resorts in several South Asian cities, are a constant reminder of the scale of both poverty *and* opulence in their midst.

Until recently, few issues have received as much attention as poverty; this is reflected in the large volume of literature on the topic.[99] Three inter-linked views undergird the discussion on poverty amongst state managers and scholars, perhaps forcing a convergence in thinking and policy: the idea of subsistence, poverty as an object of policy (not political economy), and poverty alleviation as an extension of welfare.[100] Taken together, these assumptions match the current neoliberal propensity to view poverty as an *externality*, not as a social relation. Hence, the poor are those who fall below the poverty-line, a benchmark of bare subsistence. The poor are not seen as a class of people in relation to the sources of social wealth, lacking in the capacity 'to sustain a physical and emotional life' and the opportunity afforded by wealth to 'live a life informed by self-determination and the regard of others in a secure environment'.[101] Poverty is basically approached in biological, not social terms.

Second, the poor are the object of public policy, rarely of political economy.[102] In alternative NGO thinking, the participation by the poor in their own uplift is accorded centrality, in self-help organisations, financial activities,[103] or grassroots alleviation exercises.[104] Yet, NGO thinking does not escape the 'policy' approach to poverty. Condemnations of existing social and class structures, power imbalances, or hierarchies accentuated by international relations *per se* do not necessarily embody radically different approaches to development.[105] For the most part, NGOs work within established political and social structures, rather than working to dislodge them.[106]

Finally, linked to the above, the relational aspects of poverty are subordinated to its welfare dimension. The conception of poverty as a welfare problem, an alternative to a political economy formulation, draws its rationale from the historical perception of the poor as 'a threat' to the social order,[107] or a fetter to the smooth functioning of a market economy.[108] Reform is the essence of most poverty alleviation programmes, not the restructuring of society.[109] The persistence and reproduction of poverty are usually attributed to over-population or fiscal deficits; they are not seen as an *integral* feature of a market-based economy.[110] Policy considerations barely involve the capacity of dominant social structures to skew the gains of economic growth.[111] The interests of dominant propertied classes, themselves entrenched in the state, ensure that structural questions bypass poverty alleviation measures.[112]

With this background, traditional approaches to poverty alleviation in South Asia become explicable. The solution to the 'vicious circle of poverty' is productive investment or an increase in productivity.[113] The massive problem of over-population requires strategies of population control.[114] 'Traditional' culture, especially as it informs higher fertility rates, demands a 'modern' reordering of habits and preferences.[115] The culture of poverty, in turn, necessitates the education of the poor to escape destitution.[116] The burden of history is clearly at odds with policy.[117] This is not to suggest that structural determinants of poverty – asset ownership or access to employment – have been neglected;[118] these elements simply do not inform the core aspects of policy.

Broadly, three statist strategies of poverty alleviation have been advocated in South Asia: policies that have attacked poverty indirectly via macroeconomic growth, 'maximizing the rate of growth of GNP [Gross National Product]';[119] policies targeting the poor as a distinct group requiring special treatment 'through rural development, small industries and labour-intensive rural works programmes'; and policies calling for a 'radical redistribution of assets through land reforms, nationalization of big industries, and so on'.[120] Invariably, the 'trickle-down' approach has been followed, producing uneven effects.[121] The explosion of the urban poor in South Asian cities can be attributed in part to these effects, which appear in the form of rural landlessness and overall diminished possibilities on the land.[122]

Unable to generate requisite levels of employment or to distribute assets, the state has been largely incapable of defying dominant class interests, with familiar consequences. For instance, the existence of tenancy (either of the fixed-rent or share-crop variety) affects the distribution of social assets.[123] Patterns of land distribution are discernably connected to poverty.[124] Without assets, the majority of the poor have been unable to participate in the market. Given social rigidities, economic growth in South Asia has not produced 'a silent revolution.'[125]

Direct assaults on poverty usually take the form of measures to help the most vulnerable groups, especially women and children.[126] Food subsidies and health care (for example, immunisation) have been the chief form of anti-poverty intervention.[127] Yet, gender-based inequities have ensured that these measures lag behind the growing incidence of poverty, especially among women. Evidence shows that there have been appreciable increases in the number of female-headed households.[128] Migration of male family members in search of employment, the disintegration of the 'joint family system', divorce, widowhood, separation, or desertion may be some of the reasons.[129] Gender-based poverty is also more immediately linked to inequality in food consumption between men and women (with less food intake for women).[130]

Key to the globalising logic now operative in South Asia is the restructuring of the state and the emphasis on agents in civil society and their transnational linkage *via* an emerging GCS.[131] The twin processes of liberalisation and privatisation necessitate a restructuring of the state.[132] Ironically, the state is implicated in its own demotion. With a background of over-centralised planning, often resulting in fiscal crises, poor management of the economy, economic waste in the public sector, and an inability to deliver services, the state must now accommodate private agents of capital, both domestic and global.[133] Stagnation in the development budgets of the state provides a natural window of opportunity for NGOs to step in.[134] On the other hand, direct links to NGOs facilitate globalisation by creating transnational bridgeheads *outside* the state.

Congealed in *structural adjustment*, as elsewhere, South Asians listen to the same tune: liberalisation of the 'national' economy, privatisation or denationalisation, and devaluation.[135] Undeterred by domestic opposition, the state in South Asia is not only spearheading adjustment, it is also being reconstituted.[136] Key to the transformation is the realignment of the national economy to the global economy and the role of the state as a facilitator for market processes. Significantly, the role of development planning itself is in question.[137] In the new order, planning is reduced to a set of measures to enforce fiscal discipline, to create possibilities for integrating the national to the global economy, and to soften the impact of globalisation.

To contextualise, poverty alleviation is coming under heavy strain. The effects of globalisation on poverty in the region can be linked to the specific form of economic restructuring promoted by global financial institutions. Two areas where the impact is perceptible concern the role of labour and social programmes. The 'unprotected' worker seems to be the new vanguard of reform.[138] On the other hand, debt burdens and IMF conditionality impel changes in welfare regimes. Although there are regional and country-wide variations,[139] there are also common elements to the character of restructuring under conditions of globalisation. These include a reduced state capacity in economic matters, especially in the area of employment *via* public spending, and greater subordination of 'national' decision-making to international financial institutions or to global capital.[140] In a broader sense, globalisation also involves economic liberalisation under regimes of procedural democracy; denationalisation and elevation of both the (official) private and informal sector; and greater receptivity towards global capital, information technology, and West-centred cultural norms and practices.[141] Though supportive of democratic political practice, the new orthodoxy makes few demands for reducing military expenditures, relaxing political surveillance, or curtailing the coercive apparatus of the state.[142]

Within the framework of macro management and institutional change, structural adjustment programmes (SAPs) hinge upon the market for the provision of solutions to economic and social problems.[143] In South Asia, SAPs have consisted of the now familiar package of economic reforms: deregulation of the economy and privatisation; fiscal discipline, which usually means reduced public expenditures; new trade regimes premised on devaluation to propel exports; and 'open door' policies towards global capital.[144] Given the highly unequal structures of asset ownership, access to education, and political power, *adjustment* has produced skewed results.[145]

The *social* aspect of these reforms reveals a picture of uneven impact.[146] Those who can be valorised in the burgeoning global market have successfully adjusted, including big industrialists, large land owners, and highly skilled professionals.[147] On balance, the burden has fallen heavily on social groups least able to join the race to the market.[148]

The burden of cuts in public expenditure has hit social programmes (for example, health care and education) that benefit the poor.[149] While defence budgets remain healthy, the reduction in subsidies on food items, transportation, utility charges, and fertilisers, for instance, have adversely, if unevenly, affected the urban poor and poor farmers and tenants.[150] Deregulation of the economy has revitalised some sectors of the economy, but also driven out local firms in the face of stiff foreign competition.[151] Efficiency considerations have generated unprecedented levels of unemployment and underemployment in both the public and private sectors.[152] On the other hand, industrial upgrading, wage cuts, and the retrenchment of workers in the public sector reveal a bias against labour.[153]

Conclusion

The root of economic restructuring lies in the dismantling of the post-colonial social compact between state and society, and between dominant classes and the vast majority of the dispossessed.[154] A new transnational alliance is being constructed involving global capital, a neoliberal state, and the dominant classes.[155] Unlike the previous era in which labour and trade unions were important *political* players in virtually all South Asian nations, the new hegemony makes no such pretensions.

Economic globalisation in South Asia assigns NGOs of different hues a new role in development.[156] Yet, given the limitations of these organisations, they are unlikely to replace the state as the mainstay of poverty alleviation. Unable to question the structures of power and inequality, their role cannot escape their reformist character.[157] Paradoxically, attempts to reduce the role of the state in development produce the conditions that enhance the need for greater state intervention. This may also be the case for South Asia.

In the era of globalisation, social polarisation and social indifference go hand in hand.[158] Reinforcing a new mood of indifference is the deepening *cultural* polarisation between the globalising few and the marginalised many.[159] Resistance to globalisation, therefore, appears inextricably tied to a repudiation of West-centred cultural homogenisation.

The cultural divide in South Asia gives poverty an entirely new character. Deprivation and destitution are not expressed only in lower food intake or the absence of shelter, clothing, clean water, or access to medicine and education, but also in the awareness of a potential disintegration in the idea of community itself; the logic of market globalisation and its local counterpart in exchange-based social relations undermine cohesion. The capacity for self-determination is likely to diminish with a breakdown in social connectedness.

Pre-dating global integration, poverty has been a durable feature of South Asian society.[160] Under new conditions, however, it assumes a distinctive form. Though material want remains the central dimension of poverty, in a globalising *cultural* context, deprivation becomes more palpable. Poverty is crystallised in the context of attempts by the upper and middle echelons of society to seek validation in the idiom of a globalising culture.[161] Indigenous resources of consolation are solicited,[162] while received rationalisations of under strain.[163] Non-material dimensions of poverty accentuate its material properties, as globalisation makes cultural polarisation an inseparable attribute of deprivation. In short, the race to competitiveness is likely to produce a new kind of social indifference, undermining social cohesion.

NOTES

I am indebted to Ritu Vij and two anonymous reviewers for valuable comments and suggestions on this paper. Tyler Attwood provided useful assistance; his help is duly acknowledged.

1.   V.G. Kulkarni, 'The Middle Class Bulge', *Far Eastern Economic Review*, (Vol. 156, No. 2, 1993), pp. 44–6.

2.   In 1992, the Human Development Index (HDI) ranking of the five major nations of South Asia was as follows: Sri Lanka=97; Pakistan=128; India=134; Bangladesh=146; and Nepal=151. See *Human Development Report 1995* (New York: Oxford University Press, published for the United Nations Development Programme, 1995), p. 20.

3.   According to one estimate, 'India has the largest concentration of rural poverty of any country in the world'. See Robert Chambers, N.C. Saxena, and Tushaar Shah, *To The Hands Of The Poor* (Boulder, CO: Westview Press, 1990), p. 3.

4.   Kartik Roy, 'Rural-Urban Migration in South Asia', *Journal of Contemporary Asia* (Vol. 22, No. 1, 1992), pp. 57–72.

5. Throughout the first two decades since Independence, poverty occupied a central place in academic and policy discussions. The preoccupation today is with reform. See Romesh Diwan, 'Economic Reforms as Ideology', in Special Section: Review of Political Economy, *Economic and Political Weekly* (Vol. 30, No. 30, 1995), pp. 73–86.

6. See Atul Kohli, *Democracy and Discontent: India's Growing Crisis of Governability* (Princeton, NJ: Princeton University Press, 1990), and Ayesha Jalal, *Democracy and Authoritarianism in South Asia: A Comparative and Historical Perspective* (Cambridge: Cambridge University Press, 1995).

7. , *op. cit.*, in note 5, pp. 77–81. There also appears to be convergence among different paradigms of liberalisation. See E. Sridharan, 'Economic Liberalisation and India's Political Economy: Towards a Paradigm Synthesis', *Journal of Commonwealth and Comparative Politics* (Vol. 31, No. 3, 1993), pp. 1–31.

8. For instance, in the Indian context, this sentiment is reflected in the 'There Is No Alternative' (TINA) group. See T. Krishna Kumar, 'Management of Development in the Newly Emerging Global Economic Environment', *Economic and Political Weekly* (Vol. 31, No. 25, 1996), p. 1598.

9. According to Robert Cox, internationalisation of the state refers to 'the global process whereby national policies and practices have been adjusted to the exigencies of the world economy of world production'. Robert W. Cox, *Production, Power, and World Order: Social Forces in the Making of History* (New York, NY: Columbia University Press, 1987), p. 253.

10. The literature on globalisation is vast. For useful critical perspectives and for various aspects of global restructuring, see Stephen Gill, 'Globalisation, Market Civilisation, and Disciplinary Neoliberalism', *Millennium: Journal of International Studies* (Vol. 24, No. 3, 1995), pp. 399–423, and James H. Mittelman (ed.), *Globalization: Critical Perspectives* (Boulder, CO: Lynne Rienner, 1996). On social forces, see Cox, *op. cit.*, in note 9. Time-space compression and the proliferation of new identities are best captured by David Harvey, *The Condition of Postmodernity* (Oxford: Basil Blackwell, 1989), and Mike Featherstone (ed.), *Global Culture: Nationalism, Globalization and Modernity* (London: Sage Publications, 1990), respectively.

11. Stephen Gill, 'Political Economy and Structural Change: Globalizing Elites in the Emerging World Order', in Yoshikazu Sakamoto (ed.), *Global Transformation: Challenges to the State System* (Tokyo: United Nations University Press, 1994), pp. 169–99.

12. John Gray, *After Social Democracy* (London: Demos, 1996). For a contrary view, see Paul Hirst and Grahame Thompson, *Globalisation in Question: The International Economy and the Possibilities of Governance* (Cambridge: Polity Press, 1996).

13. In the context of the hegemony of global capital, the political idiom of this order, 'new constitutionalism', also seems more permissible than expansive constructions of democratic governance. See Gill, *op. cit.*, in note 10, pp. 412–14.

14. On the link between globalisation and localisation, see Jonathan Friedman, 'Being in the World: Globalization and Localization', in Featherstone (ed.), *op. cit.*, in note 10, pp. 311–28.

15. Gill, *op. cit.*, in note 10.

16. he market is closed to those with nothing of (market) value'. David P. Levine, *Wealth and Freedom: An Introduction to Political Economy* (Cambridge: Cambridge University Press, 1995), p. 114. The poor, as Zillur Rahman notes, are 'enmeshed in varying ties of dependence and unequal power relations which have the effect of severely circumscribing the fundamental assumptions of free choice and perfect competition'. Hossain Zillur Rahman, 'Rethinking the Poverty Debate', in Hossain Zillur Rahman and Mahabub Hossain (eds.), *Rethinking Poverty: Bangladesh as a Case Study* (New Delhi: Sage Publications, 1995), p. 24.

17. is appears to be the central objective of liberalisation, promoted by international disciplinary institutions such as the World Bank and the International Monetary Fund. See Michel Chossudovsky, 'India Under IMF Rule', *The Ecologist* (Vol. 22, No. 6, 1992), pp. 271–5.

18. Arjun Appadurai, 'Disjuncture and Difference in the Global Cultural Economy', in Featherstone (ed.), *op. cit.*, in note 10, pp. 295–310.

19. Bhikhu Parekh, 'Nehru and the National Philosophy of India', *Economic and Political Weekly* (Vol. 26, Nos. 1 and 2, 1991), pp. 35–48.

20. Chossudovsky, *op. cit.*, in note 17, p. 272.

21. Mark A. Robinson, 'Assessing the Impact of NGO Rural Poverty Alleviation Programmes: Evidence from South India', *Journal of International Development* (Vol. 4, No. 4, 1992), pp. 397–417.

22. S.P. Gupta, 'Economic Reform and Its Impact on Poor', *Economic and Political Weekly* (Vol. 24, No. 22, 1995), pp. 1305–6.

23. Mark W. Zacher, 'The Decaying Pillars of the Westphalian Temple: Implications for International Order and Governance', in James N. Rosenau and Ernst-Otto Czempiel (eds.), *Governance Without Government: Order and Change in World Politics* (Cambridge: Cambridge University Press, 1992), pp. 58–101. For a critique of the shrinking of the state in development, see Paul Streeten, 'Markets and States: Against Minimalism', *World Development* (Vol. 21, No. 8, 1993), pp. 1281–98.

24. On recent discussions of civil society, see David L. Blaney and Mustapha Kamal Pasha, 'Civil Society and Democracy in the Third World: Ambiguities and Historical Possibilities', *Studies in Comparative International Development* (Vol. 28, No. 2, 1993), pp. 3–24. Key liberal proponents of GCS include Richard Falk, *Explorations at the Edge of Time: Prospects for World Order* (Philadelphia, PA: Temple University Press, 1992); Ronnie D. Lipschutz, 'Reconstructing World Politics: The Emergence of Global Civil Society', *Millennium* (Vol. 21, No. 3, 1992), pp. 389–420; Martin Shaw, 'Civil Society and Global Politics: Beyond a Social Movements Approach', *Millennium* (Vol. 23, No. 3, 1994), pp. 647–67; and Paul Ghils, 'International Civil Society: International Non-Governmental Organisations in the International System', *International Social Science Journal* (Vol. 44, No. 133, August 1992), pp. 417–29. Authors of a different (Gramscian) persuasion include Cox, *op. cit.*, in note 9; Stephen Gill and David Law, *The Global Political Economy: Perspectives, Problems and Policies* (Baltimore, MD: The John Hopkins University Press, 1988); and Laura Macdonald, 'Globalising Civil Society: Interpreting International NGOs in Central America', *Millennium* (Vol. 23, No. 2, 1994), pp. 267–85.

25. For GCS in IR theory, see note above. For the new mood in DS concerning NGOs, see the Special Issue of *World Development* (Vol. 15, Supplement, 1987). Relevant here are also celebrations of new social movements. For an excellent critique of some recent discussions of social movements, see R.B.J. Walker, 'Social Movements/World Politics', *Millennium* (Vol. 23, No. 3, 1994), pp. 669–700.

26. David C. Korten and Antonio B. Quizon, 'Government, NGO and International Agency Cooperation: Whose Agenda?', in Noeleen Heyzer, James V. Riker, and Antonio B. Quizon (eds.), *Government-NGO Relations in Asia: Prospects and Challenges for People-Centred Development* (London: Macmillan Press, 1995). pp. 131–64.

27. On the new orthodoxy, see see Rajni Kothari, *Poverty: Human Consciousness and the Amnesia of Development* (London: Zed Books, 1993), pp. 1–31. On the elevation of NGOs as providers of security nets, see Kothari, 'Under Globalisation: Will Nation State Hold?', *Economic and Political Weekly* (Vol. 30, No. 26, 1995), pp. 1593–1603.

28. On the fragmentation of coalitions, see Kothari, 'Under Globalisation', *op. cit.*, in note 27. On the deepening of debt peonage, see Kothari, *Poverty, op. cit.*, in note 27.

29. On the revision of the social compact, see Parekh, *op. cit.*, in note 19. On the issue of political tolerability, see Kothari, 'Under Globalisation', *op. cit.*, in note 27, p. 1593.

30. On liberal IR theories, see David Long, 'The Harvard School of Liberal International Theory: A Case for Closure', *Millennium* (Vol. 24, No. 3, 1995), pp. 505, and David Lond and Peter Wilson (eds.), *Thinkers of the Twenty Years' Crisis: Inter-War Idealism Reassessed* (Oxford and New York, NY: Clarendon Press, 1995). For a review of development theories, see Arturo Escobar, *Encountering Development: The Making and Unmaking of the Third World* (Princeton, NJ: Princeton University Press, 1995).

31. The most notable sentiment here is reflected in Immanuel Kant, *On Perpetual Peace: A Philosophical Essay*, trans. F. Trueblood (Boston, MA: American Peace Society, 1897 [1795]). For a recent statement, see Michael Doyle, 'Kant, Liberal Legacies, and Foreign Affairs', Parts I and II, *Philosophy and Public Affairs* (Vol. 12, Nos. 3–4, 1983), pp. 205–35, and 323–53.

32. This line of thinking can be traced back to Adam Smith, *An Inquiry into the Nature and Causes of The Wealth of Nations* (New York, NY: The Modern Library, 1937 [1776]).

33. Arturo Escobar, 'Imagining a Post-Development Era? Critical Thought, Development and Social Movements', *Social Text* (Vol. 10, Nos. 2–3, 1992), pp. 20–56.

34. In realist discourse, the metaphor of anarchy naturalises the world order. By contrast, the liberal idea of progress relegates poorer regions to a near-natural state. For an earlier formulation of this position, see Smith, *op. cit.*, in note 32.

35. On the former, see Kenneth N. Waltz, *Man, State, and War: A Theoretical Analysis* (New York, NY: Columbia University Press, 1959). On the latter, see Ronald L. Meek, *Social Science and the 'Ignoble Savage'* (Cambridge: Cambridge University Press, 1976).

36. Hedley Bull's conception of the 'state of nature', it must be stressed, is more Lockean than Hobbesian. See Hedley Bull, *The Anarchical Society: A Study of Order in World Politics* (New York, NY: Columbia University Press, 1977).

37. Tzvetan Todorov, *The Conquest of America: The Question of the Other*, trans. R. Howard (New York, NY: Harper and Row, 1984).

38. The recent epithet 'quasi-states', used and developed by Robert H. Jackson, echoes this sentiment. See Robert H. Jackson, *Quasi-States: Sovereignty, International Relations, and the Third World* (Cambridge: Cambridge University Press, 1990). Similarly, the terminology of 'underdeveloped', 'developing', or 'emerging' areas in DS continues the old tradition.

39. R.B.J. Walker, *Inside/Outside: International Relations as Political Theory* (Cambridge: Cambridge University Press, 1993), especially pp. 1–25 and 104–24.

40. On this reading, the corporate structure of DS would be unimaginable without a 'developing' part of humanity, a part in need of progress to deliver it from its natural condition. On the relation between time and otherness, see Johannes Fabian, *Time and the Other: How Anthropology Makes Its Object* (New York, NY: Columbia University Press, 1983).

41. Walt W. Rostow, *The Stages of Economic Growth: A Non-Communist Manifesto* (Cambridge: Cambridge University Press, 1960).

42. Frans J. Schuurman (ed.), *Beyond the Impasse: New Directions in Development Theory* (London: Zed Books, 1993). Also, see Escobar, *op. cit.*, in note 33.

43. For a rereading of the anarchy *problématique*, see Alexander Wendt, 'Anarchy Is What States Make Of It: The Social Construction of Power Politics', *International Organization* (Vol. 46, No. 2, 1992), pp. 391–425.

44. Charles W. Kegley, Jr., and Eugene R. Wittkopf, *World Politics: Trend and Transformation*, Third Edition (New York, NY: St. Martin's Press), Part III, pp 177–348.

45. Before *dependencia* writings, development theorists had been quite content with the idea of territorially self-contained, 'national development'.

46. Charles W. Kegley, Jr., 'The Neoidealist Moment in International Studies? Realist Myths and the International Realities', *International Studies Quarterly* (Vol. 37, No. 2, 1993), pp. 131–46.

47. Lipschutz, *op. cit.*, in note 24.

48. See Björn Hettne, 'Introduction: Towards an International Political Economy of Development', Special Issue on 'The International Political Economy of Development', *The European Journal of Development Research* (Vol. 7, No. 2 1995), pp. 223–32.

49. James N. Rosenau, *Turbulence in World Politics: A Theory of Change and Continuity* (Princeton, NJ: Princeton University Press, 1990), p. 36. See also Joseph A. Camilleri and Jim Falk, *The End of Sovereignty: The Politics of a Shrinking and Fragmenting World* (Aldershot: Edward Elgar, 1992).

50. This assumption is challenged by Wendt, *op. cit.*, in note 43.

51. Liberal protagonists of GCS as diverse as Ronnie D. Lipschutz, James N. Rosenau, and Richard Falk self-consciously take human agency as a central tenet of transnational politics. See Lipschutz, *op. cit.*, in note 24; Rosenau, *op. cit.*, in note 49; and Falk, *op. cit.*, in note 24.

52. Gene M. Lyons and Michael Mastanduno (eds.), *Beyond Westphalia: State Sovereignty and International Intervention* (Baltimore, MD: John Hopkins University Press, 1995), especially Chapter 1.

53. Falk, *op. cit*, in note 24. See also Miguel Darcy de Oliveira and Rajesh Tandon, 'An Emerging Global Civil Society', in *Citizens: Strengthening Global Civil Society* (Washington, DC: CIVICUS World Alliance for Citizen Participation, 1994), pp. 1–17.

54. Lipschutz, *op. cit.*, in note 24, p. 390.

55. *Ibid.*, pp. 391–2.

56. See M.J. Peterson, 'Transnational Activity, International Society and World Politics, *Millennium* (Vol. 21, No. 3, 1992), p. 371–88.

57. *Ibid.*, pp. 377–8.

58. See Martin Shaw, 'Global Society and Global Responsibility: The Theoretical, Historical and Political Limits of "International Society"', *Millennium* (Vol. 21, No. 3, 1992), pp. 431–44.

59. Again, Falk appears to be fully cognizant of global capitalism. Yet, he does not explicitly link GCS to capitalism, but only as a reaction against it, or simply as a parallel form of transnational life. See Richard Falk, 'The Making of Global Citizenship', in Jeremy Brecher, John Brown Childs and Jill Cutler (eds.), *Global Visions: Beyond the New World Order* (Boston, MA: South End Press, 1993), pp. 39–50.

60. The classic statement here is that of Milton Friedman, *Capitalism and Freedom* (Chicago, IL: University of Chicago Press, 1962).

61. Howard H. Frederick, *Global Communication and International Relations* (Pacific Grove, CA: Brooks/Cole Publishing Co., 1992).

62. Falk, *op. cit.*, in note 59.

63. Walker, *op. cit.*, in note 39.

64. See Walker, *op. cit.*, in note 25.

65. Lipschutz, *op. cit.*, in note 24.

66. For an explicit statement of this compromise, see Shaw, *op. cit.*, in note 24.

67. Lipschutz, *op. cit.*, in note 24.

68. This point is more fully explored in Mustapha Kamal Pasha and David L. Blaney, 'Global Civil Society and Democracy in the Third World', unpublished mimeo. An earlier version of this paper was presented by Pasha at the Third Annual Conference on Democracy and Democratic Transitions, Graduate School of International Studies, University of Denver, Denver, Colorado, 15–16 April 1994.

69. Ellen Meiksins Wood correctly sees '[private] property as a distinct and autonomous locus of social power'. Ellen Meiksins Wood, 'The Uses and Abuses of Civil Society', *Socialist Register 1990* (London: Merlin Press, 1990), p. 61.

70. The prominent exception here is Falk, *op. cit.*, in note 24. However, Falk, too, tends to supply norms and practices from the West as the modular form for universal practice.

71. For instance, Lipschutz's idea of global civil society fails to acknowledge the existence of durable structures of inequality that divide rich and powerful from the poor and weak areas. Recent efforts to 'bring the Third World back' into IR theory, though eschewing a naturalised image *via* conversations of cultures, also

tend to abstract out problems of poverty or inequality. Hence, in recognizing 'difference', a new form of essentialism is advanced. See, for instance, Yosef Lapid and Friedrich Kratochwil (eds.), *The Return of Culture and Identity in IR Theory* (Boulder, CO: Lynne Rienner Publishers, 1996).

72. Falk seems to be an important exception. See Falk, *op. cit.*, in note 59.

73. Macdonald, *op. cit.*, in note 24.

74. See Stephen Gill and David Law, 'Global Hegemony and the Structural Power of Capital', *International Studies Quarterly* (Vol. 36, No. 4, 1989), pp. 475–99.

75. David Williams and Tom Young, 'Governance, the World Bank and Liberal Theory', *Political Studies* (Vol. XLII, No. 1, 1994), pp. 84–100, and Tom Young, '"A Project to be Realised": Global Liberalism and Contemporary Africa', *Millennium* (Vol. 24, No. 3, 1995), pp. 527–46.

76. See Gill, *op. cit.*, in note 10. For a background on these disciplinary institutions, see Susan George and Fabrizio Sabelli, *Faith and Credit: The World Bank's Secular Empire* (Boulder, CO: Westview Press, 1994).

77. James H. Mittelman and Mustapha Kamal Pasha, *Out From Underdevelopment Revisited* (Basingstoke: Macmillan Press, 1997), pp. 49–79.

78. Cox, *op. cit.*, in note 9, pp. 253–65.

79. Gill and Law, *op. cit.*, in note 24, especially pp. 71–80.

80. Thomas W. Dichter, 'The Changing World of Northern NGOs: Problems, Paradoxes, and Possibilities', in John P. Lewis, *et al.*, *Strengthening the Poor: What Have We Learned?* (New Brunswick, NJ: Transaction Books, 1988), pp. 177–88.

81. Lyons and Mastanduno, *op. cit.*, in note 52.

82. Recently, for instance, the World Bank and other UN agencies have elected to lend their blessing to several Third World NGOs. Other transnational actors, often with local affiliation, have also become the principal channel of Official Development Aid from rich to poor nations. See World Bank, *Annual Report 1995* (Washington, DC: Oxford University Press, 1995). Also, see Williams and Young, *op cit.*, in note 75.

83. 'At least 2,500 Northern NGOs with a Third World focus exist in the donor countries. Ten per cent of this total (about 200 organizations) have annual budgets of $1,000,000 or more'. Dichter, *op. cit.*, in note 80, p. 182.

84. Williams and Young, *op. cit.*, in note 75.

85. Dichter, *op cit.*, in note 80.

86. These may include social action groups interested in mobilizing the poor rather than implementing programmes. See Robinson, *op. cit.*, in note 21, p. 401.

87. Julie Fisher, 'Third World NGOs: A Missing Piece of the Population Puzzle', *Environment* (Vol. 36, No. 7, 1994), pp. 6–11 and 37–41.

88. As Neil Webster notes, 'contemporary arguments for decentralised democracy and non-governmental organisations taking on a greater role in rural development also have powerful ideological assumptions behind them; assumptions that reflect theories of social change and development whose roots lie primarily in western liberal philosophy'. Neil Webster, 'The Role of NGDOs in Indian Rural Development: Some Lessons from West Bengal and Karnataka', *The European Journal of Development Research* (Vol. 7, No. 2, 1995), pp. 407.

89. For instance, the World Bank instructed Bangladesh to abrogate rules that discourage the establishment of NGOs. Aubrey William, 'A Growing Role for NGOs in Development', *Finance and Development* (Vol. 27, No. 4, 1990), pp. 31–3. However, it is also fair to note that relations between the international financial institutions and Third World NGOs are not always one of collusion, collaboration, and harmony. See, for instance, Bishwapriya Sanyal, 'Antagonistic Cooperation: A Case Study of Nongovernmental Organizations, Government and Donors' Relationships in Income-generating Projects in Bangladesh', *World Development* (Vol. 19, No. 10, 1991), pp. 1367–79.

90. Webster, *op. cit.*, in note 88, p. 413.

91. Williams and Young, *op. cit.*, in note 75.

92. Aloysius P. Fernandez, 'NGOs in South Asia: People's Participation and Partnership', *World Development* (Vol. 15, Supplement, 1987), pp. 39–49.

93. S. Ambirajan, *Classic Political Economy and British Policy in India* (Cambridge: Cambridge University Press, 1978), pp. 1–26. For a more exoticised view of pre-colonial South Asia, see Arnold Lupton, *Happy India: As It Might Be If Guided By Modern Science* (London: George Allen and Unwin, 1992).

94. World Bank, *Bangladesh: From Stabilization to Growth* (Washington, DC: The World Bank, 1995), p. 12. According to one group of Indian economists, poverty is the absence of ability 'to provide a minimum nutritional diet in terms of calorie intake as well as to allow for a modest expenditure on items other than food'. See EPW Research Foundation, 'Poverty Levels in India: Norms, Estimates and Trends', *Economic and Political Weekly* (Vol. 28, No. 34, 1993), p. 1748.

95. By the most conservative estimates, between seven and eight million Nepalis live in absolute poverty. See David Seddon, 'Democracy and Development in Nepal', in Michael Hutt (ed.), *Nepal in the Nineties: Versions of the Past, Visions of the Future* (Delhi: Oxford University Press, 1994), p. 146.

96. These figures are based on the World Bank's *World Development Report 1995* (New York, NY: Oxford University Press, 1995).

97. Around 1990, the proportion of the rural population of Bihar living in poverty was about 58 per cent, over three times the proportion of the rural poor in the northwestern states of the Punjab and Haryana (18 per cent). See Gaurav Dutt and Martin Ravallion, *Why Have Some Indian States Done Better Than Others At Reducing Rural Poverty* (Washington, DC: The World Bank, 1996), pp. 1–2. For Pakistan, see Naved Hamid and Akmal Hussain, 'Regional Inequalities and Capitalist Development: Pakistan's Experience', in S. Akbar Zaidi (ed.), *Regional Imbalances and the National Question in Pakistan* (Lahore: Vanguard Books), pp. 1–42. On country comparisons, see Poona Wignaraja and Akmal Hussain (eds), *The Challenge in South Asia: Development, Democracy and Regional Cooperation* (New Delhi: Sage Publications, 1989).

98. Chossudovsky, *op. cit.*, in note 17, p. 271.

99. Recent studies include Robert Chambers, *Poverty in India: Concepts, Research, and Reality* (Brighton: Institute of Development Studies at the University of Sussex, 1988); Attar Chand, *Poverty and Underdevelopment* (Delhi: Glan Publishing House, 1987); Pramod K. Chaubey, *Poverty Measurement: Issues, Approaches, and Indices* (New Delhi: New Age International Publishers, 1995); Nona Grandea, *Adjustment and Poverty in South Asia* (Ottawa: The North-South

Institute, 1993); A.E. Punit, *Profiles of Poverty in India* (Delhi: B.R. Publishing Corporation, 1982); K.R. Ranadive, *The Political Economy of Poverty* (Hyderabad: Orient Longman, 1990); Sushma Sagar, *Poverty Measurement: Some Issues* (Jaipur: RESA Publishers, 1988); Joop Wijnandus Wit, *Poverty, Policy, and Politics in Madras Slums: Dynamics of Survival, Gender, and Leadership* (Amsterdam: Vrije Universiteit, 1993).

100. For a good summary of studies on poverty in the South Asian, and notably Indian, context, see EPW Research Group, *op. cit.*, in note 94.

101. Levine, *op cit.*, in note 16, p. 115.

102. On the need to broaden the concept, see Robert Chambers, 'Poverty in India: Concepts, Research and Reality', in Barbara Harriss, Sanjivi S. Guhan, and Robert H. Cassen (eds.), *Poverty in India: Research and Policy* (Oxford: Oxford University Press, 1992), pp. 301–32. Chambers, however, fails to avoid the pitfalls of 'measuring' poverty in fairly conventional ways.

103. Susan Holcombe, *Managing to Empower: the Grameen Bank's Experience of Poverty Alleviation* (Atlantic Highlands, NJ: Zed Books, 1995).

104. Singh Inderjit, *The Great Ascent: The Rural Poor in South Asia* (Baltimore, MD, and London: The John Hopkins University Press/Published for the World Bank, 1990); Frances Stewart, *Adjustment and Poverty: Options and Choices* (London: Routledge, 1995); Richard Jolly, 'Poverty and Adjustment in the 1990s', in John P. Lewis, *et al.*, *op. cit.*, in note 80, pp. 163–75; Tony Killick, Tony Addison, and Lionel Demery, 'Poverty, Adjustment and the IMF', in Khadija Haq and Uner Kirdar (eds.), *Human Development, Adjustment and Growth* (Islamabad: North-South Roundtable, 1987), pp. 112–37.

105. Despite rhetorical assaults on globalisation, the conception of poverty entertained in alternative statist designs has not been dissimilar; only the 'solutions' are different.

106. See Mittelman and Pasha, *op. cit.*, in note 77.

107. Bronislaw Geremek, *Poverty: A History* (Oxford: Blackwell, 1994), p. 246.

108. Martin Ravallion and Gaurav Att, 'How Important to India's Poor is the Sectoral Composition of Economic Growth?', *The World Bank Economic Review* (Vol. 10, No. 1, 1996), pp. 1–25.

109. Gupta, *op. cit.*, in note 22.

110. In radical critiques, however, there is considerable scope for challenging existing structures of inequality and treating those structures as the primary source of poverty. See A.R. Desai, (ed.), *Agrarian Struggles in India After Independence* (Delhi: Oxford University Press, 1986).

111. As John P. Neelsen notes, 'stratification structures as structures of domination imply, besides inequality of power and appropriation potential, corresponding relative opportunities for retaining or acquiring power by the particular holders of position'. John P. Neelsen (ed.), *Social Inequality and Political Structures: Studies in Class Formations and Interest Articulation in an Indian Coalfield and its Rural Heartland* (New Delhi: Manohar Publications, 1983), p. 6.

112. On resistance against land reform in Pakistan, for instance, see Hamid and Hussain, *op. cit.*, in note 97.

113. Punit, *op. cit.*, in note 99.

114. South Asia has been spared its variant of neo-Malthusian ideology in both its 'life-boat' and 'triage ethics' versions. For a statement of 'life-boat' ethics, see Garret Harden, 'The Case Against Helping the Poor', *Psychology Today* (Vol. 8, No. 4, 1974), pp. 38–43 and 123–6. The discussion of 'triage ethics' can be found in William and Paul Paddock, *Famine 1975! America's Decision: Who Will Survive* (Boston, MA: Little, Brown and Co., 1967).

115. Chaubey, *op. cit.*, in note 99.

116. Oscar Lewis, *Village Life in Northern India: Studies in a Delhi Village* (Urbana, IL: University of Illinois Press, 1958).

117. For a useful historical overview of the relation between class and economic growth in South Asia, see Angus Madison, *Class Structure and Economic Growth: India and Pakistan Since the Moguls* (London: George Allen and Unwin, 1971).

118. G.K. Kadekodi and G.V.S.N. Murty (eds.), *Poverty in India: Data Base Issues* (Delhi: Vikas Publishing House, 1992), p. 29.

119. C.H. Hanumantha Rao, *Agricultural Growth, Rural Poverty and Environmental Degradation in India* (Delhi: Oxford University Press, 1985), p. 85. This policy has included measures for labour absorption through an increase in agricultural growth or expansion of the industrial sector.

120. *Ibid.*

121. Jean Dreze, 'Poverty in India and the IRDP [Integrated Rural Development Programme] Delusion', Special Section: Review of Agriculture, *Economic and Political Weekly* (Vol. 25, No. 39, 1990), pp. 95–104.

122. Ronald J. Herring, *Land to the Tiller: The Political Economy of Agrarian Reform in South Asia* (New Haven, CT, and London: Yale University Press, 1983).

123. *Ibid.*

124. Amitava Mukherjee, *Structural Adjustment Programme and Food Security* (Aldershot: Avebury, 1994).

125. Frida Johansen, *Poverty Reduction in East Asia: The Silent Revolution* (Washington, DC: World Bank, 1993).

126. Dreze, *op. cit.*, in note 121.

127. Gupta, *op. cit.*, in note 22.

128. K. Shanthi, 'Female Poverty: Data Constraints and Issues', in Kadekodi and Murty (eds.), *op. cit.*, in note 118, pp. 210–26.

129. *Ibid.*

130. *Ibid.*

131. Kothari, 'Under Globalisation', *op. cit.*, in note 27.

132. Dalip S. Swamy, *The Political Economy of Industrialisation: From Self-Reliance to Globalisation* (New Delhi: Sage Publications, 1994), p. 256.

133. On this issue see, for instance, the World Bank-sponsored study on democracy and adjustment by Stephan Haggard and Steven B. Webb, (eds.), *Voting for Reform: Democracy, Political Liberalization, and Economic Adjustment* (New York, NY: Oxford University Press, 1994). For a critical appraisal of the Bank-sponsored democratic projects, see Williams and Young, *op. cit.*, in note 75.

134. Gupta, *op cit.*, in note 22. For a different view, see S. Guhan, 'Social Expenditures in the Union Budget: 1991–96', *Economic and Political Weekly*, (Vol. 30, Nos. 18 and 19, 1995), 1095–1101. Historically, India, for instance,

has had one of the largest NGO communities in the world. According to one author, 'NGOs engaged in rural development number around 15,000'. Robinson, *op. cit.*, in note 21, p. 399.

135. For a distinction between 'stabilisation' and 'adjustment measures', see Mukherjee, *op. cit.*, in note 124, pp. 1–17.

136. For instance, the IMF plan requires the Indian state to curtail social spending, and state subsidies and price supports; dispose of profitable public enterprises to big domestic and foreign capital, while shutting down ailing enterprises; devalue currency to spur exports and liberalise imports; reform banking and finance; and reduce capital gains tax for the rich. See Chossudovsky, *op. cit.*, in note 17, p. 46. Similar plans have been developed for Pakistan, Sri Lanka, Bangladesh, and Nepal. See Grandea, *op. cit.*, in note 99.

137. Kothari, 'Under Globalisation', *op. cit.*, in note 27.

138. Both the IMF and the World Bank have sought the repeal of minimum wage legislation and the decoupling of income from inflation. See Choussudovsky, *op. cit.*, in note 17, p. 273.

139. Haggard and Webb, *op. cit.*, in note 133.

140. Kothari, 'Under Globalisation', *op. cit.*, in note 27.

141. *Ibid.*

142. Wignaraja and Hussain (eds.), *op. cit.*, in note 97.

143. Diwan, *op. cit.*, in note 5.

144. Grandea, *op. cit.*, in note 99.

145. *Ibid.*

146. Diwan, *op. cit.*, in note 5.

147. Grandea, *op. cit.*, in note 104.

148. Economists at the IMF admit that poverty increased in the 'initial adjustment phase' in India. See Ajai Chopra, Charles Collyns, Richard Hemming, and Karen Parker, with Wousik Chu and Oliver Fratzscher, *Economic Reform and Growth*, Occasional Paper 134 (Washington, DC: International Monetary Fund, 1955), p. 23.

149. Swamy, *op. cit.*, in note 132, pp. 256–81. On the differential impact of structural adjustment on social spending, see K. Seetha Prabhu, 'The Impact of Structural Adjustment on Social Sector Expenditure: Evidence from India', in C.H. Hanumantha Rao and Hans Linnemann (eds.), *Economic Reforms and Poverty Alleviation in India* (New Delhi: Sage Publications, 1996), pp. 228–54.

150. Although subsidies on food, fertiliser, and electricity in India have still not been removed and are, in absolute terms, much larger in every case in 1996 than in 1991, in real terms, they have declined. See Guhan, *op. cit.*, in note 134. In Sri Lanka, for instance SAP reduced coverage of food stamp recipients by 50 per cent. Grandea, *op. cit.*, in note 99, p. 17.

151. Grandea, *op. cit.*, in note 99, p. 17.

152. Gupta, *op. cit.*, in note 22, p. 1300.

153. World Bank, *Jobs, Poverty, and Working Conditions in South Asia* (Washington, DC: World Bank, 1995).

154. Rajni Kothari, 'Capitalism and the Role of the State', in Ghanshyam Shah (ed.), *Capitalist Development: Critical Essays* (Bombay: Popular Prakashan, 1990) pp. 115–36.

155. *Ibid.*

156. Anil Bhatt, 'Voluntary Action in India: Role, Trends and Challenges', *Economic and Political Weekly* (Vol. 24, No. 16, 1995), pp. 870–3.

157. Shashi Pandey, 'Role of Voluntary Action in Rural India', *South Asia Bulletin* (Vol. 4, No. 2, 1984), pp. 38–47.

158. Kothari, *Poverty, op. cit.*, in note 27.

159. *Ibid.*

160. Sanjivi S. Guhan and Barbara Harriss, 'Introduction', in Harriss, Guhan, and Cassen (eds.), *op. cit.*, in note 102, p. 1.

161. On the new hedonism amongst Pakistan's moneyed upper class, see Samina Ibrahim, 'Let the Good Times Roll', *Newsline* (Vol. 3, No. 7, 1992), pp. 69–73, and Sairah Irshad Khan, 'Days of Wine and Roses', *Newsline* (Vol. 3, No. 7, 1992), pp. 74–8.

162. 'As the state, in effect, withdraws from its responsibility and surrenders its autonomy, civil society in these lands is thrown on its own resources.' Kothari, *op. cit.*, in note 153, p. 130.

163. In a palpably Social Darwinist context, it becomes virtually impossible to sustain a fatalist belief in naturally hierarchical orders of abject destitution and obscene affluence.

8. Globalisation, Poverty, and the Promises of Modernity

Julian Saurin

Those who have eaten their fill speak to the hungry of the wonderful times to come.[1]

Recall the face of the poorest and weakest man whom you may have seen and ask yourself if the step you contemplate is going to be of any use to him. Will he gain anything by it? Will it restore him to a control over his own life and destiny?...then you will find your doubts and your self melting away.[2]

It has become a truism that the study of international relations, and, consequently, the types of explanations of international action and behaviour which have been put forward, have almost exclusively submitted to the deference of the already-powerful. In general terms, the study of international relations, including World Order Studies, has proceeded with only cursory attention to the so-called 'developing states'.[3] The persistent focus upon 'great powers' remains as strong as ever. There has been almost no reference to the international analysis of poverty. Thus, when some conclude that, 'with all these theories...the bodies keep piling up',[4] one may derive two immediate conclusions: first, that it is *because* of these theories that the bodies keep piling up; and second, that the normal and routinised way in which the bodies keep piling up, that is, through poverty, is disregarded or considered to be outside the frame of the IR theoretical discourse.

Thus, we may begin with a simple indictment of International Relations (IR): how can one give credence to a discipline which purports to explain international action and international order, when it has *almost nothing* to say about seventy-five per cent of the world's states, and simply discounts from its analysis eighty-five per cent of the world's population? What philosophy of history, what theory of social change, what notion of human agency does such a staggering omission entail? Should we understand from such a systematic exclusion that the existence and actions of eighty-five per cent of the world's population do not, in actual fact, matter to the proper and adequate explanation of international relations? Is this exclusion and invisibility mere oversight?

It is generally acknowledged that, in addition to its claim to the monopoly of legitimate violence,[5] the state's attempted monopolisation of the means of legitimate representation is self-serving; that is, the state portrays forced social change in a manner both favourable to itself and which effects the subversion of alternatives. Whilst important interpretative disputes continue unabated over the politics of representation and the deconstruction of discourse, the raw material for the study of IR has remained these self-representations.[6] This neutralisation of criticism[7] is evident to the extent that, in normal IR discourse, the lives of the poor and powerless – who are no less constitutive of the real world – are systematically ignored or are abandoned to 'the enormous condescension of posterity'.[8]

We have traditionally understood IR to be the study of interstate relations. Slowly, the disciplinary gatekeepers have reluctantly extended the terms of enquiry to include relations between states and intergovernmental organisations, and even to state-firm relations.[9] Notwithstanding more catholic understandings of IR, it is clear that the state remains the irreducible constituent of IR and the almost exclusive object of enquiry for IR. Other agents are usually taken into consideration only to the extent that they impinge upon the operation of the state.

Prompted by John Davis,[10] when posing the question of who are the agents of social change in IR, and when admitting the possibility that states (particularly those states occupying the north-west quadrant) are not the only agents, we should ensure that the agents which are admitted to this new history and this new explanation of social change are not admitted *only because they are implicated in the dominant history*. Instead, we need to recognise the autonomous history they possess and experience. Very briefly, I wish to put forward and then assume the case that we should not rely upon an interpretive strategy of deconstruction which purports to reveal to us that the powerful continue to represent themselves in a favourable light, and, in so doing, marginalise (and construct) the alien Other. Rather, we need to show, first, why 'underdogs' do not themselves insert their lives into the orthodox 'narrative home'; and, second, how, by uncovering the lives of subordinated peoples and collectivities, we may understand the more complex construction of world order and the particular experience of development and poverty. By so doing, we should be in a better position to address the questions 'what is development' and 'what is poverty', but also to understand how globalisation reconstitutes development and poverty, as well as to demonstrate the common experience of a global modernity.

Following Davis' warning, the more inclusive IR that will be proposed in this article should not be based on '[a] purely interpretive account of history, maintaining that social order came to be so because people construed their history in one way or another, [because this] seems to miss the uninterpretably determining power of the past'.[11] We have to locate world development, and, hence, international relations, with a keen sense of history which recognises the powerful structuring forces of the capitalist world economy[12] and the continuing legacy of classical imperialism.[13] In drawing this analysis out of the development of the world economy and the history of imperialism – which are not reducible to state policy – we can begin to understand IR as the study and explanation of the way that social life *tout court* is organised globally. To do this, however, I argue that we must develop a method which examines both how people organise the production and reproduction of their own lives, and how people *understand* and *articulate* their understanding of that production and reproduction of their own lives, including the global structuring of production and reproduction.[14] In this way, one is able to recognise and use the vast real history of international relations which has been lost due to the obsession with the state. This is a lost history – the lost eighty-five per cent – which is made up of the global organisation of the lives of 'ordinary' peoples.[15] This loss has not occurred through some epistemological trickery or absent-minded negligence, but as a result of a clear organisation of knowledge and a readily discernible division of intellectual labour which can be explained through a materialist sociology of knowledge.[16]

This article, therefore, has two main purposes. The first is to identify *how* the 'people without history', to use Eric Wolf's uncompromising phrase, have been lost to IR.[17] From an examination of the official accounts of development, one is readily able to understand how IR has absorbed a particular and exclusionary narrative of development, that is, development expressed in a definite ideological form. Of course, as noted above, mainstream IR has paid little explicit attention to questions of development. Nevertheless, mainstream IR has proceeded with an implicit and unspoken idea of development, expressed in such broad terms as the primacy of economic growth, international competitiveness, the expansion of international trade, and the regulation of interdependence.[18] In questioning the origin, portrayal, and derivation of the narrow and partial 'public transcript' of development which is used in IR, we will be able to see how the transference of ideas and knowledge about the world – from Development Studies (DS) to IR – has served to reinforce the refusal to accord time and space to the analysis of subordinate peoples.

Having identified the origin and form of this neglect, the second part of the article seeks to develop and identify why it is important to be able to recover this lost history, and to *propose a distinct approach* to the study of global development which draws on critical realist interpretations. In this respect the proposal entails the 'reinsertion of moral values and political purpose into social theory', which, at the same time, is scientific, normative, and emancipatory in intent.[19]

In the first part, then, I wish to demonstrate that the 'lived experience' of development fails to correspond with the official story of development.[20]

Borrowing from E.P. Thompson, I argue that there is now, and has been for some time, a process – to which we typically give the name 'development' – of global organisation or global ordering

> of the daily experience of working people, of the structural transformations and dislocations that produced industrial capitalism, its modes of expropriation and exploitation manifested in changing patterns of work, leisure and communal solidarity, together with the cultural and political responses engendered by them.[21]

This global organisation is characterised by the articulation of power through a host of social agents and structures, amongst which one can count the state and the states-system. The objective, then, in the second part is to propose a way in which we can begin to comprehend, record, interpret, and act politically upon the daily experience of working people in a manner which relies upon sub-altern accounts of the concrete conditions and potentialities of life.[22]

Ideology and Development: The Development of the State

This first part of this article sets out the official or 'public transcript' by which we have come to recognise development and the condition of poverty. Though drawing on a wide body of literature, a number of key arguments are compressed here to indicate the critical direction of the argument. First, with respect to the constitution of modernity, one needs to place in the foreground the experience of rapid and permanent social change which has been constitutive of capitalist transformation across three centuries, and which provoked not just a radically new unilinear sense of history (in contrast to pre-modern society), but the very idea of progress itself.[23] Second, capitalism is, historically speaking, the first world order, in so far as capitalism as a mode of socio-economic organisation encompasses the entire geographic space of the globe (albeit neither comprehensively nor with equal intensity).[24] The worldwide states-system, which post-dates the global spread of capitalism, can be seen as largely derivative of capitalism. That is to say that the worldwide states-system has emerged as the *political* form through which capitalism is regulated.[25] It is an order which, in an important sense, is not the consequence of individual will or of policy, that is to say, the outcome of a deliberate act or acts, but needs to be explained in terms of specific historical structures of accumulation.[26] It is within this first universal project that a reflexive temporalisation, which distinguished qualitatively[27] (and not just chronologically) between the modern and the pre-modern, and which thereby entailed a sense of its own historicity and self-realisation, became possible. Whatever the contending ideas of progress – whatever political fraction held the upper hand at any given moment – the new common arrogance of the modernist aspiration and the presumption of the modernist projects[28] were not in doubt: the world could be made a better place (hope was this-worldly rather than other-worldly) and, crucially, political-economic programmes devised through systematic (and violent) abstraction would guarantee these improvements.[29] The historical development of the modern state is not just coincidental with the rise of capitalism, but as the political form of capitalism, it bears witness to the necessary wilful regulation of capitalist accumulation.

A reminder of the recorded results of the world organisation of daily life is necessary but difficult, in view of the typically abstract evidence available to us. The UNDP 1992 *Human Development Report* is a useful starting point. The poorest 60 per cent of the world's population receives no more than 5.6 per cent of total world income, whilst the richest fifth benefits from at least 82.7 per cent of world income.[30] Absolute as well as relative disparities in income are becoming even more accentuated across the world (including in the UK, where inequality of income is the most acute for over a century).[31] In an apparently transformed globalised world, celebrating the victory of capitalism, the poorest 20 per cent of the world's population receives only 0.2 per cent of global commercial bank lending, 1.3 per cent of global investment, 1 per cent of global trade and 1.4 per cent of global income.[32] As US consumers spend $7.5 billion on 'lawn care' products and $9 billion on children's video games per year, US overseas aid stood at £10.1 billion per year (1989–91).[33] A quarter of the world's population does not have access to safe water; at least 12 million infants died before the age of five in 1992, with a further 175 million under-fives suffering malnutrition.[34] Brazil, the eighth 'richest' economy in the world, has two-thirds of its rural population and over one-third of its urban population classified as poor.[35] The UNDP classifies poverty through an 'absolute poverty line' whereby 'the income or expenditure level below which a minimum, nutritionally adequate diet plus essential non-food requirements are not affordable'.[36] Thus, on a statistical reading alone, the close of the twentieth century confounds the promise of all that capitalist modernity claims to bring. Contrary to the *fin de siècle* celebrants to the holy trinity of liberalism, capitalism, and possessive individualism, for most people around the world, the daily experience of capitalist development is of growing poverty and increasingly acute poverty. It is this tragic reality 'of capitalist world development which comprises the lost history of international relations'.[37]

Whilst such data provides some broad indications of the scale of the inequalities characteristic of the world order, development statistics should be treated with caution. The discourse of development has been strongly shaped by the politics of indicators, which, in turn, reflect foundational questions of evidence, epistemology, and the burden of proof. Thus, for example, the use of GNP growth rates and GNP per capita as measures of developmental well-being have been described as 'the most powerful indicators of development to date'.[38] *Au contraire*, such data is not only extremely limited as a measure of the human condition, but often grossly misleads both the enquiry into, and the description of, that condition, not least because of the tendency to fetishise the question of development.[39] These important abstractions are unable to record the insecurities which characterise capitalist development, nor to reflect the permanent revolt against development.[40] For example, though indicators of household food security (calculated by the UNDP as a percentage of total household consumption) may point to the scale of the problem, the crucial particular local and global social relations which constitute the problem are overlooked.[41] If the path of development is marked by abstract indicators, then the consequence is to confuse the symbolic representation for the substantive experience.

The disputes in the discourse of development appear, at first sight, to derive from differences in semantic use. For example, the long-running debate over the utility and accuracy of phrases such as 'third world', or the dualism invoked in the terms 'South-North' or 'developing' and 'developed', or even the terms 'rich' and 'poor', suggests a narrow problem of classification or definition that can ultimately be resolved empirically, by asking where different states rank on key economic indicators.[42] I want to argue, however, that the dualistic vocabulary which characterises these disputes cannot be resolved semantically, but reflect more fundamental political commitments and a sense of world historical change.

There are essentially two stories that can be told about development, and by contrasting their recent history, both the substantive experiences of development and the implied senses of agency and change may be discerned. It is upon this contrast that the argument here focuses. The first story is that from which orthodox IR takes its evidence, and can be characterised as the 'official' story. Insofar as the official story is also the public record of historical change, it reflects the centrality of the state in the organisation of development. The official story of development is recounted at a considerable level of abstraction, which, in itself, reflects a fundamental violence in the name of development.[43] A telling and pervasive example of the role of the state in the unfolding of development is the universal practice of classifying indicators of development in state (or national) league tables, as if the essential contours of development were self-evidently contained within sovereign territorial spaces.[44] Thus, a universal presumption has been that progress could be measured through comparative sets of abstracted national statistics. 'Development', understood as a national and nationalist project of the modern state, is, of course, a key aspect of the discourse of development.[45] Further, a key assumption of the official story is that development is a benign project for benevolent motives, directed at the collective good. In this way, for example, massive displacements and relocations of people in the name of development and the collective good has marked the *transmigrasi* of Indonesia, the Narmada dam projects of India, and the Three Gorges Dam project in China.[46] Thus, the ills of the world are, in this view, reduced to policy failures, mistakes, or obstacles and impediments to be removed or overcome. Certainly, the idea that it is development policy itself which may systematically produce the ills of the world is an alien notion.

However, another story of development is to be told which is sub-altern in provenance and hidden from scrutiny unless wilfully sought. The story of development, as expressed through 'infrapolitics', or 'resistance that avoids any open declaration of its intentions',[47] to use James Scott's analysis, is all the same *real* politics,

> [but] under the conditions of tyranny and persecution under which most historical subjects live, it *is* political life. And when the rare civilities of open political life are curtailed or destroyed, as they so often are, the elementary forms of infrapolitics remain as a defense in depth of the powerless.[48]

It is only through a close examination of such infrapolitics that one will find wholesale evidence and testimony that contradicts the claim that, with the exception of notable development failures and mistakes, the world is being made into a better place.[49] In this second story, the prevailing notion that the poor – that is, most of the world's population – are simply hapless victims of fate, devoid of any historical agency, and marginal to the constitution of modern capitalist society, is refuted. This is not an attempt to diminish, let alone deny the profound weakness and insecurity which is constitutive of poverty. It serves instead, to demonstrate the central contradiction that modern poverty is a direct consequence of the organisation of the exploitation of labour and the transformation of nature, in which the state is severely implicated.[50] Thus, while state policy as public policy has attenuated the more extreme effects of global capitalism in social democratic states since about 1945 (albeit by transferring many excesses beyond its borders),[51] its primary function has been, and continues to be, the attempted reconciliation and legitimation of an historically-specific mode of accumulation.

The Development of Poverty

Having outlined the terms of the enquiry, and having sought to indicate the broad claims for the centrality of an 'infrapolitical' analysis, I want to turn to a characterisation of world development from which the public transcript can be recognised, but from within which the hidden transcript of infrapolitics can be drawn.

In common parlance, development is strongly associated with a strategy which takes polities from conditions of poverty to situations of wealth. Invariably, this is understood as a material change, a material improvement. The liberal conception of the state held that public policy is formulated for the public good and that poverty is the stimulus for development policy. The historical moment – the inter-War period – in which development strategies were formalised is quite clear:[52] the introduction of the Soviet planned economy, the promotion of New Deal programmes in the USA, and the establishment of Western European social democratic institutions, were all confirmed internationally through the post-War Keynesian orthodoxy. For example, the arrival of the 'science' of development, namely, development economics, 'did not arise as a formal theoretical discipline, but was fashioned as a practical subject in response to the needs of policy makers to advise governments on what could and should be done to allow countries to emerge from chronic poverty'.[53]

Colin Leys accurately identifies, through the distinctive rhetorical fashions, the sequence of development trends from the 1950s onwards, as passing from an objective of 'high-mass consumption', to the less ambitious 'catching-up', to the modest 'redistribution with growth', to the altogether resigned 'basic needs' approach.[54] This last phase, overseen by the man who had endeavoured to cluster bomb and napalm any needs – basic or otherwise – out of the Vietnamese, nevertheless gave way to a development strategy which entailed the complete abandonment of any commitment to equity or democracy, and which presaged the thorough naturalisation of the market and the final surrender of development to the whim of the market.[55] Whether 'development' was to be applied to war-torn Europe or to the colonial world, two ideological presuppositions that were evident at the outset were gradually subverted over four decades: first, that poverty could, in principle, be eliminated through the implementation of dedicated policies; and second, that the state was the agent responsible for such policies and the agent most able to implement them.

In the first presupposition, poverty was generally understood as a vestige of lack of development, or as the innate limitation on demand characteristic of pre-modern, that is, pre-capitalist, social organisation.[56] In a direct sense, poverty revealed a society that was under-developed. The foundation of development policy lay in a diagnosis of 'backwardness', wherein underdevelopment reflected a generalised lack of demand and capital scarcity.[57] Policies ranging from Keynesian counter-cyclical demand management, to import-substituting industrialisation, to the creation of regional economic communities have been premised on the drive to simultaneously stimulate and regulate the increase in aggregate demand. The underlying assumption of development economics – from neoclassics to orthodox Marxism – has been that an increase in physical output will, *mutatis mutandis,* yield greater economic welfare.[58] A necessary corollary of this foundational assumption has been that economic growth is an essential precondition of greater economic welfare.[59] Invariably, this type of macro-economic assumption has been, through a process of reduction, applied to the diagnosis and prescription of the local, familial, or individual economy.

In the second presupposition, development strategy was predicated on the public regulation of capital accumulation on a national basis. Its international twin was the Bretton Woods system, notwithstanding its extremely patchy record and a host of inconsistencies. Having identified the key attributes of the underdeveloped condition, and the requirements of development, world development proceeded through a politics of copying.[60] Thus, Gerald Meier argues that '[public] planning was viewed as a mechanism to overcome deficiencies of the market price system and as a means of enlisting public support to achieve national objectives', and that, '[f]rom the emphasis on capital accumulation, industrialisation and planning, there emerged a case for foreign aid. The resource gap between the domestic investment required to fulfil the development plan's target growth rate and the possible amount of domestic savings would be filled by foreign aid'.[61] Poverty reduction was to be achieved primarily through policies which stimulated economic growth, and only secondarily through minor redistribution. Mark Rupert puts the matter succinctly: 'the core of the world economy was reconstructed on the basis of a limited generalisation of affluence made possible by institutionalising mass production and mass consumption in the advanced industrial economies'.[62] At no time was the root cause of poverty addressed, nor was the notion entertained that economic growth itself generated poverty. Furthermore, both presuppositions share the notion that development is, first and foremost, a material and *economic* problem, and that the primary (if not exclusive) role of the state is in the regulation of economic activity.[63]

Just as the inter-War and post-War periods represented the reorganisation of the institutional and production exchange relations of capitalism through inter-*national* regulation,[64] so the restructuring arising in the late 1970s, and continuing through the 1980s and 1990s, has entailed a reorganisation *via global* regulation. This global regulation, which has been characterised by privatisation and the reassertion of private interest, has not entailed the retreat or erosion of the state. As Leys argues,

[t]he era of national economies and national economic strategies is past – for the time being, at least. With capital free to move where it wishes, no state (and least of all a small poor one) can pursue any economic policy that the owners of capital dislike. Economic planning, welfare systems and fiscal and monetary policies all became subject to control, in effect, by the capital markets, signalled, in the case of Third World countries, by the conditions attached to IMF/World Bank

lending – *precisely the situation the Bretton Woods system was designed to prevent.*[65]

A measure of this degree of global transformation is the nostalgic and faintly nonsensical hope contained in the appeal to 'Keynesianism in one country'. Massive public support (or subsidy) as part of the regulatory programme had been vital for the accumulation process of private capital. With privatisation and the accelerating global centralisation of capital, the public subsidy has not been removed, but often massively increased.[66] Thus, our attention should not be deflected into a discourse on the state which seeks to contrast a pristine private realm against a pure public realm in which the terms of debate are limited to discussing transfer of ownership techniques: these are the terms of ideological propaganda. Rather, examination should be led by what is currently

> entirely missing from the picture [are]...the actual centres of concentrated wealth and power, the people and institutions that determine what happens in the social and economic order and largely dominate the state, either by direct participation or imposition of narrow constraints on political choice, converting governmental authority into a powerful and interventionist 'nanny state' that cares for their needs with much solicitude.[67]

The terms of enquiry are not set by an attempt to explain the supposed decline of state power or the demise of the interventionary state. Instead, the enquiry should be prompted by the question of how state power has been transformed, and how capital – particularly in the form of corporate power – has secured to itself the nannying services of the state.

Not for the first time, the poor were the barometer of political economic restructuring. The rise to prominence of a highly interventionary IMF during the 1970s as a *de facto* regulator of development, followed by the widespread introduction of structural adjustment programmes under the direction of the World Bank,[68] represented a reshaping of international capital regulation, whose first and permanent casualty was the global poor. As Keith Griffin and John Knight rightly observed, where a cut in public expenditure is absolutely unavoidable, the costs of this should be borne by those most able to do so.[69] This priority had been one of the achievements of the democratic labour and socialist movements of the first half-century in the construction of polities that approximated a welfare state. However, over the last two decades, almost exclusively the opposite has occurred: that is, 'human development programmes have been savagely cut and the brunt of the adjustment have fallen on the poor. This has weakened long-run prospects for development while increasing inequality and poverty'.[70]

The subversion of public policy by, on the one hand, international governmental development organisations with a neoliberal agenda, and, on the other hand, by domestic and international private capital, has had the effect of undermining the premise of post-War development strategy. Ley writes that,

> [b]y the mid-1980s the real world on which 'development theory' had been premissed had...disappeared. Above all, national and international controls over capital movements have been removed, drastically curtailing the power of states everywhere, but especially in the Third World. As a result most states could no longer be the prime movers of development that 'development theory' had hitherto always presupposed, and none of the alternative candidates (such as social movements or communities) proposed by 'development theorists' as the field unravelled were very convincing.[71]

This subversion, or global political-economic reconstruction, has, according to the neoliberal orthodoxy, ensured that production, allocation, and distribution of resources is to be determined principally by the 'market' and not by the 'state'. If one supposes for just one minute that this is a plausible option, then a brief reflection on the history of development – essentially economic development – will demand that the economic function of the state is, in future, assigned a marginal role in development. If so, what is left for that state in the promotion of development?

Against the new orthodoxy, following Trevor Blackwell and Jeremy Seabrook, the defining aspiration of institutionalised critics of neoliberalism (that is, official opposition parties, or new 'Labour' governments), is not to attack capitalism as the cause of poverty, but only to manage the economy.[72] However, even this responsibility has been surrendered to the market. Writing about the official British opposition, though applicable to almost all social democratic parties in OECD states, Larry Elliott comments that,

> [a]s far as the opposition is concerned, the days when a national government could manage demand or ensure full employment are long gone. Globalised capital markets mean that all 'centre left' government can offer is some education, some training and a bit more research and development, then let the market get on with it.[73]

The ideological reaction of recent years has been marked by a profound restoration of the naturalisation of poverty coincident with the naturalisation of the market. By 'naturalisation', I mean that poverty has come to be understood as both inevitable and irremovable, part of the natural, even eternal, order of things. Thus conceived, state attempts to regulate or ameliorate the condition of poverty are reconstructed as futile obstacles to progress. Elliott identifies this shift in the policy emphasis of the state, which has corresponded to political changes across the world, as follows:

> having decided that it can no longer regulate the economy, [the state is] left with a bit of a vacuum. Governments have to do something. So Labour has a new idea. It will regulate people instead, imposing a panoply of social controls to ensure that the problems caused by an uncontrollable deregulated economy – crime, juvenile delinquency, family breakdown – don't threaten the comfortable lifestyles of its new middle-class constituency.[74]

Concluding Discussion: Development as Political Struggle

To summarise so far, the foundations of post-War development policy were premised on the central role of the state in the economic development of national economies. The post-War convention held that poverty could be, in principle, reduced – possibly even eliminated – through the implementation of appropriate public policy. Today, however, the foundations of this development order have been subverted by the neoliberal assault on the state and the naturalisation of the market, which have resulted in the denial of public responsibility for poverty alleviation. The pivotal question in contemporary development is identified by Leys:

> [w]hat is at stake is…nothing less than whether human beings can act, collectively, to improve their lot, or whether they must once again accept that it is ineluctably determined by forces – nowadays 'world market forces' – over which they have, in general, little or no control (and least of all those who need it most).[75]

If the terms of public policy are indeed set by the social protection of the few, itself contingent upon the abandonment of the many, then the central questions of development are thrown into sharp relief. If the indicators of progress remain gross material gains, overall rates of growth, and relative competitiveness, irrespective of the social relations and social conditions upon which such growth is predicated, then not only are fundamental normative issues of development brought to the fore, but essential questions of legitimation are raised. Amartya Sen, prompted by Immanuel Kant's injunction to see human beings as ends in themselves and not to regard them instrumentally, critically notes that the analysis of development frequently takes the form of focusing on production and prosperity as the essence of progress, treating people as the means through which that productive progress is brought about, rather than seeing the lives of people as the ultimate concern and treating production and prosperity merely as means to those lives.[76]

In this respect, development, conceived as a national and international project, resulted in the production of a set of public, or official, accounts, or 'transcripts', telling the story of development. The failure of the state to eliminate poverty has not been because, as the neoliberals claim, it sets public policy an impossible task. Instead, the failure of public policy to eliminate poverty arises from two principal errors. First, the failure arises through the disregard by public policy of the 'real' experience of development, that is, the conduct and change in daily livelihoods. The apparent silence of the poor should not be taken as evidence either of their absence, or of their consent to the benign neglect of development policy. The abstract history of development does not deal with real lives. As Raff Carmen writes,

> [p]eople, after all, have always been present in their own lives; their consciousness need not be 'raised' by an external lever; nor do they need 'empowering' by an external source. People are only too aware what their problems and their sufferings are: they live them, breathe them, bear them every day. Their culture of silence is not the silence of those who cannot talk or cannot act. If they are silent, it is because they have been made silent, not by acts of God, but by acts of man.[77]

Second, public policy has failed because the official story of development – whether of the post-War Keynesian orthodoxy or the later neoliberal reaction – fails to acknowledge that the combined and uneven development of capitalism across the world itself produces, of necessity, extremes of inequality and pervasive poverty. Such poverty is not natural but social, and insofar as it reflects historically particular social relations, it is neither permanent nor inevitable. Thus, development, properly understood, must be viewed as a global process of the historical transformation of capitalism and beyond.

Whereas the official story of development, complete with the neoliberal *volte-face*, is an account shot through with the assumptions and logic of capitalism, we need, in Ellen Meiksins Wood's phrase, to 'distance ourselves from the assumptions of capitalism and reveal its structures in the daily transactions of social life'.[78] From these daily transactions, we will be able to acknowledge 'that subordinates can fully recognise the full extent to which their claims, their dreams, their anger is shared by other subordinates with whom they have not been in direct touch'.[79]

Since development policy has been predicated on a mistaken analysis of the nature of (capitalist) economic growth, and has based policies and programmes on abstracted data, the assumptions of capitalism have been internalised or naturalised. The result has been the failure to ask foundational questions. The continuing crisis in development and the failure to fulfil the promises of development have simply led to the implementation of yet more and more measures and remedies which were at the root of failure in the first place. A central part of the official story entails the dismissal of the real lives of people as substantive evidence of development, or rather, maldevelopment. Whereas the official story of development, of 'progress from above' which 'describes the open interaction between subordinates and those who dominate'[80] may be termed the 'public transcript', the disregarded evidence can be termed, following James Scott, the *hidden transcript*. The hidden transcript 'characterizes discourse that takes place offstage beyond direct observation by powerholders'; it is that activity which is composed of the frustration, anger, contempt, despair, hope, and dreams which underlie the 'conformity in the face of domination...[which is] a question of suppressing a violent rage in the interest of oneself and loved ones'.[81] It is here, then, where, if we take the trouble of distinguishing the public transcript from the hidden transcript, we would not only be able to identify active sites of resistance, but would also be able to recognise the host of immanent alternatives to capitalism.

In adopting Scott's analysis, one can see that the neglect of infrapolitics and the hidden transcript is in large part a reflection of the articulation of material and representative power contained in the public transcript. He argues that

> [t]he 'official transcript' as a social fact presents enormous difficulties for the conduct of historical and contemporary research on subordinate groups.... [T]he great bulk of events, and hence the great bulk of archives, is consecrated to the official transcript. And on those occasions when subordinate groups do not put in an appearance, their presence, motives, and behaviour are mediated by the interpretation of dominant elites.[82]

Indeed, the modernist assumption that a vital element of social progress is the expansion of knowledge is contradicted by the politics of development where the growth of ignorance is a necessary corollary. On what basis can this claim be made?

First, if, as Quarles van Ufford rightly maintains, '[t]he official statements are part of a power struggle, with the government trying to impose a standardised representation of what is happening in local society on to the people in question', it follows that, '[a]s political statements, the images of the local scene also serve to legitimise the role of government itself'.[83] Thus, the representation of backwardness, conservatism, idleness, helplessness, and 'basket cases' provides the context within which external agents are obliged to act. Ignorance of the reality of local history is thereby a prerequisite of such self-styled 'benign' intervention, whether by state or by market. As Karl Marx pointedly remarked, the bourgeois error lay in its belief 'that the particular conditions of its liberation are the only general conditions within which modern society can be saved'.[84]

Second, the treatment of history as that which is laid open by the public transcripts – self-serving representations of the progress of development[85] – is the *modus operandi* of IR, the consequence of which is to elevate historical agency as the monopoly of the rich and powerful, and, correspondingly, to deny identity, let alone agency, to the poor and 'powerless'. One consequence of this is to portray progress as the realisation of the desiderata and grace and favour of the rich, rather than as the hard-fought and permanent struggle of the poor.

For example, agricultural innovation, which has been most successfully exploited by already economically and politically powerful landholders, does indeed raise productivity.[86] Moreover, the official transcripts record this as evidence of development. However, as many investigations have shown, in so doing, not only is the gulf in market competitiveness between the small- and medium-size landholders and the wealthy exacerbated, but it results in often permanent land expulsions, household insecurity, exclusion, and abandonment.[87] However, '[i]gnorance…becomes an important asset for those who are engaged in policy processes. Lack of insight into what is actually going on [in the daily lives of people] in the 'implementation' process in fact becomes of paramount importance'.[88] Consider, for example, Marx's careful commentary on the tension between increased production and the impoverishment of labour:

> [t]he worker becomes poorer the more wealth he produces, the more his production increases in power and extent. The worker becomes an ever cheaper commodity the more commodities he produces. The *devaluation* of the human world grows in direct proportion to the *increase in value* of the world of things. Labour not only produces commodities; it also produces itself and the worker as a *commodity*.[89]

The public development transcript addresses the increase in production as the measure and record of development. The proportionate devaluation of the worker – experienced as pay cuts, forced migration, seasonal poverty, unemployment, longer working hours, job insecurity, bullying, 'compelled dullness', hazardous working conditions, and ill health, together with the subjection to wage slavery – which is experienced and contained in the hidden transcript, does not conventionally form the evidence of development.

The ease with which analysis is drawn towards the consideration of official development is a function of the availability of the public transcript. It is the public transcript as the domain of the development statistics – from growth in manufacturing output to average male earnings, from per capita expenditure on primary education to hospital waiting lists – to which we are bound to refer that simultaneously deters us from the often inaccessible, difficult to interpret, often 'subjective' hidden transcripts which reflect the development of real lives. 'In social investigation and measurement', as Sen wisely advises, 'it is undoubtedly more important to be vaguely right than to be precisely wrong'.[90] To be vaguely right here is to attempt to place in the foreground the immediate experience of development.

Third,

> [t]aking a long historical view, one sees that the luxury of relatively safe, open political opposition is both rare and recent. The vast majority of people have been and continue to be not citizens, but subjects. So long as we confine our conception of *the political* to the activity that is openly declared we are driven to conclude that subordinate groups essentially lack political life or that what political life they do have is restricted to those exceptional moments of popular explosion. To do so is too miss the immense political terrain that lies between quiescence and revolt and that, for better or for worse, is the political environment of subject classes. It is to focus on the visible coastline of politics and miss the continent that lies beyond.[91]

It is in the pursuit of the exploration of the lost continent of subordinated groups that one may redirect the purpose and mode of IR enquiry. Thus, if we seek to comprehend how and why loss of control and autonomy, loss of freedom, loss of self-realisation, and loss of self-determination has grown apace, at the same time as the achievements of world capitalist development are trumpeted, the answers lie, surely, in the organisation of the daily lives of ordinary people. To adopt Eduardo Galeano's metaphor of world development, '[t]hey train you to be paralysed, and then sell you crutches'[92]; it is as if the public transcript is the marketing department's pitch for the sale of crutches. The analysis of the hidden transcript will tell us how and why paralysis came about, how it is resisted, and how paralysis may be overcome without resort to the technical fix.

To a very large extent, the arguments that are now commonly deployed with respect to globalisation, which emphasise the novelty and intensity of complex relationships and exchanges and which allegedly radically constrain the autonomy of sovereign and other actors, are plausible only on the basis of a profound historical amnesia. That is to say, most states and most national economies have always been subject to strong disciplining and intervention from external agents and processes. Such interpretations have succeeded in transforming – in sharp contradiction to the lived experience of subordinate classes across the world – the curious historical oversight of five centuries of imperialism into an irrelevant intellectual anachronism.

One can readily acknowledge that the contemporary reformation of the world, perhaps bearing the epithet 'post-Westphalian', is a strikingly unsurprising acceleration of '[a] market-driven and multidimensional process, [in which] globalisation renders obsolete invented divisions of the world into developed and developing countries, industrialised and industrialising nations, and core and periphery'.[93] The material divisions which mark the lives of people are poorly reflected by the implied binary logics of 'North-South', 'developed-developing', and so on. Indeed, this dualistic discourse which characterises DS exemplifies the obscuring of real lives which is the consequence of abstraction. Derek Sayer categorically identifies the violence of abstraction to which this article has sought to draw attention, when he writes that 'the ultimate measure of the awesome power, and the fundamental violence, of unfettered abstraction is to be found in the millions upon millions of nameless corpses which this most vicious of centuries has left as its memorial'.[94] DS and IR must be conducted with a keen sense of history which means locating the debates within the rise and development of capitalism, which is essentially an uneven yet combined process. This article has argued that IR has proceeded on the basis of an extremely partial history of development which has considered only the dubious public transcript. Second, this article has suggested a distinct approach to promote an understanding of development which proceeds on a twofold basis: (1) that IR should address the *global organisation* of social life, and (2) that it should do so primarily through the use of hidden transcripts as the raw material by which development is comprehended and appreciated. For IR to continue to neglect questions of development, and then to heed only the public transcript when attention is paid to questions of development, is indefensible. This is not a question of obeying or resisting the intellectual division of labour. Why should we, in IR, be bothered about development? Again, returning to Leys, as he borrows from Marx, '*[d]e te fabula narratur*' – this story is about you.[95]

NOTES

This article represents one strand of the research pursued by the author, under the title 'Globalisation, Modernity and Environmental Degradation: The International Relations of Knowledge and Causation of Global Environment Change', whilst Research Fellow of the ESRC's Global Environmental Change Programme. The support of the Programme is gratefully acknowledged. In addition I would like to thank John Simpson and Caroline Thomas of the Mountbatten Centre, University of Southampton, for providing me with an opportunity to present an early version of this paper. I have also benefited greatly from discussions with my Sussex colleagues Marc Williams, Laura Chrisman, and Pinar Bedirhanoglu.

1. This line from Bertolt Brecht forms the epigraph to *The Indian Economy* (London: Granada, 1978), written by my respected Sussex colleague, Pramit Chaudhuri, who died in summer of this year.

2. Mahatma K. Gandhi, quoted in 'The Faces of Poverty' in *International Year for the Eradication of Poverty* (New York, NY: UN Department of Public Information, 1996).

3. One indicative set of evidence showing this neglect can be found in the publishing record of three core IR journals. A rapid survey of *International Organisation, International Studies Quarterly*, and the *Review of International Studies* reveals that, since 1990, of approximately 450 articles published, only 60 contained reference to developing states. Of these references, only 10 dealt explicitly with development related questions very broadly interpreted. Where reference to developing states did occur it was typically of an extremely cursory and superficial nature, with external intervention, security analysis, and questions of sovereignty dominating such references. With notable exceptions, references to developing states were limited to the portrayal of these states as passive objects of international action: zones of intervention, or zones of instability and crisis requiring management. This pattern of exclusion was punctuated by interesting work by Ted Gurr, 'People Against States: Ethnopolitical Conflict and the Changing World System', *International Studies Quarterly* (Vol. 38, No. 3, 1994), pp. 344–78; Peter Uvin, 'Regime, Surplus and Self-interest: The International Politics of Food Aid', *International Studies Quarterly* (Vol. 36, No. 3, 1992), pp. 293–312; and Bruce Moon and William Dixon, 'Basic Needs and Growth Welfare Trade Offs', *International Studies Quarterly* (Vol 36, No. 2, 1992), pp. 191–212. Of course, there are notable exceptions to this dominance: for example the work of Marc Williams and Caroline Thomas. See Williams, *International Economic Organisations and the Third World* (Hemel Hempstead: Harvester Wheatsheaf, 1994), and Thomas, *In Search of Security: The Third World in International Relations* (Boulder, CO: Lynne Rienner, 1987). Even the studies on 'world order' and international structure were scant in their consideration of 'developing states'. For example, the special issue of *International Studies Quarterly* (Vol. 40, No. 3, 1996) on 'Evolutionary Paradigms in the Social Sciences', most notably the article by George Modelski, 'Evolutionary Paradigms for Global Politics', pp. 321–42, pays no explicit attention to developing states and their specific constitution of world order. Needless to say, where developing states received even cursory treatment, the world's poor receive no mention at all.

This reflects the complete invisibility of poverty to IR.

4. Marysia Zalewski, 'All These Theories Yet the Bodies Keep Piling Up: Theories, Theorists and Theorising', in Steve Smith, Ken Booth, and Marysia Zalewski (eds.), *International Theory: Positivism and Beyond* (Cambridge: Cambridge University Press, 1996), pp. 340–53.

5. See, amongst many others, Max Weber, *From Max Weber*, ed. and trans. H. Gerth and C. Wright Mills (London: Routledge, 1970); F.H. Hinsley, *Sovereignty* (Cambridge: Cambridge University Press, 1986); and Janice Thomson, 'State Sovereignty in International Relations: Bridging the Gap Between Theory and Empirical Research', *International Studies Quarterly* (Vol. 39, No. 2, 1995), pp. 213–33.

6. For example, the work by Cynthia Weber, *Simulating Sovereignty* (Cambridge: Cambridge University Press, 1995); James Der Derian and Michael Shapiro (eds.), *International/Intertextual Relations: Postmodern Readings of World Politics* (Lexington, KY: Lexington Books, 1989); and Jim George, *Discourse of Global Politics: A Critical (Re)Introduction to International Relations* (Boulder, CO: Lynne Rienner, 1994). However, the claimed radicalism of the deconstructionists has to be treated with considerable scepticism, insofar as they too, *start* their analysis with the self-representation of the powerful. Though the error may be mine, my research to date has failed to identify any original empirical research conducted by scholars in this tradition. Where is the empirical investigation of the real lives of the 'powerless'? One is left in a state of alarm when a leading advocate of the post-modernist turn in IR prefaces a leading example of this method with the licence, '[o]ur method...allows us to emphasize interpretation without concern for the constraints of evidence'. James N. Rosenau, in Rosenau (ed.), *Global Voices: Dialogues in International Relations* (Boulder, CO: Westview, 1993), pp. ix–x.

7. I argue that this is a cooption or neutralisation to the extent that such criticism can easily be rendered safe by dismissing the analysis as one of 'talking about talking'. See, for example, William Wallace, 'Truth and Power, Monks and Technocrats: Theory and Practice in International Relations', *Review of International Studies* (Vol. 22, No. 3, 1996), pp. 301–22. Fred Halliday also exhorts higher calibre research as the foundation of theory when he bemoans the 'bad IR *and* bad philosophy of social science' of the last decade which he dismisses as 'meta-babble'. See Fred Halliday, 'The Future of International Relations: Fears and Hopes', in Steve Smith, Ken Booth, and Marysia Zalewski (eds.), *op. cit.*, in note 4, pp. 340–53. Instead of the meta-babble test, one might apply an inelegant but critical test to deconstruction by asking the question, 'what has this got to do with the price of butter?' In other words, what can the new scholasticism tell us about the capacity of, say, the poor to exercise effective demand or retain entitlements to staple foods. Aijaz Ahmad provides an effective criticism of post-modern scholarship with respect to literary and cultural theory, though it has striking resonance in IR as well. See Aijaz Ahmad, *In Theory: Nations, Classes, Literature* (London: Verso, 1992).

8. This is E.P. Thompson's phrase from *The Making of the English Working Class* (Harmondsworth: Penguin, 1980), quoted in Ellen Meiksins Wood, 'Custom Against Capitalism', *New Left Review* (No. 195, 1992), p. 21.

. Susan Strange and John Stopford, *Rival States, Rival Firms: Competition for World Market Shares* (Cambridge: Cambridge University Press, 1991).

0. John Davis, 'History and the People Without Europe', in Kirsten Hastrup (ed.), *Other Histories* (London: Routledge, 1992), pp. 14–28.

1. *Ibid.*, p. 16.

2. See, amongst many others, Kees van der Pijl, 'Ruling Classes, Hegemony and the State System', *International Journal of Political Economy* (Vol. 19, No. 3, 1989), pp. 7–35; Michel Aglietta, 'World Capitalism in the Eighties' *New Left Review* (No. 136, 1982), pp. 25–35; Robert Cox, *Production, Power and World Order* (New York, NY: Columbia University Press, 1987); Immanuel Wallerstein, *The Capitalist World Economy* (Cambridge: Cambridge University Press, 1979); Alain Lipietz, *Miracles and Mirages: The Crises of Global Fordism* (London: Verso, 1987); Andrew Sayer and Richard Walker, *The New Social Economy: Reworking the Division of Labour* (Oxford: Blackwell, 1992); Michael Redclift, *Wasted: Counting the Costs of Global Consumption* (London: Earthscan, 1996); and Joni Seager, *Earth Follies: Feminism, Politics and the Environment* (London: Earthscan, 1993).

3. See, for example, Victor Kiernan, *America: The New Imperialism, From White Settlement to World Hegemony* (London: Zed, 1978); Victor Kiernan, *The Lords of Human Kind: European Attitudes to the Outside World in the Imperial Age* (London: Weidenfeld and Nicolson, 1967); Edward Said, *Orientalism* (Harmondsworth: Penguin, 1978); Edward Said, *Culture and Imperialism* (London: Vintage, 1993); Mark Curtis, *The Ambiguities of Power: British Foreign Policy Since 1945* (London: Zed, 1995); Frank Furedi, *The New Ideology of Imperialism* (London: Pluto, 1994); Basil Davidson, *The Black Man's Burden: Africa and the Curse of the Nation-State* (London: James Currey, 1992); or the many works of Noam Chomsky, for example, *World Order: Old and New* (London: Pluto, 1994).

4. The inspiration is clearly Marxist in origin, and has recently been well expressed for students of IR in Hazel Smith, 'The Silence of Academics: International Social Theory, Historical Materialism and Political Values', *Review of International Studies* (Vol. 22, No. 2, 1996), pp. 191–212.

5. In part, this article parallels some of the arguments made by Justin Rosenberg in 'Isaac Deutscher and the Lost History of International Relations', *New Left Review* (No. 215, 1996), pp. 3–15. Not least of the similarities is the explicit rejection of the post-modern and post-structuralist turn. This is evident in Rosenberg's article when he insists that the concrete and impersonal expressions of capitalism will disappear as a result of 'a process of social transformation, not one of cognitive reformulation' (p. 14).

6. Broadly stated, a materialist sociology of knowledge rests on the Marxist notion of the manner in which knowledge about the social world is constructed and deployed. The construction and deployment of this knowledge reflects definite material interests and modes of production. It stems, in general terms, from Karl Marx's claim that 'consciousness must be explained from the contradictions of material life, from the conflict existing between the social forces of production and the relations of production'. See Karl Marx, *A Contribution to a Critique of Political Economy* (London: Lawrence and Wishart, 1970), p. 20.

17. Eric Wolf, *Europe and the People without History* (Berkeley, CA: University of California Press, 1982).

18. See, for example, Robert O. Keohane, *After Hegemony: Cooperation and Discord in the World Economy* (Princeton, NJ: Princeton University Press, 1984); Stephen Krasner, *Structural Conflict: The Third World against Global Liberalism* (London: University of California Press, 1985); and Susan Strange, *States and Markets* (London: Pinter, 1988).

19. Smith, *op. cit.*, in note 14, p. 193.

20. The purpose and approach that I propose here, which seeks to recover the 'real experience' of development, should *not* be confused with that which purports to express hitherto marginalised 'global voices'. James N. Rosenau asks, '[a]mong the many global voices claiming to depict what moves the course of events, how does one go about selecting the most coherent, the most incisive, the most meaningful?' His method is to 'allow ourselves the license to posit some of the main voices presently seeking to be heard'. See Rosenau, *op. cit.*, in note 6, p. ix. This license extends no further than safe, imaginary, professional intellectuals, but dares not give voice to uncontrollable, real, labour organisers, trade unionists, community workers, housemaids, slum dwellers, farm hands, and assembly plant operators, amongst others.

21. Wood, *op. cit.*, in note 8, p. 21.

22. 'Subaltern' refers to the generality of subordinated classes or groups that represent a challenge to the hegemonic order of society. Thus, following Kirsten Hastrup, attention to the accounts and explanations of political, economic, and social action from subaltern groups follows from the recognition of the need 'to rewrite world history as a non-domesticated multiple history'. See Hastrup (ed.), *op. cit.*, in note 10, p. 3.

23. For a range of fine discussions see Barbara Adam, *Time and Social Theory* (Cambridge: Polity Press, 1990); Zygmunt Bauman, *Modernity and Ambivalence* (Cambridge: Polity Press, 1991); William Connolly, *Political Theory and Modernity* (Oxford: Blackwell, 1988); Anthony Giddens, *The Consequences of Modernity* (Cambridge: Polity Press, 1990); and Ellen Meiksins Wood, 'Part 1 Historical Materialism and the Specificity of Capitalism', in *Democracy against Capitalism: Renewing Historical Materialism* (Cambridge: Cambridge University Press, 1995), pp. 19–180. It is worth picking out here two central attributes of modernity. First, that the modern project was characterised, in Bauman's words, by the 'legislative ambitions of philosophical reason, the gardening ambitions of the state [weeding out aliens], and the ordering ambitions of applied sciences'. See Bauman, pp. 15–16. The legislative ambitions of modernity are nonetheless impossible to attain, since fragmentation, recategorisation, and problem-solving planning produce, in Bauman's words, the false hope of the ever receding *foci imaginarii* which 'like all horizons, the quicker is the walking the faster they recede. Like all horizons they never allow the purpose of walking to relent or be compromised. Like all horizons, they move continuously in time and thus lend the walking the supportive illusion of destination, pointer and purpose'. See Bauman, p. 10. See also Immanuel Wallerstein, 'Development: Lodestar or Illusion?', in Leslie Sklair (ed.), *Capitalism and Development* (London: Routledge, 1994) pp. 3–20.

24. The incompleteness and the uneven penetration of capitalist relations is an important part of the vitality of capitalism, and a central part of the account of resistance to capitalism and the possibility of alternatives to capitalism. Thus, the 'internal' incompleteness of capitalist relations forms the major distinctiveness of the household economy and the domestic labour question. The external incompleteness of these relations is marked by the longevity of that political-economic practice known as the peasantry.

25. For example, see Michel Aglietta, *A Theory of Capitalist Regulation* (London: New Left Books, 1979), and Robert Brenner and Mark Glick, 'The Regulation Approach: Theory and History', *New Left Review* (No. 188, 1991), pp. 45–70.

26. The constraints of space prevent elaboration of this important point, but structures of accumulation are understood here to refer to the organisation of routines of life, habitual practices, and rhythms of production and reproduction. See, amongst others, the arguments developed by Marshall Sahlins, *Culture and Practical Reason* (Chicago, IL: Chicago University Press, 1976).

27. 'Modernity' must be distinguished primarily in qualitative terms, as a distinctive quality of social experience, rather than in chronological terms, not least to make sense of uneven world development. See Peter Osborne, 'Modernity is a Qualitative, Not a Chronological, Category', *New Left Review* (No. 192, 1992), pp. 65–84. For an excellent excursus of Marx and Weber see Derek Sayer, *Capitalism and Modernity: An Excursus on Marx and Weber* (London: Routledge 1991).

28. See Bauman, *op. cit.*, in note 23.

29. For details of international policy and programmes see, for example, Edward A. Brett, *International Money and Capitalist Crisis* (London: Heinemann, 1983); Eric Helleiner, *States and the Reemergence of Global Finance* (Ithaca, NY: Cornell University Press, 1994); and Alastair I. Macbean and P.N. Snowden, *International Institutions in Trade and Finance* (London: Allen and Unwin, 1987).

30. UNDP, *Human Development Report, 1992* (Oxford: Oxford University Press, 1992), p. 35.

31. Peter Townsend, *The International Analysis of Poverty* (Hemel Hempstead: Harvester Wheatsheaf, 1993), especially Chapter 10.

32. UNDP, *op. cit.*, in note 30, p. 3.

33. World Resources Institute, *World Resources, 1994–1995: A Guide to the Global Environment* (Oxford: Oxford University Press for World Resources Institute, UN Environment Programme, UN Development Programme, 1994), p. 5.

34. UNDP, *Human Development Report, 1995* (Oxford: Oxford University Press, 1995), especially Table 3: 'Profile of Human Deprivation', pp. 160–1.

35. *Ibid.*, Table 12: 'Wealth, Poverty and Social Investment', pp. 178–9.

36. *Ibid.*, p. 223.

37. Rosenberg, *op. cit.*, in note 15, p. 10.

38. World Bank, *World Development Report* (Washington, DC: World Bank, 1992).

39. 'Fetishism' as 'forms of appearance' is used here in the Marxist sense. Norman Geras provides a relatively clear understanding of fetishism when he writes that 'the peculiar relationships of capitalism wear a mask. This gives rise to illusions concerning the natural provenance of these powers. Yet the mask is no illusion....they are objective social forms, simultaneously determined and

obscuring the underlying social relations. This is how capitalism *presents itself:* in disguise'. See Geras, in Tom Bottomore, Laurence Harris, Victor Kiernan, and Ralph Miliband (eds.), *A Dictionary of Marxist Thought* (Oxford: Blackwell, 1983), p. 165. In this context, the familiar indicators of development mask the real relations of exploitation which constitute those abstract data, and serve to deflect enquiry and even recognition from those central social relations.

40. See, for example, Trevor Blackwell and Jeremy Seabrook, *The Revolt against Change: Towards a Conserving Radicalism* (London: Vintage, 1993), and Raff Carmen, *Autonomous Development: Humanising the Landscape* (London: Zed, 1996). The International Labour Organisation has recently coined a new descriptor of development: 'jobless growth', that is, 'when a country's GDP grows with no substantial job growth'. See the ILO Press Releases, 'Global Unemployment Crisis Continues: Wage Inequalities Rising Says ILO', 26 November 1996, http://www.ilo.org/english/235press/pr/96-40.htm.

41. For a range of studies, see, for example, Helen Young and Susan Jaspars, *Nutrition Matters: People, Food and Famine* (London: Intermediate Technology, 1995); Mark Hubbard, *Improving Food Security* (London: Intermediate Technology, 1995); Jane Pryer and Nigel Crook, *Cities of Hunger: Urban Malnutrition in Developing Countries* (Oxford: Oxfam, 1988); Mohsuddin Alamgir and Poonam Arora, *Providing Food Security For All* (London: Intermediate Technology, 1991); Susan Stonich, *'I Am Destroying the Land': The Political Ecology of Poverty and Environmental Destruction in Honduras* (Boulder, CO: Westview, 1993); David Keen, *The Benefits of Famine: The Political Economy of Famine and Relief in Southwestern Sudan, 1983–1989* (Princeton, NJ: Princeton University Press, 1993); Bill Rau, *From Feast to Famine: Official Cures and Grassroots Remedies to Africa's Food Crisis* (London: Zed, 1991); Philip McMichael, *Food and Agrarian Orders in the World Economy* (Westport, CN: Greenwood, 1994); Philip McMichael (ed.), *The Global Restructuring of Agro-food Systems* (Ithaca, NY: Cornell University Press, 1994); and Harriet Friedmann, 'The Political Economy of Food: A Global Crisis', *New Left Review* (No. 197, 1993), pp. 29–57.

42. For the politics of indicators, see, amongst others, Peter Bartelmus, *Environment, Growth and Development: The Concepts and Strategies of Sustainable Development* (London: Routledge, 1994). Also see the explanatory notes by which indicators are calculated or derived in UNDP, *Human Development Report* (various years), and World Bank, *World Development Report* (various years).

43. See Joeke Schrijvers, *The Violence of 'Development': A Choice for Intellectuals* (Utrecht and New Delhi: INDRA and Kali for Women, 1993).

44. The tension evident in recording indicators of development in national league tables is instructive of the dialectics of development; at the same time that globalised capitalist socio-economic relations are increasingly acknowledged, the anachronistic form of territorialist recording persists. For the outline of this argument, see Julian Saurin, 'The End of International Relations? The State and International Theory in the Age of Globalisation', in John Macmillan and Andrew Linklater (eds.), *Boundaries in Question: New Directions in International Relations* (London: Pinter, 1995), pp. 244–61.

45. See Immanuel Wallerstein, *Unthinking Social Science: The Limits of Nineteenth-Century Paradigms* (Cambridge: Polity Press, 1991), especially Part 2.

46. Edward Goldsmith and Nicholas Hildyard (eds.), *The Social and Environmental Effects of Large Dams* (Camelford: Wadebridge Ecological Centre, 1992).
47. James Scott, *Domination and the Arts of Resistance: Hidden Transcripts* (London and New Haven, CT: Yale University Press, 1990) p. 220.
48. *Ibid.*, pp. 200–1.
49. Though this is an uncompromising and categorical portrayal of the hegemonic claim, it is not made for rhetorical effect. For example, the ease with which the phrase 'the lost decade of development' has entered our language, as though it was 'mislaid', has rendered the entire continent of Africa a 'basket case' or, more frequently, simply forgotten. See Colin Leys, 'Confronting the African Tragedy', *New Left Review* (No. 204, 1994), pp. 33–47. Africa features in IR primarily as a zone of anarchy, hunger, and 'intervention'. As Lady Bracknell may have been prompted to say, '[t]o lose one decade can be said to be a misfortune, but to lose two is downright carelessness'. See Oscar Wilde, *The Importance of Being Earnest* (London: Benn, 1980).
50. See the excellent work of Peter Dickens, *Society and Nature: Towards a Green Social Theory* (London: Harvester Wheatsheaf, 1992), and especially Dickens, *Reconstructing Nature: Alienation, Emancipation and the Division of Labour* (London: Routledge, 1996). See also Ted Benton, 'Marxism and Natural Limits: An Ecological Critique and Reconstruction', *New Left Review* (No. 178, 1989), pp. 51–86, and David Goodman and Michael Redclift, *Refashioning Nature: Food, Ecology and Culture* (London: Routledge, 1991).
51. See, by way of example, Redclift, *op. cit.*, in note 50, and Wolfgang Sachs (ed.), *Global Ecology.* (London, Zed, 1990).
52. See Colin Leys, *The Rise and Fall of Development Theory* (London: James Currey, 1996); John Toye, *Dilemmas of Development* (Oxford: Blackwell, 1993); and David Moore and Gerald Schmitz (eds.), *Debating Development Discourse: Institutional and Popular Perspectives* (Basingstoke: Macmillan, 1994).
53. Gerald Meier, 'Introduction: The Formative Period', in Meier and Dudley Seers (eds.), *Pioneers in Development* (London: IBRD/Oxford University Press, 1984), p. 4.
54. Leys *op. cit.*, in note 52, pp. 3–44.
55. One useful indicator of the broad shifts in international development strategy are the annual *World Development Reports* compiled by the World Bank.
56. See Leys, *op. cit.*, in note 52, *passim.*
57. Diana Hunt, *Economic Theories of Development: An Analysis of Competing Paradigms* (New York, NY: Hemel Hempstead, 1989).
58. See Meier (ed.), *op. cit.*, in note 53.
59. As Blackwell and Seabrook critically observe, '[m]uch of what passed for socialism effectively said "[i]f you want us to go along with this, you'll have to make it worth our while". This was sometimes glorified as the struggle at the point of production, but any serious alternatives to such bargaining were banished to the realm of dreams, of utopias, of visions'. Blackwell and Seabrook, *op. cit.*, in note 40, p. 15.
60. For useful critiques, see Ozay Mehmet, *Westernising the Third World: The Eurocentricity of Economic Development Theories* (London: Routledge, 1995); Cristovam Buarque, *The End of Economics? Ethics and the Disorder of Progress* (London: Zed, 1993); Carmen, *op. cit.*, in note 40; and Paul Ekins and Manfred

Max-Neef (eds.), *Real-life Economics: Understanding Wealth Creation* (Routledge: London, 1992). Specifically on copying, see Immanuel Wallerstein's numerous works, especially Wallerstein, *op. cit.*, in note 45.

61. Meier, *op. cit.*, in note 53, pp. 15, and 18–19. For the relationship between state policy, accumulation in agro-industry, and the development of the international politics of aid, see Harriet Friedmann and Philip McMichael, 'Agriculture and the State System: The Rise and Decline of National Agricultures, 1870 to the Present', *Sociologia Ruralis* (Vol. 29, No. 2, 1989), pp. 93–117; Harriet Friedmann, 'Distance and Durability: Shaky Foundations for the World Food Economy', *Third World Quarterly* (Vol. 13, No. 2, 1992), pp. 371–83; and Harriet Friedmann, 'The Political Economy of Food: The Rise and Fall of the Post-War International Food Order', *American Journal of Sociology* (Vol. 88, Special Supplement, 1982), pp. S248–86.

62. Mark Rupert, *Producing Hegemony: The Politics of Mass Production and American Global Power* (Cambridge: Cambridge University Press, 1995) p. 59.

63. See, amongst many others, Ian Roxborough, *Theories of Development* (Basingstoke: Macmillan, 1979); Dudley Seers, *The Political Economy of Nationalism* (Oxford: Oxford University Press, 1983); Ben Crow, Henry Bernstein, Maureen Mackintosh, and Charlotte Martin, *Survival and Change in the Third World* (Cambridge: Polity Press, 1988); and Anthony Brewer, *Marxist Theories of Imperialism: A Critical Survey* (London: Routledge, 1980).

64. Philip McMichael argues this with respect to global agro-industry in 'Agro-food System Restructuring – Unity in Diversity', in McMichael (ed.), *op. cit.*, in note 41, p. 2.

65. Leys, *op. cit.*, in note 52, pp. 23–4, emphasis added.

66. Once again, the case of state support for private agro-industrial accumulation is instructive.

67. Chomsky, *op. cit.*, in note 13, p. 88.

68. See, for example, Bade Onimode (ed.), *The IMF, the World Bank and the African Debt: The Economic Impact* (London: Zed, 1989), and Onimode, *The IMF, the World Bank and the African Debt: Social and Political Impact* (London: Zed, 1989); Stephanie Griffith-Jones and Osvaldo Sunkel, *Debt and Development Crises in Latin America: The End of an Illusion* (Oxford: Clarendon Press, 1986); and Caroline Thomas, *op. cit.*, in note 3.

69. Keith Griffin and John Knight, 'Introduction', in Griffin and Knight (eds.), *Human Development and the International Development Strategy for the 1990s* (London: Macmillan, 1990), pp. 1–7.

70. *Ibid.*, p. 2.

71. Leys, *op. cit.*, in note 52, p. 7.

72. Blackwell and Seabrook, *op. cit.*, in note 40.

73. Larry Elliott, 'Labour's Mean Streets', *The Guardian*, 4 June 1996, p. 17.

74. *Ibid.*, p. 17.

75. Leys, *op. cit.*, in note 52, p. 1. An abridged version of the principal arguments advanced by Leys in the first chapter of this book can be found in his article, 'The Crisis in "Development Theory"', *New Political Economy* (Vol. 1, No. 1, 1996), pp. 41–58.

76. As a reminder, Sen quotes Immanuel Kant: '[s]o act as to treat humanity, whether in thine own person or in that of any other, in every case as end withal, never as means only'. Amartya Sen, 'Development as Capability Expansion', in Griffin and Knight (eds.), *op. cit.*, in note 69, p. 41.

77. Carmen, *op. cit.*, in note 40, pp. x–xi.

78. Wood, *op. cit.*, in note 8, p. 22.

79. Scott, *op. cit.*, in note 47, p. 223.

80. *Ibid.*, p. 2.

81. *Ibid.*, p. 37.

82. *Ibid.*, p. 87.

83. Quarles van Ufford, 'Knowledge and Ignorance in the Practices of Development Policy', in Mark Hobart (ed.), *An Anthropological Critique of Development: The Growth of Ignorance* (London: Routledge, 1993) p. 141.

84. Karl Marx, 'The Eighteenth Brumaire of Louis Napoleon', in *Surveys from Exile: Political Writings: Volume II*, trans. B. Fowkes (London: Penguin Classics, 1992), p. 176.

85. Public transcripts are not just the expressions of the powerful, they are also the versions of life to which the subordinate subscribe, but only to the extent that 'it is frequently in the interests of both parties to tacitly conspire in misrepresentation', not least because 'subordinate groups are complicitous in contributing to a sanitised official transcript [as] one way of covering their tracks'. See Scott, *op. cit.*, in note 47, p. 5.

86. See, for example, Michael Lipton, *New Seeds, Poor People* (London: Unwin Hyman, 1989).

87. Billy Dewalt and Katherine Dewalt, 'The Results of Mexican Agricultural and Food Policy: Debt, Drugs and Illegal Aliens', in Scott Whiteford and Anne E. Ferguson (eds.), *Harvest of Want: Hunger and Food Security in Central America* (Boulder, CO: Westview, 1991), p. 202.

88. van Ufford, *op. cit.*, in note 83, p. 157.

89. Karl Marx, *Economic and Philosophical Manuscripts* (London: Penguin Classics, 1992), pp. 323–4.

90. Sen, *op. cit.*, in note 76, p. 45.

91. Scott, *op. cit.*, in note 47, p. 199.

92. Eduardo Galeano, quoted in Carmen, *op. cit.*, in note 40, p. x.

93. James H. Mittelman, 'Rethinking the International Division of Labour in the Context of Globalisation', *Third World Quarterly* (Vol. 16, No. 2, 1995), p. 273.

94. Sayer, *op. cit.*, in note 27, p. 155.

95. Karl Marx, *Capital, Volume I* (Harmondsworth: Penguin Classics, 1990), p. 90. The full extract from Marx's 'Preface to the First Edition' is as follows: '[i]f however, the German reader pharisaically shrugs his shoulders at the condition of the English industrial and agricultural workers, or optimistically comforts himself with the thought that in Germany things are not nearly so bad, I must plainly tell him: De te fabula narratur !', quoted in Leys, *op. cit.*, in note 49, p. 47.

Index

democratisation of, 92, 96, 97, 108, 112, 113–4

IMF and civil society dialogue, 21, 91–114
   constraints on, 106–113
   limitations to, 98–106
   motivations for, 96–8

industrialisation, 2, 16, 18, 211, 212

'infrapolitics', 210, 217

international community, 38, 60, 74, 78, 79, 80

International Relations (IR), 2, 3, 26, 35, 39, 119, 129, 134, 181–3, 184, 186, 204–6, 209, 218, 219, 220

intervention, 18, 59–60, 62, 69, 70, 74, 76, 79, 106, 158, 189, 192, 213, 218, 220

legitimacy, 3, 17, 22, 39, 44, 49, 51, 62, 66, 68, 69, 111–2, 150, 165, 168, 181, 205, 210, 215

Marx, Karl, 72, 218, 220

modernisation, 2, 18, 73

modernity, 8, 119, 185, 204, 205, 207, 208

moral background, 35, 44–51

neoliberalism, 3, 4, 17, 20, 21, 26, 109–10, 129, 149, 157, 159, 164, 167, 180–2, 186, 188, 191, 214, 215–16

Netwok Women in Development Europe (WIDE), 119, 120, 129, 132–4, 136, 139

nongovernmental organisations (NGOs), 19, 50, 51, 52, 60, 76, 80, 91, 97, 99–101, 102, 103, 104, 105, 107, 108, 112–13, 131, 148–68, 181, 182, 186–7, 188, 190, 191
   environmental, 151–2, 156–7, 160–1
   international (INGO), 47, 150, 152, 155, 156, 166
   and participation, 156–8, 161–3
   poverty, 152–3, 157
   structural adjustment, 153–4, 157–8, 163–6
   and World Bank, 25–6, 148–68

participation, 1, 3, 7, 18, 21, 25–6, 93, 99–100, 103, 111, 113, 148–68, 187, 188, 213

powerlessness, 78, 205, 210, 218

progress, 12, 17, 19, 36, 44, 51, 53, 69, 187, 207, 209, 215–8

race, 2, 6, 7, 13, 14, 26, 120, 123, 125, 135, 137, 139

responsibility, ethical, 13, 18, 37, 41, 48, 50, 52, 59, 70, 77–8, 80, 215

Self-Employed Women's Association (SEWA), 23, 53, 131

Sen, Amartya, 23–4, 59, 61–2, 63, 64, 65–8, 70–4, 78, 215, 219

social movements, 2, 50, 51, 120, 214